INNOVATIVE CORPORATE TURNAROUNDS

INNOVATIVE CORPORATE TURNAROUNDS

Pradip N. Khandwalla

SAGE Publications
New Delhi/Newbury Park/London

First published in 1992 by

Sage Publications India Pvt Ltd
M-32, Greater Kailash Market, Part I
New Delhi 110 048

Sage Publications Inc
2455 Teller Road
Newbury Park, California 91320

Sage Publications Ltd
6 Bonhill Street
London EC2A 4PU

Published by Tejeshwar Singh for Sage Publications India Pvt Ltd, photo-typeset by Jayigee Enterprises, and printed at Chaman Enterprises.

Library of Congress Cataloging-in-Publication Data

Khandwalla, Pradip K.
    Innovative corporate turnarounds/Pradip N. Khandwalla.
       p.   cm.
    Includes index.
    1. Corporate turnarounds—Management. I. Title.
  HD58.8.K497 658.1′6–dc20 1992 92–9828

ISBN   81–7036–282–2 (India-hbk)   0–8039–9426–5 (US-hbk)
            81–7036–283–0 (India-pbk)   0–8039–9427–3 (US-pbk)

To
Ma
the best regenerator of all

CONTENTS

LIST OF TABLES, DIAGRAMS AND CHARTS

PREFACE

In my career as a researcher of organisations and their management I have seldom found any enquiry as exhilarating as that of studying how they revive from sickness. I encountered turnarounds in the late seventies when I was looking at some government-owned enterprises. Later, in the mid-eighties I was asked by a consortium of financial institutions to coordinate case studies of a number of successful and less successful turnarounds. The rich insights that field work yielded were supplemented by the reading of the published work on turnaround and of a large number of cases from around the world. The result is this book.

In this book I have sought to explore the phenomenology of turnarounds—the sorts of actions that characterise turnarounds, the causes of sickness, the inter-relationships between different turnaround actions, innovative versus conventional actions, different types of turnaround, the situational shapers of turnaround action, etc. Most of all I have tried to highlight certain critical choices in turnaround management that have a bearing on the cost of turnaround, the speed of recovery, and the magnitude of redemption. With the help of data from 65 corporate cases of recovery from a loss situation from all over the world, I have sought to examine the consequences of surgical versus non-surgical turnarounds, participative versus technical turnarounds, and innovative versus conventional turnarounds. The results have been startling: non-surgical, participative, innovative turnarounds not only 'work'; they seem to best the usual surgical turnarounds so popular in the West, especially in the USA, on all three criteria of turnaround effectiveness.

Although the research reported in this book is on corporate turnarounds, the implications for other often moribund collectivities—institutions, communities, governments—may be significant. We live in a world whose problems have grown so complex that perforce we have to rely on collectivities to tackle them; but the competencies of the latter commonly fall far short. The result often is widespread frustration, culminating at times in violence and rebellion, at others in the sullen alienation of stakeholders. The underlying processes of effective corporate turnaround may well be useable in reviving other malfunctioning collectivities. I have also discussed significant implications for organisation theory, organisational dynamics, change agentry, and collective creativity.

Corporate sickness—and the malfunctioning of other forms of organisation and collectivity—is getting to be so 'hot' all over the world that all kinds of people may find this book interesting. Scholars of turnaround management and managers of sick or anaemic units should, of course, read this book. So also should stakeholders in sick units, such as managers of financial institutions, unions, and government agencies. But turnaround management is quintessential management, management of crisis situations at its dynamic best. There is much of interest in this book for any student, practitioner, or scholar of management. This is one of a handful of management books in which the study sample is truly international, with cases from the developed world (USA, Britain, Canada, Germany, Japan) as well as the Third World (India, Sri Lanka, several African countries, the Caribbean). The insights the book has to offer are not confined to narrow cultural or economic domains. At the same time the book does report differences between private sector and public sector turnarounds, Western and non-Western turnarounds, turnarounds of large versus smaller companies, etc.

Chapter 1 introduces the reader to the magic transformations that effective turnaround management has yielded all over the globe. Chapter 2 expounds on the general structure of turnarounds. Chapter 3 describes the surgical turnaround and highlights a couple of alternatives of this mode of turnaround. Chapter 4 describes the non-surgical turnaround without tears and a couple of alternative forms of this mode. Chapter 5 examines the contextual conditions that influence the mode of turnaround, such as size, ownership, depth and duration of sickness, causes of sickness, etc. Chapter 6 illumines the nature and effectiveness of management creativity during turnaround. Chapter 7 looks at how turnarounds unfold, their phases, and other phenomena of turnaround dynamics. Finally, Chapter 8 offers some ruminations on the turnaround phenomenon and its implications for organisation theory, regeneration of collectivities in general, public policy (particularly related to privatisation), change agentry in an unfamiliar operating context, and training for turnaround.

Many have contributed to this work. Alfred Kieser made useful comments on an earlier draft. Dr. Narayan Sheth nudged me to give the L & T Chair lecture in September 1988 in which I first conceptualised many of the ideas I have developed in this book. Ram Mohan Rao conducted a valiant search for turnaround cases published in the eighties in a number of magazines, books, and journals. He and Punya Upadhyay prepared the indexes. Savithriamma struggled amiably with countless tables and other esoteric scribbles for producing a typescript. Needless to add that any blemishes in the book are all my fault.

Ahmedabad   **Pradip N. Khandwalla**

1. THE MAGIC OF TURNAROUND

Corporate life is eventful. Some events, however, are more exciting than others, such as the launching of new divisions and departments, expansion and diversification, a change of guard at the top, fresh campaigns of market conquest, changes in management systems, corporate reorganisation, and so forth. But even among these charged events, few match the excitement of a turnaround from a shattering corporate decline. The emotions roused range from a thankful disbelief to champagne-toasting joy; for, the turnarounds of sick organisations often border on the miraculous.

Consider some examples from around the globe. The Bharat Heavy Plate and Vessels, set up by the Government of India in the late sixties to produce sophisticated equipment for the petrochemical, fertiliser, and other process industries, had not, even once, made a profit in the ten years of its existence.[1] In 1978–79 it made an abnormally large loss. Morale was low, there had been no chief executive for six months, and anarchy and industrial unrest were afoot. Then in walked a new chief executive. In a year, the company reported its first-ever profit. From earning Rs 6 million in that eventful year, the company went on to triple its turnover in the next four years and to increase its profit fifteen times.

Chrysler Corporation affords another example of a miraculous turnaround.[2] Operating in a fiercely competitive market and mired in an industrial recession, Chrysler's accumulated losses by 1981 were $3,500 million. But by 1985, under Lee Iacocca's dynamic leadership, it was earning around $2,000 million a year.

Italtel, the Italian telecommunications company, was losing an astonishing 46 per cent on sales in 1980.[3] Despite this haemorrhage, it succeeded in breaking even by 1983, and was earning a respectable 4 per cent on sales by 1984.

Can Cel, a Canadian producer of timber and pulp, was a loss-making company.[4] Earlier owned by an American multinational, it was taken over by the Government of British Columbia in 1973.

During 1968–72 it lost $70 million. However, the company broke even under government management in 1973 itself and quadrupled its profit to $50 million next year.

The State Timber Corporation of Sri Lanka lost 12 per cent on sales during 1977 and 1978.[5] It turned in a profit in 1979 and by 1981 it had increased its sales nine times over the 1977 level; its profits were six times the 1979 level. Jaguar, the British maker of luxury cars, lost 28 and 19 per cent on sales in 1980 and 1981 respectively.[6] The company broke even in 1982 and by 1985 it was earning 12 per cent on sales. Between 1980 and 1985 its sales grew nearly five times.

Turnarounds are organisational recoveries from declines. However, there has yet been no agreement on what constitutes decline. Some have thought of organisational decline in relative terms—for example, a lower rate of earning than in the past or a lower rate relative to the industry's rate, or even relative to the economy's growth.[7] But, then, how far lower? Since the sample used in the research reported in this volume was an international one, relative measures of decline were rather difficult to secure or justify. Thus, the decision was made to define corporate decline as a loss situation, and turnaround as equivalent to reaching at least a break-even from a loss situation. Two types of turnaround cases were encountered. Some case stories terminated at the point in time the company broke even. These were called break-even turnaround cases. The other cases continued their stories of recovery beyond break-even to at least one year (and often more) beyond the break-even year. These were called complete turnarounds. Conceptually, while a break-even turnaround culminated in the year in which a loss-making company broke even, a turnaround was deemed to be complete when the company reached a profitability normal to its industry or operating context or equal to its normal profitability before decline.

In order to have an international cast of turnarounds, a number of journals, business magazines, and books, written in English and published in several countries, were scanned. To ensure contemporary relevance, the search was confined to publications in the eighties (even though some of the turnarounds in fact took place in the seventies). The journals scanned for case stories included *Abhigyan, Academy of Management Journal, Administrative Science Quarterly, ASCI Journal, Business Horizons, Decision, Harvard*

Business Review, Indian Management, Journal of Management Studies, Long Range Planning, Organization Studies, and *Vikalpa.* Relatively serious business magazines, such as, *Business India, Business Week, Business World, Fortune,* and *Management Today,* were also studied. Books on turnarounds, like those by Slatter, Kharbanda and Stallworthy, and Potts and Behr, also yielded a few cases.[8] Another source was papers presented at conferences on turnarounds. About half of the cases were written by journalists, while the rest were written by scholars and participant observers. In the case of journalistic accounts especially, an attempt was made to locate multiple accounts. Where multiple accounts were available, any contradictory material was discarded. A further precaution taken was that only those cases were finally included that (*a*) gave some background information on the company and why it had turned sick; and (*b*) gave a fairly detailed account of actions taken by the management to turn it around.

Sixty-five cases were identified from all over the world. There must surely be many times this number that were unreported or reported in inaccessible books and periodicals. Nonetheless, the cases assembled exhibit a wide range of national moorings, over several industries and products, vary considerably in size and so on. Table 1.1 presents 65 cases, categorised by industry. The Table provides information on the country, approximate size, and turnaround performance. It also indicates whether the turnaround reported was up to break-even point or complete.

There are several cases from India, the UK and the USA. There are also cases from Italy, Japan, Nigeria, Zambia, the Carribbean, Sri Lanka, and Canada. Although large parts of the world are unrepresented, the sample is more representative of the world than any assembled previously.[9] Small firms have been excluded so as to capture the richness of turnaround dynamics in sizeable organisations. Even so, the variation in size is striking. Included are some of the world's great corporations, such as Imperial Chemical Industries, the world's fifth largest chemical company, USX, British Steel, and Steel Authority of India, the largest steel producers respectively in the USA, UK and India, IRI, one of the world's largest government-owned enterprises with a staff of nearly half a million, General Motors, Volkswagen, Chrysler Corporation, Fiat, and Toyo Kogyo, five of the biggest car makers in the world, and several other corporations earning billions of dollars in sales,

Table 1.1

Turnaround Miracles Round the World

	Country	Approx. Size	Turnaround Performance	Extent of Turnaround
A. Accounting and Business Machines and Office Equipment				
Docutel[10] (automatic teller machines)	USA	$ 70 m.sales	Loss of $ 8.5 m. in 1977; profit of $ 6.8 m. in 1980. Profit expected to double in 1981.	Complete
Olivetti[11] (office equipment, computers)	Italy	$ 4,000 m. sales, 47,000 employees	Lost $ 72 m. in 1978. Profit of $ 201 m. in 1984, $ 264 m. in 1985 on sales of $ 2,600 m. and $ 3.900 m. respectively.	Complete
Sweda International[12] (cash registers)	USA	$ 300 m. sales	Losses during 1974–78. Broke even in 1979. Earned 10% on sales in 1980; 15% expected in 1981.	Complete
B. Automobiles, Two-wheelers, etc.				
Chrysler[13] (cars)	USA	$ 20,000 m. sales; third largest US producer	Accumulated losses of $ 3,500 m. up to 1981. Lost $ 1,700 m. in 1981, broke even in 1982, Earned $ 2,400 m. in 1984.	Complete
Enfield[14] (two-wheelers, agro-engines)	India	Rs. 300 m. sales	Losses from 1975 to 1977. Profit of Rs. 9 m. on sales of Rs. 200 m. in 1978, Rs. 13 m. in 1980 on sales of Rs. 275 m.	Complete

Table 1.1. (Contd.)

	Country	Approx. Size	Turnaround Performance	Extent of Turnaround
Fiat[15] (cars)	Italy	One of the world's largest producers— produced 1.4 m. cars in 1983	Return on sales of −1.9% in 1980, −3.4% in 1981; broke even in 1983. Earned 2.2% on sales in 1984.	Complete
General Motors[16] (cars, other products)	USA	The world's largest car producer. $ 80,000 m. sales	1980 loss of $ 760m. Broke even in 1981. 1983 earnings of $ 3,800 m. on sales of $ 80,000 m.	Complete
Jaguar[17] (luxury cars; government-owned during turnaround)	UK	£ 500 m. sales	Lost 28% and 19% on sales in 1980 and 1981. Broke even in 1982. Earned 10% on sales in 1983. 1983 sales three times that of 1980.	Complete
Standard Motors[18] (cars, light commercial vehicles)	India	Rs. 240 m. sales	Lost Rs.13 m. by 1975. Broke even in 1976. Earned Rs. 17 m. in 1981 and sales nearly triple of 1976 sales.	Complete
Toyo Kogyo[19] (cars and trucks)	Japan	$ 5,000 m. sales; ninth largest auto maker in the world	Losses from 1975 to 1978. Earned $ 91 m. in 1981, up 27% over 1980. Productivity in 1981 2.3 times that of 1975.	Complete

Table 1.1. (Contd.)

	Country	Approx. Size	Turnaround Performance	Extent of Turnaround
Volkswagen[20] (cars)	Germany	DM 54,000 m. sales, over 2 m. cars	Profit decline after 1979 culminating in losses in 1982 and 1983. Broke even in 1984, profits of DM 600 m. on sales of DM 54,000 m. in 1985.	Complete

C. Chemicals, Fertilisers, and Pharmaceuticals

	Country	Approx. Size	Turnaround Performance	Extent of Turnaround
Celanese Corporation[21] (petrochemicals, synthetic fibres, plastics)	USA	Annual sales of $ 3,500 m.	Loss of $ 34 m. in 1982; first half 1983 profit of $ 24 m.	Break-even
Fertilisers and Chemicals Travancore[22] (government-owned; chemicals and fertilisers)	India	Rs. 2,000 m. annual sales	Accumulated losses of Rs. 720 m. as of 1983. 1981 and 1982 losses averaged Rs. 88 m. Broke even in 1984.	Break-even
Imperial Chemical Industries[23] (chemicals and dyes)	UK	World's fifth largest chemical company; $ 13,000 m. sales	1980 loss of £ 48 m. 1984 profits of £ 734 m., up 55% over 1983.	Complete
Searle[24] (drugs and health care)	USA	$ 900 m. sales	Lost 3.3% on sales in 1977; earned 10.5% on sales in 1981.	Complete
Southern Petro-chemicals and Industries[25] (government-owned; fertilisers, chemicals, electronics)	India	Rs. 5,000 m. sales	Loss of Rs. 272 m. in 1976–77 on sales of Rs. 600 m. Turned profitable in 1978–79. 1981–82 profit three times 1978–79 profit of Rs. 78 m.	Complete

Table 1.1. (Contd.)

	Country	*Approx. Size*	*Turnaround Performance*	*Extent of Turnaround*
Travancore Cochin Chemicals[26] (government-owned; miscellaneous chemicals)	India	Rs. 150 m. in sales	Lost 43% on sales in 1976. Broke even in 1979. Earned 17% on sales in 1980.	Complete

D. Computers, Electronics, Telecommunications

	Country	*Approx. Size*	*Turnaround Performance*	*Extent of Turnaround*
Ferranti[27] (electronics and computers)	UK	£ 160 m. sales	Losses in 1975 and 1976. Profit of £ 4 m. in 1977 and in 1978 £ 9 m. on sales of £ 157 m.	Complete
ICL[28] (computers)	UK	£ 1,000 m. sales	Lost £ 133 m. in 1980–81. Profit of £ 24 m. in 1981–82 on sales of £ 710 m. Sales of £ 1,000 m. in 1985–86 and profit of £ 54 m.	Complete
Italtel[29] (telecommunications equipment; government-owned)	Italy	L 1,200 b. sales	Lost 46% on sales in 1980. Broke even in 1983. Earned L 25 b. in 1984	Complete
Osborne[30] (portable computers)	USA	At its peak sold 120,000 computers a year	Filed for bankruptcy but regained positive cash-flow in 1985.	Break-even
Ultra Electronic Holdings[31] (wide range of electronic products)	UK	£ 7 m. sales	Losses during 1970–72. Broke even in 1973. Profit 67% higher in 1974.	Complete

Table 1.1. (Contd.)

	Country	Approx. Size	Turnaround Performance	Extent of Turnaround
Wang Labs[32] (computers peripherals, computers software)	USA	$ 3,000 m. sales	Losses of $ 30 m. and $ 70 m. in 1986 and 1987. Profit of $ 33 m. on first-quarter sales of $ 770 m. in 1988.	Break-even

E. Conglomerates

	Country	Approx. Size	Turnaround Performance	Extent of Turnaround
EID Parry[33]	India	Rs. 1,500 m. sales	Losses up to 1984–85 totalled Rs. 50 m. Earned Rs. 23 m. on sales of Rs. 1500 m. in 1985–86. 1986–87 profits 15% higher, and thereafter much higher.	Complete
Henley Group[34]	USA	$ 3,000 m. sales	Lost $ 426 m. in 1986 and loss also expected in 1987 but subsidiaries expected to earn $ 314 m. in 1987.	Break-even
IRI[35] (government-owned)	Italy	L 47,000 b. sales, 470,000 employees	Losses during 1980–85 totalled L 14,000 b. 1986 profit of L 3,000 b.	Break-even

F. Household Goods

	Country	Approx. Size	Turnaround Performance	Extent of Turnaround
Black and Decker[36] (power tools, home appliances)	USA	$ 1,800 m. sales	Lost $ 158 m. in 1985. Earned $ 6 m. on sales of $ 1,800 m. in 1986.	Break-even

Table 1.1. (Contd.)

	Country	Approx. Size	Turnaround Performance	Extent of Turnaround
Epe Plywood[37] (government-owned; plywood doors, furniture etc.)	Nigeria	N 7 m. sales	Lost N 0.2 m. in each of 1984 and 1985 on sales of N 3 m. Broke even in 1986. Earned N 1.3 m. on sales of N 6.7 m. in 1987.	Break-even
Sylvania and Laxman[38] (lamps and related products)	India	Rs. 160 m. sales	Losses during 1974–77 totalled Rs. 51 m. Earned Rs. 6 m. in 1978. In 1979 sales double of 1977 and earning of Rs. 16 m. on sales of Rs. 160 m. 1980 profits double of 1979 profits.	Complete
Toro[39] (lawn mowers, snow throwers etc.)	USA	$ 350 m. sales	Lost $ 30 m. in 10 quarters preceding 1983. Broke even in 1983.	Break-even

G. Packaging, Containers

	Country	Approx. Size	Turnaround Performance	Extent of Turnaround
Metal Box[40] (packaging materials)	UK	£ 1,300 m. sales	Incurred loss during 1980–82. Profit of £ 70 m. in 1983–84.	Complete
Rockware Group[41] (glass containers)	UK	4,500 employees	Lost £ 13 m. in 1983, earned £ 3 m. in 1984.	Break-even
Tinplate[42] (tinplated containers)	India	Rs. 600 m. sales, 5,000 employees	Lost Rs. 28 m. in 1979, Rs. 56 m. in 1980. Earned Rs. 11 m. in 1981.	Break-even

Table 1.1. (Contd.)

	Country	Approx. Size	Turnaround Performance	Extent of Turnaround
H. Plant, Machinery, Equipment, Engineering Products				
Bharat Heavy Electricals[43] (government-owned; power plants and allied equipment)	India	45,000 employees, $ 450 m. sales	Loss of $ 22 m. on sales of $ 200 m. in 1972–73; broke even in 1974–75; profit of $ 35 m. on sales of $ 450 m. in 1975–76.	Complete
Bharat Heavy Plate and Vessels[44] (government-owned; sophisticated heavy engineering products like pressure vessels and heat exchangers)	India	Rs. 600 m. sales, 4,000 employees	Loss from inception until 1978–79. Broke even in 1979–80. Net profit rose from Rs. 3 m. in 1979–80 on sales of Rs. 270 m. to Rs. 6 m. in 1982–83, Rs. 44 m. in 1983–84 and Rs. 89 m. in 1984–85.	Complete
Jaipur Metals[45] (former sick private co. later government-owned; electrical meters, conductors, wire products)	India	Rs. 120 m. sales, 1,750 employees	By 1984 losses totalled three times equity. From a loss of Rs. 9.4 m. on sales of Rs. 85 m. in 1983–84, the company broke even in 1984–85 and earned 10% on sales in 1984–85. Rs. 29.9 m. earned in 1986–87 on sales of Rs. 181.2 m.	Complete

Table 1.1. (Contd.)

	Country	Approx. Size	Turnaround Performance	Extent of Turnaround
Lucas[46] (engineering, autoparts, aerospace parts, electrical machines)	UK	£ 1,500 m. sales	Lost £ 21 m. in 1981. Earned £ 58 m. in 1985.	Complete
Mining and Allied Machinery Corpn.[47] (government-owned; mining and bulk material handling equipment. conveyors, coal beneficiation plants etc.)	India	7,700 employees, Rs. 800 m. sales	Lost 21% on sales in 1985–86; earned 4% on sales in 1986–87 and increased sales by 35%	Break-even
RFD Group[48] (life-saving equipment)	UK	£ 15 m. sales	Loss in 1974. Profit of £ 1.4 m. in 1975 on sales of £ 12 m. Earned 50% higher profits in 1976 on sales of £ 15 m.	Complete
Redman Heenan[49] (specialised engineering products and ancillary services)	UK	£ 22 m. sales	Losses in 1970 and 1971. 1971 loss 12% on sales. Broke even in 1972. Earned 3% on sales in 1974 and rising trend thereafter.	Complete

Table 1.1. (Contd.)

	Country	Approx. Size	Turnaround Performance	Extent of Turnaround
Richardson and Cruddas[50] (former sick co. taken over by government; structurals, different sorts of machineries)	India	Rs. 200 m. sales, 4.000 employees	Losses in 1977–78, 1978–79. Increased turnover by 27% in 1979–80 and broke even.	Break-even
Staveley Industries[51] (machine tools, foundry and abrasives, chemical extraction, electrical services)	UK	£ 50 m. sales	Losses in 1969, 1970. 1970 loss £ 1.1 m. on sales of £ 53 m. Break-even in 1971. Earned 5% on sales in 1973, with rising profits thereafter.	Complete

J. Steel

	Country	Approx. Size	Turnaround Performance	Extent of Turnaround
British Steel[52] (government-owned)	UK	One of the world's largest steel producers, 14 m. ton production capacity	Lost £ 530 m. in 1979–80. Loss-making until 1984–85. Profits rose in 1986–87 to £ 206 m. from £ 76 m. in 1985–86.	Complete
Steel Authority of India[53] (government-owned)	India	Rs. 60,000 m. sales. 250,000 employees, 10 m. ton capacity	Lost Rs. 2,000 m. during 1980–84. Broke even in 1984–85 Profit of Rs. 1,500 m. in 1985–86; profit of Rs. 3,600 m. in 1988–89.	Complete
USX[54] (formerly US Steel) (steel, oil, chemicals)	USA	$ 17,000 m. sales; largest US producer of steel	Lost $ 279 m. in 1979; losses in 1982, 1983. Broke even in 1984. Earned $ 670 m. in 1988, triple 1987 profits.	Complete

Table 1.1. (Contd.)

	Country	Approx. Size	Turnaround Performance	Extent of Turnaround
J. Textiles, Fibres, Apparel				
Dawson International[55] (textiles)	UK	£ 110 m. sales	Loss in 1974–75. Break-even in 1975–76. 1980–81 sales nearly tripled to £ 113 m. with a profit of £ 18 m.	Complete
ICI Fibres Division[56] (synthetic fibres)	UK	£ 450 m. sales	Losses totalled £ 280 m. during 1975–83. Expected profit of £ 10–15 m. in 1984.	Break-even
Munsingwear[57] (apparel)	USA	$ 100 m. sales	Lost $ 15 m. in 1982. Earned $ 3 m. in 1983.	Break-even
Warnaco[58] (apparel)	USA	$ 500 m. sales	Lost $ 23 m. in 1976. Earned $ 21 m. in 1981	Complete
K. Timber and Pulp				
Can Cel[59] (former multi-national sub-sidiary, govern-ment-owned in 1973; timber and pulp)	Canada	C $ 160 m.	Lost nearly C $ 70 m. during 1968–72. Lost 20% on sales in 1971. Profit-making after 1972. Earned 27% on sales in 1974. 1974 sales 60% above 1972 sales.	Complete
State Timber Corporation[60] (government-owned; timber and pulp)	Sri Lanka	SL Rs. 350 m.	Lost SL Rs. 5 m. a year during 1977 and 1978 on sales of around SL Rs 40 m. Earned Rs. 15 m. in 1979 and SL Rs. 84 m. in 1981, and sales increased nine times between 1977 and 1981	Complete

Table 1.1. (Contd.)

	Country	Approx. Size	Turnaround Performance	Extent of Turnaround
L. Trade and Services				
Burton Group[61] (retailing chains for apparel, office supplies. Manufactured apparel. Property holding)	UK	£ 140 m. sales	Losses in 1976 and 1977. Earned 5% on sales in 1978, 11% in 1979.	Complete
Gambia Produce Marketing Board[62] (government-owned; marketing of oilseeds etc.)	Gambia	No information	Lost D 21 m. in 1984–85, lost D 38 m. in 1985–86. Earned D 20 m. in 1985–86.	Break-even
Getz Corporation[63] (international trader)	USA	$ 500 m. in sales.	Loss in 1981. Break-even in 1982. 1983 earnings 30% above 1982 and 1984 earnings 20% over 1983 earnings.	Complete
Wickes[64] (retailer)	USA	$ 3,000 m. sales	Lost $ 250 m. in 1981 and also in 1982. 1983 July-quarter profit of $ 10 m.	Break-even
M. Transportation				
Eastern Airlines[65]	USA	$ 4,800 m. revenue, 38,000 employees	Lost $ 380 m. during five years up to 1983. Broke even in 1984.	Break-even
Air India[66] (government-owned)	India	Rs. 12,000 m. revenue, 20,000 employees	Lost Rs. 430 m. on revenue of Rs. 10,240 m. in 1987–88. Expected to earn Rs. 400 m. on revenues of Rs. 12,050 m. in 1988–89.	Break-even

Table 1.1. (Contd.)

	Country	Approx. Size	Turnaround Performance	Extent of Turnaround
Jamaica Railways[67] (government-owned)	Jamaica	1,500 employees; revenue of J $ 45 m.	Accumulated losses up to 1985 of J $ 57 m. 1986 profit of J $ 7.5 m.	Break-even
Zambia Railways[68] (government-owned)	Zambia	K 400 m. revenue	Losses up to 1985. 1985 loss K 2.4 m. 1986 profit K 4.3 m. 1987 profit K 11.1 m.	Complete
N. Tyres				
Apollo Tyres[69] (tyres for cars and trucks)	India	Rs. 1,500 m. sales	Losses from inception up to 1980–81; loss in 1983–84 of Rs. 40 m. Broke even in 1986–87 and larger profits since.	Complete
Firestone[70] (tyres, tubes, rubber products)	USA	$ 4,500 m. sales	Negative cash flow of $ 391 m. during 1977–79. Loss in 1980. Earned $ 135 m. in 1981.	Break-even
O. Miscellaneous				
Del E. Webb[71] (leisure, real estate, construction)	USA	$ 360 m. sales	Mounting losses until 1981. Broke even in 1982. Earning of $ 6 m. on sales of $ 360 m. in 1983; expected to double in 1984.	Complete
Macmillan[72] (book publishing, information services)	USA	$ 400 m. sales	Lost $ 57 m. in 1980. Broke even in 1981. Earned $ 22 m. on sales of $ 384 m. in 1982.	Complete

Table 1.1. (Contd.)

	Country	Approx. Size	Turnaround Performance	Extent of Turnaround
NBC Radio Division[73] (radio broadcasting)	USA	$ 40 m. revenue	Chronic money loser. Earned $ 3 m. in 1980 on revenues of $ 40 m.	Break-even
Pullman[74] (rail-car maker)	USA	$ 200 m. sales	Lost $ 42 m. in 1983. Earned $ 10 m. in 1984.	Break-even

such as Wang Laboratories, the Henley group, Black and Decker, Eastern Airlines, Wickes, Firestone, Celanese Corporation, ICL, and Jaguar. But there are also many smaller corporations, with sales in millions rather than billions, names like Docutel, Travancore Cochin Chemicals, Ultra Electronic Holdings, Epe Plywood, Sylvania and Laxman, Jaipur Metals and Redman Heenan, among others.

A wide range of industries are represented. Some are distinctively 'hi-tech', such as the computer, electronics and telecommunications industries. Some are 'smoke stack' industries, like steel. Consumer goods industries are represented by the automobile, household goods, packaging and containers, and the textiles, fibres, and apparel industries. There is a fairly large number of cases of machinery manufacturers, as there is of companies producing chemicals, fertilisers, and pharmaceuticals. Included also are trading and transportation companies.

Of the 65 cases, 23 illustrate break-even turnarounds, and 42 complete turnarounds. For example, the story of Celanese Corporation describes steps culminating in a profit during the first half of 1983 after a loss in 1982, while that of Wang Laboratories records the steps taken to move from losses in 1986 and 1987 to a first quarter profit in 1988. These are examples of break-even turnarounds. The stories of complete turnarounds cover a longer period of recovery, and are generally much richer in information. The Fiat story, for instance, goes beyond the break-even situation in 1983 to the profitable operations of 1984, and the story on Enfield India describes how, after losses from 1975 to 1977, the company earned profits of Rs 9 million in 1978, and Rs 13 million in 1980.

Both sets of stories are useful. The complete turnaround stories indicate how the corporation tried to reverse decline and also how the company sought to return to 'normal' levels of profitability. They therefore provide rich insights into how organisations transit from crisis management to break-even and onto 'institution building' phase that enables them to reach and sustain normal profitability levels. Thus they yield models of overall turnaround management. The break-even turnarounds may provide a more detailed account of the first turnaround actions, and therefore yield rich insights into the crisis management aspect of turnaround management.

A Sackful of Gifts

There are some phenomena that are hyper-prolific in what they yield under a microscope—the living cell, the atom and the human mind are good examples. So is turnaround management. Whatever we know of turnaround management suggests that turnarounds are time warps in the life of an organisation: the organisation enters the turnaround process in one form, usually of high entropy, and emerges in another, of a taut boxer, ready to take on the world, muscles rippling. How is this transformation achieved? Many secrets of the organisational world may be revealed by studying this transformation. For instance, most turnarounds are catalysed by newcomers at the top. The way leaders achieve control in a chaotic situation can be illumined by studying turnarounds. Change agentry, too, can be comprehended by studying how turnaround leaders diagnose what has to be done, and mobilises the organisation to change its ways. How organisations learn—for example from being domestic in their orientation to being international, from being production-centred to being market-oriented, from being mechanistic to being lithe and organic, from being go-it-alone organisations to seeking joint ventures—is also well illustrated by many turnaround cases. And, of course, a study of turnarounds yields one or more technologies for combating organisational sickness, a major and growing menace in all modern societies.

While technological innovation is a fairly extensively researched area, management creativity is not.[75] Turnarounds are situations where management creativity should be, and often is, at its flood-tide.

This is because so much needs to be accomplished with so little in so short a time. Spectacular real-time improvements in performance are unlikely with business-as-usual management. Turnarounds can indicate the ambit and content of management creativity as a response to crisis, and also how much management creativity can contribute to improvement in organisational performance. Management creativity is alluring. But is it organisationally useful? Turnaround research can provide at least a partial answer.

It has always been difficult to study organisational dynamics, that is, the way actions and events within organisations get linked over time to produce outcomes. The intent of the framework of organisational systems is to provide a dynamic, longitudinal view of organisational functioning, but in practice few systems theorists have been able to do so.[76] To be sure some organisational simulations have attempted to do this.[77] But their artificiality limits the usefulness of the findings. However, organisational dynamics can be highly interesting, as indicated by studies of how actual organisations changed their structures over time, or how they managed transitions.[78] Because turnarounds are generally temporally compressed, it becomes easier to identify the sequences in which events take place within them, and thereby unravel cause-effect or stimulus-response linkages between the events.

But beyond these gifts are other, somewhat discomforting, ones. For example, there is a belief, held by many, that in free-market economies just as there is freedom to enter, so must there be freedom to exit. That is to say, if an organisation is not viable it should be allowed to down its shutters. There is quite a debate about this in high-unemployment, low-social security economies because closures mean immense hardships to those losing their means of livelihood.[79] If, however, it is shown that even very sick organisations can be turned around, as apparently is possible (see Table 1.1), then allowing companies to close shop becomes much less justifiable. This, in turn, has large implications for social policy, for the latter may have to block some closures rather than facilitate them, and to speed up change to a more effective management.

There is a second discomforting advantage of studying turnarounds. Privatisation of 'inefficient' public enterprises has become a rallying cry of Thatcherites in many market economies.[80] However, Table 1.1 reveals several examples (about 20) of sick public enterprises that dramatically improved their performance under public management. Indeed, there are also examples of companies that had fallen sick in private hands, were nationalised to save the employees' jobs, and dramatically improved their performance under public management (examples reported in Table 1.1 include Can Cel, a Canadian company and Jaipur Metals, an Indian company). These turnaround examples question one's faith in privatisation as a master-remedy for the ills of the public sector.

A third nettlesome windfall from studying turnarounds may be the identification of humane modes of turnaround that are alternatives to the slash-and-burn type prevalent in the West, particularly in the USA. A number of turnarounds reported in Table 1.1 involved enormous human sacrifice—the lay-off of thousands—to restore health. But, as we shall see later, there were also a large number of equally dramatic turnarounds from comparably appalling corporate sickness, in which virtually no one was fired and no plants were closed. These anomalies may well lead to a reappraisal of the surgical method of turning around sick organisations. Worse, they may turn many a current corporate hero into a villain!

For the last fifty years or more the organisational sciences (organisational behaviour, organisation theory, organisational development, industrial sociology, organisational psychology, and so on) have been trying to unravel the mystery of what determines the performance of the organisation. Initially, it was thought that diligent application of some principles of management—such as a small span of control, or specialisation by function, or division of labour—yielded a decent organisational performance.[81] Then it was thought that certain styles of management, particularly the participative style of management, improved organisational performance.[82] However, while some correlation was found between, for example, the participative style and organisational (or sub-organisational) performance, it was not clear whether the style caused the performance or *vice versa*.[83] Still later it was thought that if the organisation's design was appropriate to the context in which it operated its performance would be high. The empirical support for this hypothesis to-date has been slim.[84] Recently, attempts have been made to isolate modes of management that characterise companies with an excellent track record.[85] In one of the better-known studies, that of Peters and Waterman, the researchers identified several traits that they claimed characterised over 40 companies that had consistently performed well over a 20-year period. However, they offered no evidence that all these companies had all these traits during even one of these 20 years.

The main problem with identifying the determinants of superior organisational performance is one of antecedence. If an organisation has a certain feature and it is also known to perform well, one cannot infer that the feature has contributed to the superior performance, for good performance may, instead, have led the organisation to adopt that feature. For instance, a company that is doing well often uses its profit or 'slack' for such status, enhancing activities as institutional advertising, computerisation, community development and other good corporate citizenship activities.[86] In such situations, if an organisational feature can be shown to have immediately preceded improvement in performance, there is greater confidence in saying that the feature in question may have contributed to superior performance. This sort of antecedence is easy to establish in turnarounds. This is because the improvement in performance is usually very striking, indeed so striking that random factors can be ruled out; and vigorous action precedes relatively immediately the improvement in performance. In such situations it is easier to accept the pattern of turnaround actions as contributing to the improvement in organisational performance and thus enables us to understand better the causal forces that shape organisational effectiveness.

A study of turnarounds may change our conceptions of the nature of organisations. An influential paper in the seventies, which triggered a good deal of organisational research, argued that organisations, like living organisms, essentially have limited adaptability.[87] Operating in cosy niches, organisational forms tend to disappear when environmental conditions nurturing these niches change and become hostile. The high sickness rates in several industries in several countries would tend to support the argument; turnarounds, however, tend to controvert it. An examination of turnarounds may yield important insights into the limits of organisational adaptability and their determinants.

These and other gifts are unwrapped in the rest of the book. In Chapter 2, 27 turnaround elements have been identified, and the extent to which they occurred in complete turnarounds is reported. Also reported are elements that are basic to most turnarounds, and elements that trigger distinctive forms of turnarounds. Two major alternative turnaround designs are identified, the harsh and the humane. The harsh turnaround and its variants are examined in Chapter 3, and the humane turnaround and its variants in Chapter 4. Their relative performance is also assessed in Chapter 4. In Chapter 5 the operating context of turnarounds, inclusive of culture, size, ownership, the nature, extent, and depth of sickness, and the way these shape turnarounds, is considered. In Chapter 6 turnaround creativity and its impact on turnaround performance is investigated. Chapter 7 tries to unravel the dynamics of turnaround management, and combs the intriguing area of change agents and organisational learning. Chapter 8 restates the major conclusions and explores their implications for organisational theory and turnaround theory.

Notes and References

1. See Pradip N. Khandwalla, 'Turnaround management in the public sector', *Lok Udyog*, Vol. 17, No. 6, 1983, pp. 25–38.
2. See *Business Week*, 'Can Chrysler keep its comeback act rolling?', 14 February 1983, pp. 58–62; see also *Business Week*, 'The next act at Chrysler', 3 November 1986, pp. 48–52; and Maynard M. Gordon, *The Iacocca management technique* (New York: Bantam, 1987).
3. See Marisa Bellisario, 'The turnaround at Italtel', *Long Range Planning*, Vol. 18, No. 1, 1985, pp. 21–24.
4. See Robert W. Sexty, *Canadian Cellulose Co. Ltd.: A case study of government rescue and turnaround* (Toronto: The Institute of Public Administration of Canada, 1982).
5. See Ravi Ramamurti, 'State Timber Corporation of Sri Lanka (A) and (B)', Cases 0-382-018 and 0-382-019 (Boston: President and Fellows of Harvard College, 1981).
6. See David Chambers, 'Consumer orientation and the drive for quality', paper presented at the Roundtable on 'Public Enterprise Management: Strategies for Success' at New Delhi, 6–11 March 1988, under the auspices of the Commonwealth Secretariat and the Indian Institute of Management, Ahmedabad.
7. See Pradip N. Khandwalla, *Effective turnaround of sick enterprises (Indian experiences): Text and cases* (London: Commonwealth Secretariat, 1989); Donald C. Hambrick and Steven M. Schecter, 'Turnaround strategies for mature industrial-product business units', *Academy of Management Journal*, Vol. 26, No. 2, 1983, pp. 231–48; Dan Schendel, G.R. Patton, and James Riggs, 'Corporate turnaround strategies: A study of profit decline and recovery', *Journal of General Management*, Vol. 3, No. 3, 1976, pp. 3–11.

8. See Stuart Slåtter, *Corporate recovery: Successful turnaround strategies and their implementation* (Harmondsworth, Middlesex: Penguin, 1984); O.P. Kharbanda and E.A. Stallworthy, *Company rescue: How to manage a company turnaround* (London: Heinemann, 1987); Mark Potts and Peter Behr, *The leading edge* (New Delhi: Tata McGraw-Hill, 1987).

9. Prior studies of successful turnarounds have generally been based on within-nation samples. For example, the study by Dan Schendel, G. R. Patton, and James Riggs was of 54 US firms ('Corporate turnaround strategies: A study of profit decline and recovery', *Journal of General Management*, Vol. 3, 1976, pp. 3–11); that by Donald Bibeault was of 81 US companies (*Corporate turnaround: How managers turn losers into winners* (New York: McGraw-Hill, 1982); that by Donald C. Hambrick and Steven M. Schecter, 1983, op. cit., was of 53 US businesses; that by Charles Hofer was of a dozen US firms 'Turnaround strategies', *Journal of Business Strategy*, Vol. 1, No. 1, 1980, pp. 19–31); that by Stuart Slatter, 1984, op. cit., was of 30 British companies, those by Pradip N. Khandwalla were respectively of nine Indian companies ('Strategy for turning around complex sick organizations', *Vikalpa*, Vol. 6, 1981, pp. 143–66) and five Indian companies (1989, op. cit.). However, there was a study by Manjunath Hegde of 17 American, European and Japanese companies ('Western and Indian models of turnaround management', *Vikalpa*, Vol. 7, No. 4, 1982, pp. 289–304), and by O.P. Kharbanda and E.A. Stallworthy, 1987, op. cit., of turnarounds from a number of countries.

10. See *Business Week*, 'Docutel: Born again and counting on new vigour, in automatic tellers', 27 July 1981, pp. 48 and 50.

11. See Kharbanda and Stallworthy, 1987, op. cit., pp. 142–53; and G. Turner, 'Inside Europe's giant companies—Olivetti goes bear hunting', *Long Range Planning* , Vol. 19, 1986, pp. 13–20.

12. See *Business Week*, 'Sweda: Aggressive‡marketing produces a spirited turnaround', 31 March 1980, pp. 101–2.

13. See *Business Week*, 'The next act at Chrysler', 3 November 1986, pp. 48–52. See also *Business Week*, 'Can Chrysler keep its comeback act rolling?', 14 February 1983, pp. 58–62; and Maynard M. Gordon, 1987, op. cit.

14. See Dharni Pani, 'Enfield: Revving up again,' *Business India*, 5–18 December 1983, pp. 84, 85, 87, 89, 91 and 92, and Pradip N. Khandwalla, 1989, op. cit., pp. 197–207.

15. See Fabrizio Galimberti, 'Getting FIAT back on the road', *Long Range Planning*, Vol. 19, No. 1, 1986, pp. 25–30; Kharbanda and Stallworthy, 1987, op. cit., pp. 146–47.

16. See Kharbanda and Stallworthy, 1987, op. cit., pp. 115–27; B.O. Reilly, 'Is Perot good for General Motors?' *Fortune*, Vol. 110, No. 6, August 1984, pp. 84–85; G.G. Burck, 'Will success spoil General Motors?' *Fortune*, Vol. 108, August 1983, p. 94.

17. See David Chambers, 1988, op. cit.

18. See Sushila Ravindranath, 'Standard Motors in high gear', *Business India*, 1–14 August 1983, pp. 64–65, 67, 69, and 70–71.

19. See *Business Week*, 'Toyo Kogyo: A sure loser stages a turnaround', 25 January 1982, pp. 74–76.

20. See Kharbanda and Stallworthy, 1987, op. cit., pp. 214–29.

21. See *Business Week*, 'Celanese: Weaving a new pattern to survive a cyclical economy', 15 August 1983, p. 62.
22. See K.G. Kumar, 'The matter of FACT', *Business India*, 3–16 June, 1985, pp. 114, 115, 117, 119 and 120.
23. See *Business Week*, 'Behind the stunning comeback at Britain's ICI', 3 June 1985, pp. 48–49; Rebecca Nelson, 'ICI', pp. 83–91, in Rebecca Nelson and David Clutterback (eds), *Turnaround: How twenty well-known companies came back from the brink* (London: W.H. Allen, 1988).
24. See *Business Week*, 'Searle: Rallying a drug company with an injection of new vitality', 8 February 1982, pp. 50 and 52.
25. See Sushila Ravindranath, 'SPIC bounces back', *Business India*, 23 April–5 May 1985, pp. 110, 111, 113, 115, 117, 119 and 120.
26. See Pradip N. Khandwalla, 1989, op. cit.
27. See David Mansfield, 'How Ferranti fought back', *Management Today*, January 1980, pp. 66–70 and 128; Stuart Slatter, 1984, op. cit., pp. 354–66.
28. See D.C.L. Marwood, 'ICL: Crisis and swift recovery', *Long Range Planning*, Vol. 18, No. 2, 1985, pp. 10–21. Also see Simon Caulkin, 'ICL's Lazarus act', *Management Today*, January 1987, pp. 56–63; and Kharbanda and Stallworthy, 1987, op. cit., pp. 158–65.
29. See Marisa Bellisario, 1985, op. cit.
30. See *Business Week*, 'Three computer makers and chapter 11: Trying to write a happy ending', 4 March 1985, pp. 60–61.
31. See Stuart Slatter, 1984, op. cit., pp. 288–95.
32. See *Business Week*, 'Why the doctor's son is getting Wang back on its feet', 25 January 1988, pp. 67–68.
33. See Palakunnithu G. Mathai, 'Parry: Overhaul', *India Today*, 15 June 1987, pp. 116–17.
34. See *Business Week*, 'Mike Dingman tunes'em up, and turns'em around, spins'em off', 5 October 1987, pp. 58–60 and 62.
35. See Dilip Thakore, 'How the world's largest public sector company has been turned around', *Business World*, 22 June–5 July 1987, pp. 34–47. See also K.K. Roy, 'Italy's non-oil public sector: Prodi (gious) turnaround', *Economic Times*, 19 June 1987, p. 5; Romano Prodi, 'Instituto per la Ricostruzione Industrial (IRI)', pp. 93–101, in Nelson and Clutterback. 1988, op. cit.
36. See *Business Week*, 'How Black and Decker got back in the black', July 1987, pp. 70–71.
37. See F.J. Aboderin, 'EPE Plywood situation', paper presented at the Roundtable on 'Public Enterprise Management: Strategies for Success', held at New Delhi, 6–11 March 1988, under the auspices of the Commonwealth Secretariat, London, and Indian Institute of Management, Ahmedabad.
38. See Pradip N. Khandwalla, 1989, op. cit.
39. See *Business Week*, 'Coming to life after warm weather wilted the big plans', 10 October 1983, p. 52.
40. See Geoffrey Foster, 'The remaking of Metal Box', *Management Today*, January 1985, pp. 13–21.
41. See Anita van de Vliet, 'Why Rockware was recycled', *Management Today*, September 1985, pp. 62–69.

42. See Subrata Roy, 'Tinplate: The Tata stake', *Business India*, 11–24 April 1983, pp. 64–66 and 71.

43. See V. Krishnamurthy, 'Management of organizational change: The BHEL experience', *Vikalpa*, Vol. 2, No. 2, 1977, pp. 113–19; Ravi Ramamurti, 'National Machinery Corporation of India', a disguised case of BHEL (Boston: Northeastern University), undated.

44. See Pradip N. Khandwalla, 1989, op. cit.

45. See Sreekant Khandekar, 'JMEL: Dramatic turnaround', *India Today*, 15 December 1985, pp. 103–4. See also Surya Mookherjee, 'Industrial sickness and revival: A study of select organizations', paper presented at the 'National Seminar on Industrial Sickness in India', held at Gandhi Labour Institute, Ahmedabad, India, 3–4 June 1989.

46. See Anita van de Vliet, 'Where Lucas sees the light', *Management Today*, June 1986, pp. 38–45; Sir Godfrey Messervy, 'Lucas', pp. 195–202, in Nelson and Clutterback, 1988, op. cit.

47. See U.K. Roy, 'Mining and Allied Machinery Corporation–India'. Paper presented at the Roundtable on 'Public Enterprise Management: Strategies for Success', held at New Delhi, 6–11 March 1988, under the auspices of the Commonwealth Secretariat, London, and Indian Institute of Management, Ahmedabad.

48. See Stuart Slatter, 1984, op. cit., pp. 296–301.

49. See Stuart Slatter, 1984, op. cit., pp. 279–87.

50. See Pradip N. Khandwalla, 1989, op. cit.

51. See Stuart Slatter, 1984, op. cit., pp. 271–79.

52. See Ian MacGregor, 'Recovery at British Steel', *Journal of General Management*, Vol. 7, No. 3, 1982, pp. 5–16. See also David Chambers, 1988, op. cit. Also Kharbanda and Stallworthy, 1987, op. cit., pp. 62–69.

53. See. V. Krishnamurthy, 'SAIL blazes a new trail', *The Economic Times*, 19 November 1987. See also Subrata Roy, 'Spotlight on SAIL', *Business World*, 1–14 March 1986, pp. 43–51; 'SAIL rolling plan for 1989–90', *The Economic Times*, 29 December 1989, p. 1; 'Steel price hike unlikely', *The Economic Times*, 1 March 1989, p. 1; T.N. Ninan, 'SAIL: Dramatic turnaround', *India Today*, 30 April 1986, pp. 106–7; 'SAIL to enter chemicals', *The Economic Times*, 2 April 1987, p. 1; Subrata Roy, 'SAIL: Will it succeed?' *Business India*, 10–23 August, 1987, pp. 42–52.

54. See *Businees Week*, 'Big Steel is humming again', 8 August 1988, pp. 50–51; O.P. Kharbanda and E.A. Stallworthy, 1987, op. cit., pp. 55–61.

55. See Nicholas Newman, 'Dawson's well-knit whoosh', *Management Today*, March 1981, pp. 74–82, 165 and 168.

56. See Debra Isaac, 'ICI's new yarn', *Management Today*, February 1984, pp. 66–73

57. See *Business Week*, 'Munsingwear: Stitching together a comeback', 28 May 1984, p. 60.

58. See *Business Week*, 'Warnaco: Prospering by slimming and donning big name labels', 18 October 1982, p. 64.

59. See Robert W. Sexty, 1982, op. cit.

60. See Ravi Ramamurti, 1981, op. cit.

61. See Stuart Slatter, 1984, op. cit., pp. 302–12.
62. See Kabbe M.A. Jallow, 'The Gambia Produce Marketing Board—A case study', paper presented at the Roundtable on 'Public Enterprise Management: Strategies for Success', New Delhi, 6–11 March 1988, held under the auspices of the Commonwealth Secretariat, London, and Indian Institute of Management, Ahmedabad.
63. See *Business Week*, 'The No. 1 Yankee trader gets its ship back on course', 25 March 1985, pp. 60–61.
64. See *Business Week*, 'Wickes: Creditors question Sanford Sigoloff's crash cure', 21 November 1983, pp. 58–59.
65. See *Business Week*, 'Why Frank Borman finally has something to smile about', 29 April 1985, pp. 52–53.
66. See Vasuki and S. Tripathi, 'Air-India: Out of the woods', *India Today*, 30 June 1989, pp. 114–16; S. Narayan, 'Air India takes wing', *Business World*, 21 June–4 July 1989, pp. 42–43.
67. See Dudley Sackaloo, 'Case study on Jamaica Railway Corporation', presented at the First Pan Commonwealth Roundtable on 'Public Enterprise Management: Strategies for Success', held at Nicosia, Cyprus, 1–5 June 1987.
68. See Emanuel Hachipunka, 'Zambia Railways Limited', paper presented at the Roundtable on 'Public Enterprise Management: Strategies for Success', New Delhi, 6–11 March 1988, held under the auspices of the Commonwealth Secretariat, London, and Indian Institute of Management, Ahmedabad.
69. See K.G. Kumar, 'Apollo Tyres Ltd: No more skidding', *Business India*, 18–26 June 1988, pp. 61, 63, 67; and Pradip N. Khandwalla, 1989, op. cit., pp. 231–44.
70. See *Business Week*, 'Survival in the basic industries: A shrunken Firestone picks its turf in tires', 25 April 1982, pp. 46–50 and 52.
71. See *Business Week*, 'Del E. Webb: Back from the brink and ready to grow', 9 June 1984, p. 87.
72. See *Business Week*, 'Macmillan: Back to the schoolhouse to sustain a text book turnaround', 28 November 1983, pp. 67–68.
73. See Geoffrey Colwin, 'Freddie Silverman's secret success', *Fortune*, 14 July 1980, pp. 123–24.
74. See *Business Week*, 'Pullman's not a sleeper anymore', 22 July 1985, pp. 70–71.
75. For a review of technological innovation, see D. Hurley (ed.), *The management of technological change* (London: The Commonwealth Secretariat, 1987). For a survey of managerial creativity, see John R. Kimberly, 'Managerial innovation', p. 84 in Paul C. Nystrom and William H. Starbuck (eds.), *Handbook of organizational design*, Vol. 1 (London: Oxford University Press, 1981).
76. See Daniel Katz and Robert L. Kahn, *The social psychology of organizations* (New York: Wiley, 1966); Fremont E. Kast and James E. Rosenzweig, 'General systems theory: Applications for organization and management', *Academy of Management Journal*, December 1972, pp. 447–65
77. See Kalman J. Cohen and Richard M. Cyert, 'Simulation of organisational behaviour', pp. 305–34, in James G. March (ed.), *Handbook of organisations* (Chicago: Rand McNally, 1965); F. Smart, W.A. Thompson, I. Vertinsky, 'Diagnosing corporate effectiveness and susceptibility to crises', pp. 57–96, in C.F. Smart, and W.T. Stanbury, *Studies on crisis management* (Toronto: Institute for Research on Public Policy, 1978).

78. See Alfred D. Chandler, Jr., *Strategy and structure* (New York: Doubleday, 1966); Danny Miller and Peter H. Friesen, *Organizations: A quantum view* (Englewood Cliffs, N.J.: Prentice-Hall, 1984).
79. See V. Padaki and V. Shanbhag (eds.), *Industrial sickness: The challenge in Indian textiles* (Ahmedabad: ATIRA, 1984); S.S. Mehta, *Sick industries syndrome in India: An alternative* (Ahmedabad: Gandhi Labour Institute, 1989).
80. See Richard Hemming and Ali M. Mansoor, *Privatization and public enterprises* (Washington, D.C: IMF, 1988); T.L. Sankar and Y. Venugopal Reddy (eds.), *Privatization: Diversification of ownership of public enterprises* (Hyderabad: Booklinks Corp., 1989).
81. See Harold Koontz and C. O'Donnel, *Principles of management* (New York: Knopf, 1959). For an insightful critique of the principles of management position see Joan Woodward, *Technology and organization* (London: Her Majesty's Printery, 1958) and Herbert Simon, *Administrative behavior* (New York: Macmillan, 1960).
82. See Rensis Likert, *New patterns of management* (New York: McGraw-Hill, 1961) and *The human organization* (New York: McGraw-Hill, 1967).
83. See for example Aaron Lowin and James Craig, 'The influence of level of performance on managerial style: An experimental object lesson', *Organizational Behavior and Human Performance*, Vol. 3, 1968, pp. 440–58.
84. See Paul Lawrence and Jay Lorsch, *Organization and its environment* (Cambridge, Mass.: Harvard University Press, 1967); Pradip N. Khandwalla 'Viable and effective organizational designs of firms', *Academy of Management Journal*, Vol. 16, No. 3, 1973, pp. 481–95; Johannes M. Pennings, 'The relevance of the structural-contingency model for organizational effectiveness', *Administrative Science Quarterly*, Vol. 20, 1975, pp. 393–410; John Child, 'Organizational design and performance: Contingency theory and beyond', *Organization and Administrative Sciences*, Vol. 8, 1977, pp. 169–83; Pradip N. Khandwalla, 'Some top management styles, their context and performance', *Organization and Administrative Sciences*, Winter 1976/77, Vol. 7, pp. 21–51.
85. See Pradip N. Khandwalla, *The design of organizations*, chapters 11, 15 (New York: Harcourt Brace Jovanovich, 1977); B.L. Maheshwari, *Decisional styles and organizational effectiveness* (New Delhi: Vikas, 1980); William G. Ouichi, *Theory Z: How American business can meet the Japanese challenge* (Reading, Mass.: Addison-Wesley, 1981); Tom Peters and Robert H. Waterman, *In search of excellence: Lessons from America's best run companies* (New York: Harper, 1982); Pradip N. Khandwalla, 'Pioneering innovative management: An Indian excellence', *Organization Studies*, Vol. 6, No. 2, 1985, pp. 161–83.
86. See Richard M. Cyert and James G. March, *A behavioral theory of the firm* (Englewood Cliffs, N.J.: Prentice-Hall, 1963).
87. See Michael T. Hannan and John H. Freeman, 'The population ecology of organizations', *American Journal of Sociology*, Vol. 82, 1977, pp. 929–64.

2. METHOD BEHIND THE MAGIC

Magic is no miracle. Much hard work and skill underlie its tricks. This is also true of turnarounds. Just as there is method to magic so is there method to turnaround.

A number of turnaround researchers have sought to identify the essential elements of turnarounds. There have been basically two approaches to this. One set of researchers have looked at cases of turnarounds. They have enquired into the sorts of management actions that lift a company up from the morass of a decline. These range widely, such as pricing changes, imposition of management controls, sales campaigns, lay-offs of surplus staff, attempts at communicating with stakeholders and roping them into the turn-around effort, fixing accountability for performance, replacing incompetent or corrupt managers, adding profitable products and dropping loss-making ones, modernising plants, and so on. This approach provides rich insight into what management actually does, why, and how. The other approach looks at secondary data available on a large number of organisations, and tries to classify the data under various heads. The emphasis is on identifying and measuring quantifiable variables, such as change in the volume of advertising expense, in corporate sales coming from new products, in the volume of R and D expenditure, in new capital expenditure, the size of manpower laid off, and so forth. This approach un-covers alternative turnaround strategies. Although it is less rich than the case study approach in describing and explaining stra-tegies and how they are implemented, its inferences are based on 'objective' data. It is especially useful for conducting reliable tests of hypotheses and for testing quantitative models.

Both of these approaches have enlarged our understanding of the sorts of actions that need to be looked at to understand better the magic of turnarounds. Table 2.1 lists several studies of both types. For instance, a study by Schendel and Patton looked at

Table 2.1

Classes of Turnaround Actions in Various Studies

Schendel, Patton, Riggs[1] (1976; secondary data)	Organisation and management changes (general management changes, decentralisation and profit responsibility, change in orientation of managers, say towards marketing); marketing programme changes (new products, R and D, price changes, production changes); major plant expenditure (new plant construction, expansion of existing plant, modernisation, acquisition of new capacity); product diversification (acquisition, internal development); geographical diversification (foreign, domestic); efficiency increases (cost-cutting, new budgeting and cost-control systems, new plant and equipment, capital expenditure cutbacks); divestiture (of divisions or product-lines, plants, inventory, mines); vertical integration.
Schendel and Patton[2] (1976; secondary data)	Percentage changes in sales, invested capital, invested capital-to-sales ratio, equipment-to-sales ratio, plant and equipment age, sales per employee, ratio of cost of goods to sales, cash-flow, working capital, inventory turnover, value-added etc.
Hofer[3] (1980; case studies)	Asset-reduction, revenue-increasing, cost-cutting, change in market-share, change in key functional area emphasis (e.g. from production to marketing), change in top management, change in business.
Khandwalla[4] (1981; case studies) (1989; case studies)	Induction of change agent(s) at the top; credibility-building by the change agent(s); mobilisation of the organisation; quick pay-off actions; reprieve from external pressures; opportunistic harnessing of external environment; strengthening of mechanisms for influencing external environment; selective changes in the product-mix; selective professionalisation of management functions; motivational strategy; co-ordination strategy; performance control strategy; management style.
Hegde[5] (1982; case studies)	Structural changes; divestiture and/or diversification; technological changes (R and D); personnel policy; marketing and operations; costs/finance.
Bibeault[6] (1982; case studies)	Improving management processes (tight controls, changing attitudes, understanding the business better, absolute control to management, viable leadership, strong financial executive, more active board); having a viable core business (back to the basic core, sound strategies); financing; improving motivation (positive thinking, dealing with uncertainty).

Table 2.1 (contd.)

Hambrick and Schecter[7] (1983; secondary data)	New products, R and D, marketing, product quality, price, market-share, productivity, direct costs, receivables, inventories, new plant and equipment, capacity utilisation.
Slatter[8] (1984; case studies)	Asset reduction, change of management, financial control, cost reduction, debt restructuring/financial, improved marketing, organisational changes, product-market changes, growth *via* acquisition, investment.
O'Neill[9] (1986; case studies)	Change in management, business redefinition, policy changes, growth strategies, restructuring, planning.
O'Neill[10] (1986; secondary data)	Banking surrogates for pricing, receivables, inventories, capacity utilisation, employee productivity, relative direct costs, product quality etc.
Potts and Behr[11] (1987; case studies)	Change anticipation, exploitation of corporate strengths, management of technological change, search for alliances partnership with labour, calculated risk-taking, visioning, balancing of the immediate and the distant future etc.
Kharbanda and Stallworthy[12] (1987; case studies)	Diagnosing, doctoring, leadership, people-management, decentralisation, coping with change, planning etc.
Mukherji[13] (1989; case studies)	Diagnosing, problem-solving and troubleshooting, organisational design, short-term actions, credibility-building, organisation development, culture-management, management of change etc.

available secondary data on a sample of 36 US corporations that had turned around and a matched sample of 36 corporations that had not.[14] A later study by Hambrick and Schecter looked at 260 US 'mature' businesses that had, during a four-year period, a return on investment (ROI) during the first two years below 10 per cent.[15] Of these 53 were considered to have turned around because their ROI in the third and fourth years averaged 20 per cent. The two studies identified such quantifiable variables as: percentage changes in sales, invested capital, and age of equipment; percentage sales through new products; R and D expenditure as a percentage of sales; monetary value of new plant construction, modernisation, and related factors; foreign versus domestic sales; cutbacks in capital expenditures; amount of divestiture; changes in the ratio of marketing expense to sales; market-share changes; changes in percentage of direct to total costs; changes in the percentages of receivables and inventories to sales; changes in capacity utilisation, and so on.

While case writers may not necessarily ignore quantifiable data, they tend to notice qualitative data far more. For instance, Khandwalla noted the initial credibility-building actions of management in several Indian turnarounds, the management's attempts at mobilising the organisation for turnaround, its attempts at roping in stakeholders for the turnaround effort, the management's motivational and coordination strategies, and so on.[16] Similarly, Bibeault, in his study of 81 American cases, focussed on improvements brought about by new managements in various management processes such as control, leadership, Board supervision, and in gaining an understanding of the corporation's business.[17] Potts and Behr, in their study of a number of American turnarounds, pointed to change-anticipation and management, alliance-making and leadership, as keys, among others, to turnaround,[18] and Kharbanda and Stallworthy, in their study of a number of turnarounds from around the world, emphasised the importance of diagnosing and doctoring, leadership, coping with change and people-management.[19]

This book is a treasure hunt rather than a trial; that is, it is an exploration of the mysteries of turnaround management rather than a report of rigorously tested hypotheses. The case survey method has been adopted to probe the architecture and dynamics of various kinds of turnaround.[20] Accordingly, categories of turnaround management actions were sought to be identified that could unravel turnaround mysteries from case studies data.

Since turnaround management is a sub-species of management, the initial categories were strategic management actions (diversification, expansion, vertical integration) and operational and functional management actions (marketing, production, finance, control, personnel, R and D, and related actions).

A scan of the turnaround studies, especially the ones that dealt with turnaround cases, led to the identification of categories of specific turnaround management actions, such as personnel changes,[21] cost-cutting,[22] initial control,[23] initial diagnosis and troubleshooting,[24] organisational mobilisation,[25] stakeholder management[26] (that is, management of both external and internal stakeholders), asset-reduction,[27] among others. Thereafter, a content-analysis of a dozen of the more elaborately written cases for identifying any additional categories that could be useful in analysing turnarounds, led, ultimately, to the inductively assembled 27 variables listed in Table 2.2; these seem reasonably useful for analysing turnaround actions reported in cases. The net was cast wide enough to capture all the significant facts of all the cases but not so wide as to generate an unmanageable number of elements. The process of assembling categories of turnaround elements was inevitably an intuitive, trial-and-error process, given the relative nascence of turnaround as an area of research. But it was not a random or arbitrary process. A sort of tree of categories was built up by successively resorting to management concepts, studies based on turnaround cases, and finally, a content-analysis of a dozen cases included in this study.

Thereafter, each case was analysed in terms of the elements listed in Table 2.2 so as to summarise its actions. For the purpose of analysis, turnaround action was generally assumed to begin with the first acts of a new top management following a loss situation, and assumed to end when the company had broken even or reached normal profitability, following the break-even, in the case of complete turnarounds. Many of the ratios suggested by the secondary data using researchers could not be used because of incomplete quantitative information given in the cases.

Table 2.2

Elements for Analysing Turnaround Cases

A. Personnel Changes
1. *Change in top management* at the level of chairman, president, managing director, CEO.
2. *Fresh induction of managers, technical staff etc.*

B. Diagnosing and Troubleshooting
3. *Formal diagnostic activities* (for example, carrying out organisational surveys, getting outside consultants to diagnose problems, management retreats to diagnose corporate problems etc.).
4. *Initiation of managerial meetings* (problem-solving task-forces for trouble-shooting etc.).

C. Stakeholder or People-Management
5. *Credibility-building actions of management* (for example, the management of a public enterprise getting the government to accept sharp increases in managerial remuneration, the owner-family bringing in new equity in a large loss-making company, major public relations campaigns etc.).

Table 2.2 (contd.)

---

6. *Garnering stakeholders support* (actions to secure the support of major stakeholders like the government, financial institutions, unions, customers etc., as for example, by being helpful to them, by inviting them to participate in formulating the turnaround strategy or in financing the turnaround etc.).

7. *Increased training of managers and staff* (attempts to increase productivity, quality, efficiency etc. through training of managers, staff, workers etc.).

8. *Public articulation by management of mission, goals etc.* of the organisation (for example, by formulating and disseminating priorities for action, future strategy etc.).

9. *Management communicating with staff, lower level managers etc.* (for example, by communicating corporate issues, problems, successes etc. through meetings, workshops, newsletters, video shows etc.).

10. *Incentives, motivating, grievance redressal* (motivating through incentives to managers and/or workers: attempts at motivating them through increases in perquisites and emoluments, greater autonomy, greater job challenge, etc.; better handling of staff grievances).

11. *Example setting by top managers* (setting of personal example by top executive, as by taking to the road to sell, showing extraordinary integrity, self-discipline etc.).

12. *Disciplining* (by firing or by punishing incompetent or corrupt managers or staff, getting tough with unions etc.).

13. *Better organisational integration, participative management, emphasis on core values* (more integrated functioning, by resorting to participative decision-making, seeking better collaboration between managers, seeking better relations with staff, involvement of workers or their representatives in decision-making, team-building, attempts at building a new culture by emphasising core values etc.).

D. Operations Management

14. *Significant retrenchment* (actions to reduce costs through large-scale retrenchment and/or facilities closures, that is, closure of plants, branches etc., resulting in the lay-off of at least 10 per cent of the staff of an organisation or its sub-unit).

15. *Cost reduction measures other than retrenchment* (other reductions in costs such as, by slashing advertising, moving to cheaper quarters, negotiating lower interest rates etc.).

16. *Plant modernisation etc. for greater efficiency, quality, productivity* (actions to increase productivity, efficiency, work quality, capacity utilisation etc. by modernising the plant, automation, retooling, plant reorganisation or redesign, repairs to plant etc.).

17. *Attempts to increase efficiency, quality, productivity other than through plant modernisation etc. and training* (such as, through in-house campaigns, change of production chief etc.).

18. *Marketing related actions,* actions that increase sales (for example, price increases, advertising campaigns, product promotion, increase in sales outlets etc.).

E. Management Systems and Structure

19. *Management control enhancing actions* (actions to increase the control of

Table 2.2 (Contd.)

management over operations such as, installation or strengthening of budgetary and financial controls, management information systems, computerisation, cash-control, inventory-control etc.).

20. *Professionalisation of manufacturing management, personnel management, planning etc.* (for example, a better system of production planning and scheduling, corporate planning, career and manpower planning etc.).

21. *Restructuring decentralisation, fixing accountability, structural changes etc.* (divisionalising, setting up of profit centres, delegation of authority, establishing clearer accountability for performance etc.).

F. Financial Management

22. *Liquidation of current assets and liabilities* like debtors and stocks, reduction or liquidation of current liabilities by paying off suppliers, advances etc.

23. *Borrowings, raising equity finance etc.* (raising of long-term funds through borrowings, securing of deposits, raising of equity finance etc.).

G. Strategic Management

24. *Diversification, product-line rationalisation, expansion etc.* (dropping poorly performing products, adding profitable products, diversification, vertical integration, expansion etc.).

25. *Divestiture and liquidation of fixed assets and long-term liabilities* (for example, through sale of plants, divisions etc. and by paying off long-term loans etc.).

26. *Innovation, new product development etc.* (technological change, step up in R and D, better absorption of imported technology, technological joint ventures, attempts at indigenisation, that is, at import substitution, development of new products etc.).

H. Miscellaneous

27. *Miscellaneous* – residual management actions such as write-off of assets, prevention of take-overs, neutralising political or other opposition, protecting managers etc.

The Procedure for Analysing Cases

Each case was independently analysed by two persons. Each person allocated management *actions* specified in the case to the 27 elements of turnaround. Vague statements in the case, not backed by any details, such as 'The new chief improved morale', were ignored, as also opinions expressed by the case writer, such as 'He did a great job'. Also only actions initiated during the turnaround were coded, not those that were merely a continuation of past action, or those that were statutorily taken. In short, only actions were scored, and only those actions were scored that were voluntarily initiated du,ing the turnaround. After the scoring, an attempt was made to assess the degree of agreement between the two scorers. This turned out to be reasonably good, averaging over 80 per cent per case. Disagreements were resolved by re-reading the facts, sharpening definitions, and so on. For the few ambiguous items where disagreement could not be resolved, the author used his best judgement after close textual reading.

Next, an attempt was made to assess the overall architecture of turnarounds. For this purpose a score of 1 was given to a turnaround element if the management had taken action that could be subsumed under that element. If no such action was reported in the case, the element received a score of 0. Since the interest was in identifying the categories of turnaround action resorted to, rather than with the specifics of the action, even if several actions could be allocated to a turnaround element, the latter received a score of only 1. Thus, a binary data structure of 0s and 1s was created for each case, in which a 0 indicated that the case did not report any management actions pertinent to the relevant turnaround element, while a 1 indicated that the case facts as reported indicated one or more actions pertinent to that element.

An alternative way of scoring that was considered and rejected was to score not only whether a turnaround element was present or absent in a case, but also how much of it was present[28] and of what quality. The cases varied greatly in the detail in which actions were described. Indeed, within each case too, there was enormous variation in the detail in which different actions were described. It was felt that too much subjectivity would be injected into judging 'how much' and 'how good or bad', and since this was only a preliminary, exploratory study of turnaround architectures, it was decided to stick to the determination of simply whether a turnaround element was present or absent. Despite this limitation however, as we shall see later, the data analysis yielded a fascinating haul of turnaround designs.

The analysis of a specific case may clarify the procedure further. Warnaco, a large American producer of apparel, with sales of around $450 million, lost $23 million in 1976 but earned $7 million in 1977.[29] By 1981 it was earning $21 million on sales of $479 million. Vigorous attempts were made by its president, Mr. James C. Walker, between 1977 and 1979 to turnaround the company. Since the case reports no change in top management in the 1976–79 period, the score for element 1 in Table 2.2 for Warnaco was 0. However, several elements did get scores of 1. Since the management shifted the annual budget planning deadline to enable better cost projections and therefore more flexibility in pricing, an action aimed at better management control of costs and pricing, item 19 in Table 2.2, got a score of 1. Item 14 (retrenchment) got a score of 1 because the management reduced headquarters staff by half and cut back one of its import units by 75 per cent. It scored 1 in item 16 (plant modernisation and related actions) because Warnaco heavily invested in automating its cutting machines. It also scored 1 in item 18 (marketing related actions) because of its large investment in distribution centres. It earned 1 in item 24 (product-line rationalisation, diversification, expansion) by virtue of several actions: expansion of strong existing brands, an attempt at getting to the top end of the business, dropping inappropriate products, a company producing quality men's wear was bought for $20 million, and a product-line in knitwear, Pringle of Scotland, was added. Warnaco also scored 1 for item 25 (divestiture, liquidation of fixed assets and long-term liabilities) because it sold off several low-profit product-lines worth $200 million in annual sales, and 1 for item 21 (restructuring) because the management gave greater operating autonomy and responsibility to divisions it retained. Warnaco scored 0 for the rest of the turnaround elements.

This sort of a procedure summarises a mass of disparate information into easier-to-analyse strings of numbers. But it presupposes that the case history contains no serious errors of omission and commission. Serious errors of commission may be rare because litigation could result. Besides, they probably were rare for the cases because the sources, journals, business magazines and other publications, carried no corrections or corrective comments from the respective managements. However, serious acts of omission may be more frequent, especially in the cases written by journalists, who do not write cases with scholarly objectivity. They may highlight what they think is interesting copy material and fail to mention what they think may not be of much interest to readers. Besides, the run-of-the-mill journalists get their information from a few persons at the top, who in turn may not be very aware of many 'trivial' actions being taken in the innards of a large organisation. I recall vividly a turnaround case in which the chief executive said that the company had fallen sick because of lack of finance and when this finance was arranged the company regained in health. However, when I probed executives in various functional areas two, three, or even four levels below the chief executive, a vastly richer picture emerged—of actions related to cost control, marketing, production planning, training and so forth—that had materially contributed to the turnaround. These comments are simply made to alert the reader to the potential deficiencies of some of the analysed case data.[30]

Precautions were therefore taken. Only those cases were selected in which turnaround actions were reported in some detail. Wherever possible, multiple sources were consulted to piece together the full turnaround story. Only those business magazines or periodicals were scanned for cases, such as Fortune, Business Week, Management Today, Business India, and Business World, that were known to have reasonably high journalistic standards. Only actions were scored and the inferences and judgements of the case writer were ignored.

A troublesome problem in cross-cultural case-based research (of the kind attempted in this book) is of inter-writer and inter-cultural biases. What is considered important by the writer gets reported or highlighted, and what is not considered important tends to be downplayed or omitted.[31] All management writers, academic or journalistic, carry in their heads some model or the other of effective and ineffective management. If a writer believes in the rightness of 'Theory X' (say, 'tough management and drastic actions are needed to cure sickness'), he or she may over-emphasise the firing of executives, retrenchment of staff, closure or disposal of loss-making plants, tight controls, and so on. He or she may under-emphasise attempts at effective communications, at participative decisions, at exciting people with idealism or a vision of excellence, at delegating authority, actions that are compatible with a 'Theory Y' mind-set.[32] Writers, especially journalists in 'tough' cultures, such as that of the USA, may systematically accentuate 'Theory X' types of actions, and journalists in 'tender' cultures, such as that of India, may be predisposed to accentuate 'Theory Y' actions. Unfortunately, beyond those indicated earlier, no other precautions could be taken to mitigate this problem. However, it should be pointed out that well over half of the cases selected were published in either professional journals or books written by scholars, or were papers presented by scholars or participant observers at academic conferences, or were pieced together from multiple journalistic write-ups. The various possible biases were probably minimised by the 0–1 mode of scoring (even a 'Theory X'-minded writer may not fail to mention significant 'Theory Y' actions, although he or she may not emphasise them, and *vice versa* for a 'Theory Y'-minded writer), and by the scoring of only reported actions and ignoring the writer's inferences or interpretations. These biases were probably less troublesome for complete turnaround accounts than for break-even turnaround accounts because generally the former tended to be longer, more detailed accounts.

Given the various problems possible with case write-ups, especially acts of omission in reporting management actions, a culture-biased or convictions-biased tendency to over-emphasise certain types of actions and under-value or even ignore other types of actions and so forth, it would be safer to consider the conclusions of the book as tentative rather than definitive, that is, as hypotheses that need further consideration, refinement, and testing.

Validity of Turnaround Elements

In research dealing with organisational effectiveness, one generally begins with an assemblage of variables that prior research or theory or one's intuition suggests may be relevant to organisational effectiveness. But there is always the nagging doubt whether the variables chosen do, in fact, matter.

How do we know that the selected 27 turnaround elements do indeed contribute to turnaround? There are ways of assessing the contribution of these elements to turnaround. The first is to compare the scores (on these elements) of a group of successfully turned around companies with (ideally) a matching sample of sick companies that failed to turn around. If the scores of the successful group substantially exceed the scores of the failed group, then one can reasonably surmise that the chosen turnaround elements do in fact contribute to turnaround. Such a sample of failed turnarounds was not available for the study reported in this book but an attempt was made in some other studies to make this sort of a comparison.

For example, Stuart Slatter compared a sample of 30 successful British turnarounds with a sample of 10 unsuccessful British turnarounds on 10 turnaround elements.[33] 'Asset reduction', 'debt financial/restructuring', 'organisational changes', and 'change in management' were substantially more frequently resorted to by the successful turnarounds while 'cost reduction' was more frequently resorted to by the failed recovery cases. There was no difference in 'improved marketing' and not much of a difference in 'financial control', 'product market changes', 'growth *via* acquisition', and 'investment'. However, except in the case of 'cost reduction' (and 'improved marketing' where there was a tie), on all other eight types of turnaround actions the successful cases had higher percentages. In Khandwalla's study of ten Indian turnarounds in broadly the same industry, five were relatively successful turnarounds and five relatively less successful. Barring one case of a tie, in all other nine cases of turnaround action the more successful cases had higher scores, most notably in the case of 'initial control', 'revenue generation', 'quick pay-off projects etc.', 'quick cost reduction', 'organisational mobilisation', and 'internal co-ordination'.[34] Since the Slatter and Khandwalla turnaround elements are heavily represented in the 27 turnaround elements (albeit under somewhat different labels), there is some buttressing of the usefulness of the system of turnaround elements employed in this volume to study turnarounds.

A second way of assessing the validity of a group of explanatory variables is to correlate them with a 'criterion' or performance variable. This was possible in the present study. Although all the turnarounds were 'successful', they varied greatly in the rate of recovery. The criterion variable was the rate at which the profitability of a sick company went up as the turnaround progressed. This rate was estimated by subtracting the maximum loss (as a percentage of sales) from the profit (as a percentage of sales) during the year after the one in which the company broke even, and dividing this by the interval. As an example, if a company lost five per cent on sales in 1982, broken even in 1984, and earned four per cent on sales in 1985, the gain in profitability would be four per cent on sales—(−five percent on sales)= nine per cent on sales, and the rate of gain would be nine per cent on sales divided by three years (1985–1982), that is, three per cent on sales a year. In all but two of the 42 cases of complete turnaround enough information was available to estimate the rate of increase in profitability. Earnings-to-sales ratio was employed because information on other bases such as equity or capital employed was much less frequently available.

The measure of the rate of increase in profitability was correlated with the company's total turnaround actions score. The latter was derived simply by counting the number of turnaround elements utilised by the company (the scoring of turnaround elements has been explained earlier). The correlation was 0.44, significant at a 99 per cent confidence level. Thus, the 27 turnaround elements as a *system* of variables did seem to predict improvement in profitability. In other words, the more of these elements that were utilised by a company, the higher was the rate at which profitability increased. This finding was consistent with the results of Khandwalla's study of the five successful and five much less successful Indian turnarounds referred to earlier, where also the successful turnarounds utilised more of these elements than the less successful ones. Each of the 27 elements was also correlated with the measure of rate of profitability improvement. All but four correlations were positive, and ten equalled or exceeded 0.3, the level at which a correlation between normally distributed variables would be significant. Table 2.3 shows the results.

Table 2.3

Correlations of Turnaround Elements
with Rate of Improvement in Profitability

Sample : 40 Complete Turnarounds

1.	Attempts to increase efficiency, quality, productivity other than through plant modernisation etc. and training	.49
2.	Garnering stakeholders' support	.45
3.	Formal diagnostic activities	.42
4.	Professionalisation of manufacturing management, personnel management, planning etc.	.42
5.	Incentives, motivation, grievance-redressal	.39
6.	Better organisational integration, participative management, emphasis on core values	.38
7.	Significant retrenchment	−.36
8.	Diversification, product-line rationalisation, expansion etc.	−.33

Table 2.3 (Contd.)

9.	Initiation of managerial meetings, problem-solving task forces	.32
10.	Management control-enhancing actions	.30
11.	Borrowings, raising equity finance etc.	.28
12.	Public articulation by management of corporate mission, goals etc.	.23
13.	Credibility-building actions of management	.22
14.	Marketing related actions	.21
15.	Divestiture and liquidation of fixed assets and long-term liabilities	−.19
16.	Fresh induction of managers, technical staff etc.	.17
17.	Plant modernisation etc. for greater efficiency, quality, productivity	.16
18.	Increased training of managers and staff	.15
19.	Miscellaneous actions	.14
20.	Example-setting by top managers	.11
21.	Innovation, new product development etc.	−.11
22.	Changes in top management	.11
23.	Management communicating with staff, lower managers etc.	.11
24.	Restructuring (decentralisation, fixing accountability, structural changes etc.)	.03
25.	Liquidation of current assets and liabilities	.01
26.	Cost-reduction actions other than retrenchment	.00
27.	Disciplining	.00

A sizeable positive correlation between a turnaround element and rate of improvement in profitability means that the turnaround element is an accelerator of recovery. A small correlation does not mean that the turnaround element is unimportant to the turnaround; simply that it does not increase the speed of recovery. A negative correlation means that the element is a decelerator of recovery, so that its absence is an accelerator. It is interesting to note, and also surprising, that retrenchment, diversification, and to a lesser extent divestiture and technological innovation, can turn out to be decelerators, not accelerators. On the whole the *system* of 27 turnaround elements seems to be relevant to a study of turnaround management, although its constituents may not be equally relevant.

The Architecture of Successful Turnaround

To examine the architecture of a full turnaround from disaster to normalcy, Table 2.4 shows the scores for each of the 27 turnaround elements for the sample of 42 complete turnarounds (23 break-even turnarounds were excluded because post-break-even actions taken to restore normal profitability in their case were not generally reported). For each element the Table shows the percentage of cases that reported action under that element. For example, all the 42 cases reported actions related to diversification, product-line rationalisation, expansion and such related activity, while 21 per cent or just about one in five reported actions that could be subsumed under example-setting by top managers.

Table 2.4

Percentages of Cases Engaging in Different Turnaround Actions

Sample: 42 Complete Turnarounds

	Percentage Engaging in Action
1. Diversification, product-line rationalisation, expansion etc.	100
2. Change in top management	93
3. Marketing related actions	81
4. Restructuring (decentralisation, fixing accountability, structural changes etc.)	69
5. Cost-reduction measures other than retrenchment	64
6. Plant modernisation etc. for greater efficiency, quality, productivity	60
7. Management control-enhancing actions	57
8. Innovation, new product development etc.	57
9. Significant retrenchment	52
10. Divestiture and liquidation of fixed assets and long-term liabilities	45
11. Garnering stakeholders' support	45
12. Incentives, motivation, grievance redressal	45
13. Better organisational integration, participative management, emphasis on core values	45
14. Disciplining	43
15. Borrowing, raising equity finance etc.	40
16. Formal diagnostic activities	40
17. Fresh induction of managers, technical staff etc.	38
18. Management communicating with staff, lower managers etc.	38
19. Attempts to increase efficiency, quality, productivity other than through plant modernisation etc. and training	35
20. Public articulation by management of mission, goals etc.	33

Table 2.4 (Contd.)

21.	Professionalisation of manufacturing management, personnel management, planning etc.	29
22.	Credibility-building actions of management	28
23.	Liquidation of current assets and liabilities	26
24.	Initiation of managerial meetings, problem-solving task forces	26
25.	Increased training of managers and staff	26
26.	Example-setting by top managers	21
27.	Miscellaneous	14

Table 2.4 indicates three classes of actions. The first consists of actions that may be necessary for most successful turnarounds, such as diversification, product-line rationalisation and such related activity, changes in top management, marketing related actions, restructuring, cost reduction measures other than retrenchment, plant modernisation, and similar measures. There surely is a great variety of actions available within each of these six turnaround elements, but it would appear that a management trying to turn around a corporation must try to shuffle its products around, bring in fresh blood at the top, try and strengthen the marketing of its products or services, pay attention to cost reduction measures, decentralise with enhanced accountability, and improve operations through modernisation, and so on.

The second group consists of elements with scores in their forties and fifties. It is not necessary that actions that can be subsumed under these elements be taken; however, it may often be expedient to do so. Much would depend on the particular context of the corporation and the orientation of top management as to whether these elements are activated. That is, operating conditions and management ideology may determine whether these elements will be part of the corporation's turnaround strategy or not. These elements range from management control enhancing actions, innovation, and retrenchment, to divestiture, networking with stakeholders for support, attempts to motivate staff, participative management, disciplining, diagnostic efforts, and raising capital.

The third group consists of turnaround elements that are apparently infrequently used. It is also possible, of course, that errors of omission by case writers may be more serious *vis a vis* these elements than the others. These range across management communications, the public articulation of corporate mission and goals by management, and credibility-building action by management, to increased professionalisation of management systems, increased training, example-setting by top managers, and such like. The infrequency of their use need not mean low usefulness. These rarely used elements, compatible with 'transformational leadership', management professionalism, and a human resource development emphasis,[35] may be precisely the ones that could be sources of major innovations in turnaround management.

Relationships between Turnaround Elements

To get an overall map of the management of turnaround it is useful to know the pecking order of the various turnaround elements. It is also useful to comprehend how these elements are related to one another. That is, we need to know what happens to other elements when one of these is activated. There are several ways in which this sort of information is useful. For one thing, it prompts us to probe the causal relationships between the elements. This can secure for us a better understanding of the dynamics of turnarounds. It also helps us anticipate the consequences of taking specific turnaround actions in live situations and therefore helps us choose our actions more wisely. It can also lead to new techniques for turnarounds, new approaches to turnarounds, that is, to improved ways of turning around organisations.

In order to get some idea of how turnaround elements are related, the binary scores of the 27 elements were correlated for the sample of 42 complete turnarounds. While statistical significance for the correlations could not be established because of the gross violation of the requirement of normally distributed variables, Table 2.5 reports those correlations of each turnaround element with others that equalled or exceeded 0.30 (if the variables were normally distributed, a correlation of 0.30 would be statistically significant at the confidence level of 95 per cent two tails).

Table 2.5

Sizeable Correlations of Turnaround Elements

Sample: 42 Complete Turnarounds

1. *Incentives, motivation, grievance redressal*: Plant modernisation etc. for greater

Table 2.5 (Contd.)

---

efficiency, quality, productivity (0.55), garnering stakeholders' support (0.52), attempts to increase efficiency, quality, productivity other than through plant modernisation etc. and training (0.51), increased training of managers and staff (0.44), credibility-building actions of management (0.38), public articulation by management of corporate mission, goals etc. (0.38), management communicating with staff, lower managers etc. (0.36), divestiture and liquidation of fixed assets and long-term liabilities (−0.35), initiation of managerial meetings, problem-solving task forces (0.33), marketing related actions (0.32), formal diagnostic activities (0.32), miscellaneous actions (0.32).

2. *Garnering stakeholders' support*: Incentives, motivation, grievance redressal (0.52), credibility-building actions of management (0.48), initiation of managerial meetings, task forces (0.43), better organisational integration, participative management, emphasis on core values (0.42), formal diagnostic activities (0.42), professionalisation of manufacturing management, personnel management, planning etc. (0.38), significant retrenchment (−0.37), public articulation by management of corporate mission, goals etc. (0.37), management communicating with staff, lower managers etc. (0.37), liquidation of current assets and liabilities (0.33), attempts to increase efficiency, quality, productivity other than through plant modernisation etc. and training (0.32).

3. *Initiation of managerial meetings, problem-solving task forces*: Better organisational integration, participative management, emphasis on core values (0.54), increased training of managers and staff (0.50), garnering stakeholders' support (0.43), significant retrenchment (−0.41), plant modernisation etc. for greater efficiency, quality, productivity (0.38), innovation, new product development etc. (−0.36), professionalisation of manufacturing management, personnel management, planning etc. (0.34), incentives, motivation, grievance redressal (0.33).

4. *Increased training of managers and staff*: Initiation of managerial meetings, problem-solving task forces (0.50), incentives, motivation, grievance redressal (0.44), management communicating with staff, lower managers etc. (0.42), formal diagnostic activities (0.39), plant modernisation etc. for greater efficiency, quality, productivity (0.38), public articulation by management of corporate mission, goals etc. (0.38), example-setting by top managers (0.35).

5. *Formal diagnostic activities*: Restructuring (decentralisation, fixing accountability, structural changes, etc.) (0.45), garnering stakeholders' support (0.42), increased training of managers and staff etc. (0.39), significant retrenchment (−0.38), professionalisation of manufacturing management, personnel management, planning etc. (0.34), incentives, motivation, staff redressal (0.32), better organisational integration, participative management, emphasis on core values (0.32).

6. *Significant retrenchment*: Initiation of managerial meetings, problem-solving task forces (−0.41), better integration, participative management, emphasis on core values (−0.39), formal diagnostic activities (−0.38), garnering stakeholders' support (−0.37), professionalisation of manufacturing management,

Table 2.5 (Contd.)

---

personnel management, planning etc. (−0.35), plant modernisation etc. for greater efficiency, quality, productivity (−0.30).

7. *Better organisational integration, participative management, emphasis on core values*: Initiation of managerial meetings, problem-solving task forces (0.54), professionalisation of manufacturing management, personnel management, planning. etc. (0.49), garnering stakeholders' support (0.42), significant retrenchment (−0.39), formal diagnostic activities (0.32), restructuring (decentralisation, fixing accountability, structural changes etc.) (0.30).

8. *Professionalisation of manufacturing management, personnel management, planning etc.*: Better organisational integration, participative management, emphasis on core values (0.49), restructuring (decentralisation, fixing accountability, structural changes etc.) (0.43), garnering stakeholders' support (0.38), significant retrenchment (−0.35), management control enhancing actions (0.34), formal diagnostic activities (0.34).

9. *Plant modernisation etc. for greater efficiency, quality, productivity*: Incentives, motivation, grievance redressal (0.55), increased training of managers and staff (0.38), initiation of managerial meetings, problem-solving task forces (0.38), attempts to increase efficiency, quality, productivity other than through plant modernisation and training (0.31), significant retrenchment (−0.30)

10. *Attempts to increase efficiency, quality, productivity other than through plant modernisation etc. and training*: Incentives, motivation, grievance redressal (0.51), miscellaneous actions (0.40), management communicating with staff, lower managers etc. (0.33), garnering stakeholders' support (0.32), plant modernisation etc. for greater efficiency, quality, productivity (0.31).

11. *Management communicating with staff, lower managers etc.*: Increased training of managers and staff (0.42), public articulation by management of corporate mission, goals etc. (0.38), garnering stakeholders' support (0.37), incentives, motivation, grievance redressal (0.36), attempts to increase efficiency, quality, productivity other than through plant modernisation etc. and training (0.33).

12. *Public articulation by management of corporate mission, goals etc.*: Credibility-building actions of management (0.67), increased training of managers and staff (0.38), management communicating with staff, lower managers etc. (0.38), incentives, motivation, grievance redressal (0.38), garnering stakeholders' support (0.37).

13. *Credibility-building actions*: Public articulation by management of corporate mission, goals etc (0.69), garnering of stakeholders' support (0.48), incentives, motivation, grievance redressal (0.38), marketing related actions (0.30).

14. *Restructuring (decentralisation, fixing accountability, structural changes etc.)*: Formal diagnostic activities (0.45), professionalisation of manufacturing management, personnel management, planning etc. (0.43), management control-enhancing actions (0.35), better organisational integration, participative management, emphasis on core values (0.30).

Table 2.5 (Contd.)

15. *Liquidation of current assets and liabilities*: Innovation, new product development etc. (0.41), garnering stakeholders' support (0.33), fresh induction of managers, technical staff etc. (0.31).

16. *Fresh induction of managers, technical staff etc.*: Divestiture and liquidation of fixed assets and long-term liabilities (0.37), liquidation of current assets and liabilities (0.31), management control-enhancing actions (0.30).

17. *Innovation, product development etc.*: Liquidation of current assets and liabilities (0.41), initiation of managerial meetings, problem-solving task-forces (−0.36), cost-reduction actions other than retrenchment (−0.34).

18. *Management control-enhancing actions*: Restructuring (decentralisation, fixing accountability, structural changes etc.) (0.35), professionalisation of manufacturing management, personnel management, planning etc. (0.34).

19. *Marketing related actions*: Incentives, motivation, grievance redressal (0.32), credibility-building actions of management (0.31).

20. *Divestiture and liquidation of fixed assets and long-term liabilities*: Fresh induction of managers, technical staff (0.37), incentives, motivation, grievance redressal (−0.35).

21. *Miscellaneous actions*: Attempts to increase efficiency, quality, productivity other than through plant modernisation etc. and training (0.40), incentives, motivation, grievance redressal (0.32).

22. *Cost-reduction actions other than retrenchment*: Innovation, new product development etc. (−0.34).

23. *Example-setting by top managers*: Increased training of managers and staff (0.35).

24. *Change in top management*: Nil

25. *Borrowing, raising equity finance, etc.*: Nil

26. *Disciplining*: Nil

27. *Diversification, product-line rationalisation, expansion*: Nil

Note: Only product moment correlations of 0.30 and above are reported above.

Table 2.5 reports 110 correlations, an average of just over four per turnaround element. That is to say, on an average each element tended to activate only four other elements. The system constituting turnaround elements thus appears to be a 'loosely coupled' one, rather than a 'tightly coupled' one.[36] Limited rather than widespread bondings of the elements, as in a 'loosely coupled' system, can make it difficult to change the organisational system in a big way simply by changing one or two elements. Many elements need to be altered for creating a large impact on the system.

There is, however, all too palpable an asymmetry in how linked each turnaround element is to the others. Some elements have no appreciable linkages at all, or very few indeed, such as change in top management (element 1), product-line rationalisation, diversification expansion (element 24), cost-cutting other than through retrenchment (element 15), divestiture and liquidation of long-term liabilities (element 25), raising of capital funds (element 23), setting of personal example (element 9), disciplining (element 10), among others. Some are copiously bonded, such as incentives and staff motivation (element 8), actions to garner stakeholders' support (element 4), diagnostic activities (element 12), initiation of meetings, task forces (element 13), significant retrenchment (element 14), and increased training (element 5).

This bonding variability is not entirely unexpected. Some elements may be basic to most turnarounds and be present in almost all turnarounds. They would therefore not be correlated much with other variables. The six foundational elements identified earlier, such as, diversification, change at the top, marketing actions, cost-reduction measures (excluding retrenchment), restructuring, and modernisation and similar others averaged only two sizeable correlations apiece. On the other hand, elements that appear in just about half the turnaround situations are largely what may be called decision variables: they may or may not be resorted to by turnaround managements. Bondings should be more numerous for these because of underlying alternative managerial approaches to turnarounds. Ten of these, with Table 2.4 scores ranging from 40 per cent to 57 per cent, averaged five sizeable correlations apiece. However, the range was also pretty high, with five of them having three or less sizeable correlations each and five with six or more correlations each. The more highly bonded amongst these may be strategic decision variables in the sense that activating them could in turn activate many other turnaround elements.

The nine remaining elements averaged 4.5 sizeable correlations each. Barring two elements that had two or less sizeable correlations, the others had at least three, and three had seven or more each. Thus even these relatively infrequently encountered turnaround elements may often have the potential to trigger widespread turnaround action.

Table 2.6 summarises the foundational and strategic (that is, highly bonded) elements of turnaround management.

Table 2.6

Foundational and Strategic Turnaround Variables

A. Foundational Elements

1. Diversification, product-line rationalisation, expansion etc.
2. Change in top management
3. Marketing related actions
4. Restructuring (decentralisation, fixing accountability, structural changes etc.)
5. Cost-reduction measures other than retrenchment
6. Plant modernisation etc. for greater efficiency, quality, productivity

B. Strategic Decision Variables

1. Incentives, motivation, grievance redressal
2. Garnering stakeholders' support
3. Initiation of managerial meetings, problem-solving task forces
4. Increased training of managers and staff
5. Formal diagnostic activities
6. Significant retrenchment
7. Better organisational integration, participative management, emphasis on core values

Note: Only those elements that had scores in Table 2.3 of 60 per cent or over have been listed as foundational elements. Only those elements that had at least six correlations greater than or equal to 0.30 (see Table 2.4) have been listed as strategic decision variables.

High versus Low Cost Turnarounds

A number of researchers have tried to identify different types of turnarounds. Charles Hofer, for example, postulated strategic *versus* operating turnarounds.[37] Strategic turnarounds were those achieved through a change in the organisation's strategy for competing in its existing business, or through altering the emphasis on a key management function like marketing, finance, or production, or through diversification. Operating turnarounds were those achieved through increasing revenue, cost-cutting, and/or asset-reduction strategies. Donald Bibeault distinguished between 'management process' turnarounds, achieved through vigorous management action aimed at correcting the weaknesses of the previous management and achieving a change in company culture, and turnarounds achieved through favourable external changes such as a business upswing, reduced competitive pressures, and favourable changes in government policies.[38] Hambrick and Schecter identified three types of successful turnarounds which they labelled as asset and cost surgery, selective product and/or market pruning, and piecemeal productivity.[39] In asset and cost surgery turnaround, increased productivity and capacity utilisation were strongly emphasised, as were liquidation of receivables and inventories and pruning of R and D and marketing expenditure. In selective product and/or market pruning turnaround also, the raising of productivity and liquidation of receivables and inventories were emphasised; in addition, prices were raised and product quality was emphasised. In piecemeal productivity turnarounds, capacity utilisation and productivity were emphasised.

But all these studies have skirted the question of the cost of turnaround. Many turnarounds in the West are marked by mass firings and plant closures that impose heavy costs on staff and society. For instance, at NCR, an American company producing cash registers, the turnaround was effected by firing seven vice-presidents, 12 executives, and 17,000 employees.[40] The much-applauded turnaround at Chrysler Corporation cost 80,000 jobs[41] as also in the case of British Leyland,[42] and the turnaround of British Steel resulted in lay-offs for 200,000 and a 50 per cent reduction in Britain's steel making capacity.[43] The question is: are there alternatives to mass surgery in regenerating sick organisations?

A principal components factor analysis of the binary data on 42 complete turnarounds did yield a factor that seemed to indicate an alternative to high cost turnarounds.[44] This main factor explained 25 per cent of the variance. As Table 2.7 shows (see the first factor), this factor seems to suggest two polar types of successful turnarounds: at the high end of the score on the factor, a participative, collaborative, 'Theory Y' excellence-oriented, mission-charged, professionalist, resources development-oriented, stakeholders-oriented turnaround mode; and at the low end of the score an authoritarian, 'Theory X' surgery-oriented turnaround mode. Thus, there may well be less expensive ways of regenerating sick organisations, a point developed in the next two chapters. A later chapter discusses creative turnaround that is still another low-cost, highly effective option to turnarounds that involve high costs in human, organisational and social terms.

Table 2.7

Principal Components Factors and
Turnaround Elements Loading Heavily on Them

Sample: 42 Complete Turnarounds

		Heavily Loading Turnaround Elements	**Loading**
Factor 1	1.	Incentives, motivation, grievance redressal	.77
(accounted for	2.	Garnering support of stakeholders	.75
25% of the	3.	Initiation of managerial meetings,	
variance		problem-solving task-forces	.67
explained by all	4.	Increase training of managers and staff	.58
ten factors)	5.	Formal diagnostic activities	.57
	6.	Public articulation by management	
		of corporate mission, goals etc.	.55
	7.	Better organisational integration, participative	
		management, emphasis on core values	.54
	8.	Professionalisation of manufacturing management,	
		personnel management, planning etc.	.53
	9.	Plant modernisation etc. for greater efficiency,	
		quality, productivity	.53
	10.	Significant retrenchment	−.52
Factor 2	1.	Marketing related actions	.59
(accounted for	2.	Innovation, new product development	.56
13% of total	3.	Restructuring (decentralisation, fixing	
variance		accountability, structural changes etc.)	−.56
explained)	4.	Better organisational integration, participative	
		management, emphasis on core values	−.53
Factor 3		Fresh induction of managers, technical	
(accounted for		staff etc.	76
12% of total			
variance explained)			
Factor 4		Liquidation of current assets and	
(accounted for		liabilities	.51
10% of total			
variance explained)			

Table 2.7 (Contd.)

	Heavily Loading Turnaround Elements	Loading
Factor 5 (accounted for 9% of total variance explained)	Nil	
Factor 6 (accounted for 8% of total variance explained)	Diversification, product-line rationalisation, expansion, etc.	.62
	Changes in top management	−.55
Factor 7 (accounted for 7% of total variance explained)	Nil	
Factor 8 (accounted for 6% of total variance explained	Nil	
Factor 9 (accounted for 6% of total variance explained)	Nil	
Factor 10 (accounted for 5% of total variance explained)	Nil	

Note: Only loadings of 0.5 and more have been reported.

A Stock Taking

The analysis of 42 complete turnarounds made in this chapter has indicated the following:

1. As a group, the 27 turnaround elements (see Table 2.2) do predict corporate recovery from a decline. Some of these elements may accelerate recovery, some others

decelerate it, and still others may neither accelerate nor decelerate recovery (see Table 2.3).

2. Some of the 27 elements may be more basic than the rest. They are utilised in most turnarounds. These are listed in Table 2.6.

3. Some elements seem to be strategic in the sense of being discretionary and having the power of activating a number of other elements. Widely different turnaround strategies may be employed depending upon whether and which of these elements are utilised by the management. These elements are also listed in Table 2.6.

4. A very important choice in the design of turnaround strategies is whether the turnaround is to be humane, constructive, and participative or authoritarian and retrenchment-oriented (see Table 2.7).

How do these findings stack up against the findings of prior turnaround research? The results of other researches may not be strictly comparable with the foregoing results because of differences in the definition of a turnaround, the samples studied, research methods used, statistical analysis carried out, and so on. For instance, in this study the sample was a multi-national one of complete turnarounds, involving a return to profitability from a loss situation and growth in profitability sustained for at least one year beyond the break-even year. By contrast, in the studies by Schendel, Patton, and Riggs, Schendel and Patton, Hofer, Hambrick and Schecter, Slatter, Bibeault, O'Neill, Potts and Behr, and others (see Table 2.1), the samples were national, and the turned around business had not necessarily broken even from a loss situation. The critical factor, rather, was relative improvement in financial performance. Other studies, such as those by Hegde and Kharbanda and Stallworthy (see Table 2.1), though multi-national in character, did not discriminate between break-even and complete turnarounds, and Hegde did not insist on recovery from loss as a turnaround criterion. Patton and Riggs, Hambrick and Schecter, and O'Neill's second study looked only at secondary, quantitative turnaround variables. None of the studies listed in Table 2.1 reported correlations or factor analysis results.

Despite these differences, however, it may be useful to identify the points of convergence and divergence between the results of analysing the data on 42 complete turnarounds and prior research efforts. First of all, how many of the basic or foundational elements of turnaround shown in Table 2.5 turned out to be so in prior studies? Several studies indicate that change at the top is usually a necessary condition for turning around organisations. For instance, in Slatter's study of 30 successful British turnarounds, in all but two of the cases there was a change in management.[45] In Bibeault's study there was a new chief executive officer in 59 out of 81 cases.[46] In some 20 reported cases of successful turnarounds in India, there was a change at the top in 19 of these.[47] In the study of 54 turned around firms in the USA by Schendel, Patton, and Riggs, 39 had general management changes.[48] In Hegde's multi-national sample, in 17 out of 18 cases of turnaround there was a change in top management.[49] Thus, it would appear that change in top management is usually a pre-condition for turnaround. The reason may be the need for fresh thinking and the ability of a new chief executive to break with precedent, past strategies, 'sunk costs',[50] and such related factors. Bibeault suggests that the need for a new chief executive is particularly acute if the causes of sickness are internal to the organisation.[51]

Beyond change in top management the extent of convergence is more modest. Slatter's study indicated that financial control was strengthened in over 60 per cent of his British sample of successfully turned around companies.[52] This broadly coincides with item 7 in Table 2.4 ('management control enhancing actions'), which was undertaken by 57 per cent of the sample. While these attempts at control are systemic (better control systems), Bibeault's study indicated that strong leadership and absolute control of management, that is, asserted *personal* control by the chief executive, was resorted to in over 60 per cent of his American cases.[53] The convergence is on the need for management control during turnaround, but there is divergence on its form. Cost reduction (including that through retrenchment) was commonplace in Slatter's sample (partially corresponding with item 5 in Table 2.6, 'cost reduction actions other than retrenchment'[54]). In the Schendel, Patton, and Riggs study, new products and R and D characterised over 60 per cent of the cases, partially coinciding with item 1 of Table 2.6 ('diversification, product-line rationalisation, expansion, etc.'[55]).

In Hegde's study, decentralisation with accountability, aggressive marketing, and new market development, broadly coinciding respectively with items 4 (restructuring), 3 (marketing-related items), and 1 (diversification, etc.) in Table 2.6, were the turnaround mechanisms employed in at least three out of five sickness situations.[56] On the other hand, asset-reduction, which figured so prominently in the Slatter study,[57] was not a foundational element in Table 2.6. Broadly speaking, all but one of the six elements listed as foundational in Table 2.5 seem to be so in at least one other study.

As far as strategic elements are concerned, since none of the other studies reported correlations between turnaround elements, it is not possible to determine whether or not the elements listed as strategic in Table 2.6 were in fact so in the prior studies.

Finally, while a number of studies did indicate various kinds of turnarounds, none of them sought low-cost alternatives. This is the distinctive contribution of this book. In Chapter 3 the harsh, surgery-oriented turnaround is described. In Chapter 4, an exposition is made of the humane, low-cost alternative. In a later chapter (Chapter 6), the creative turnaround, yet another low-cost option, is discussed.

Notes and References

1. See Dan Schendel, G.R. Patton, and James Riggs, 'Corporate turnaround strategies: A study of profit decline and recovery', *Journal of General Management*, Vol. 3, No.3, 1976, pp. 3–12.
2. See Schendel and Patton, 1976, op. cit.
3. See Charles H. Hofer, 'Turnaround strategies', *The Journal of Business Strategy*, Vol. 1, No. 1, 1980, pp 19–31.
4. See Pradip N. Khandwalla, 'Strategy for turning around complex sick organizations', *Vikalpa*, Vol. 6, Nos.3 and 4, 1981, pp. 143–65, or Pradip N. Khandwalla, 'Turnaround management of mismanaged complex organizations', *International Studies of Management and Organization*, Vol. 13, No. 4, 1983, pp. 5–41. See Pradip N. Khandwalla, *Effective turnaround of sick enterprises (Indian experiences): Text and cases* (London: Commonwealth Secretariat, 1989).
5. See Manjunath C. Hegde, 'Western and Indian models of turnaround management', *Vikalpa*, Vol. 7, No. 4, 1982, pp. 289–304.
6. See Donald B. Bibeault, *Corporate turnaround: How managers turn losers into winners* (New York: McGraw-Hill, 1982).
7. See Hambrick and Schecter, 1983, op. cit.

8. See Stuart S. Slatter, *Corporate recovery: Successful turnaround strategies and their implementation* (Harmondsworth, Middlesex: Penguin, 1984).

9. See Hugh M. O'Neill, 'Turnaround and recovery: What strategy do you need?' *Long Range Planning*, Vol. 19, No. 1, 1986, pp. 80–88.

10. See Hugh M. O'Neill, 'An analysis of the turnaround strategy in commercial banking', *Journal of Management Studies*, Vol. 23, No. 2, 1986, pp. 165–88.

11. See Mark Potts and Peter Behr, *The leading edge* (New Delhi: Tata McGraw-Hill, 1987).

12. See O.P. Kharbanda and E.A. Stallworthy, *Company rescue: How to manage a business turnaround* (London: Heinemann, 1987).

13. See A.K. Mukherji, *Turnaround strategy for enterprise in crisis* (New Delhi: Papyrus, 1989).

14. See Dan Schendel and G.R. Patton, 'Corporate stagnation and turnaround', *Journal of Economics and Business*, Vol. 28, No. 1, 1976, pp. 237–41.

15. See Donald C. Hambrick and Steven M. Schecter, 'Turnaround strategies for mature industrial-product business units', *Academy of Management Journal*, Vol. 26, No. 2, 1983, pp. 231–48.

16. See Khandwalla, 1981, 1989, op. cit.

17. See Bibeault, 1982, op. cit.

18. See Potts and Behr, 1987, op. cit.

19. See Kharbanda and Stallworthy, 1987, op. cit.

20. See Robert K. Yin, *Case study research: Design and methods* (Beverly Hills: Sage, 1984, especially ch. 5). See also Danny Miller and Peter Friesen, *Organizations: A quantum view* (Englewood Cliffs, N.J.: Prentice-Hall, 1984), and Mathew J. Manimala, 'Managerial heuristics of pioneering—innovative (PI) entrepreneurs: An exploratory study'. Unpublished doctoral dissertation, Indian Institute of Management, Ahmedabad, 1988.

21. See Schendel, Patton and Riggs, 1976, op. cit., Slatter, 1984, op. cit., Bibcault, 1983, op. cit., Hegde, 1982, op. cit.

22. See Schendel, Patton, Riggs, 1976, op. cit., Hofer, 1980, op. cit., Hambrick and Schecter, 1983, op. cit., Slatter, 1984, op. cit., O'Neill, 1986, op. cit.

23. See Khandwalla, 1981, 1989, op. cit., Bibeault, 1983, op. cit., Slatter, 1984, op. cit.

24. See Kharbanda and Stallworthy, 1987, op. cit., Mukherji, 1989, op. cit.

25. See Khandwalla, 1981, 1989, op. cit., Mukherji, 1989, op. cit.

26. See Khandwalla, 1981, 1989, op. cit., Bibeault, 1983, op. cit., Potts and Behr, 1987, op. cit., Kharbanda and Stallworthy, 1987, op. cit., Mukherji, 1989, op. cit., etc.

27. See Hofer, 1980, op. cit., Hegde, 1982, op. cit., Slatter, 1984, op. cit.

28. See Miller and Friesen, 1984, op. cit, for an attempt to quantify from case data the extent to which elements were present.

29. See *Business Week*, 'Warnaco: Prospering by slimming and donning big name labels', 18 October 1982, p. 64.

30. For issues in case-based analysis, see Yin, 1984, op. cit., Manimala, 1988, op. cit., and Danny Miller and Peter Friesen, 'Archetypes of organizational transition', *Administrative Science Quarterly*, Vol. 25, 1980, pp. 268–99.

31. See Y.S. Lincoln, and E.J. Guba, *Naturalistic enquiry* (Beverly Hills, California: Sage, 1985); Van Maanen (ed.), *Qualitative methodology* (Beverly Hills, California:

Sage, 1979); Gareth Morgan, 'Paradigms, metaphors and puzzle solving in organization theory', *Administrative Science Quarterly*, Vol. 85, 1980, pp. 605–22.

32. For Theory X and Theory Y, see Douglas McGregor, *The human side of enterprise* (New York: McGraw-Hill, 1960).
33. See Slatter, 1984, op. cit., p. 121.
34. See Khandwalla, 1989, op. cit., ch. 4.
35. For transformational leadership, see James MacGregor, Burns, *Leadership* (New York: Harper and Row, 1978, especially ch. 3); Warren Bennis and Burt Nanus, *Leaders: The strategies for taking charge* (New York: Harper and Row, 1985); Pritam Singh and Asha Bhandarkar, *Corporate success and transformational leadership* (New Delhi: Wiley Eastern, 1990). For professional management, see Pradip N. Khandwalla, *The Design of organizations* (New York: Harcourt Brace Jovanovich, 1977, especially ch. 11). For human resource development, see Udai Pareek and T. Venkateswara Rao, *Designing and managing human resource systems: With special emphasis on human resource development* (New Delhi: Oxford and IBH, 1981); Wayne F. Cescio, *Managing human resources: Productivity, quality of work life, profits*, 2nd ed. (New York: McGraw-Hill, 1989).
36. For a discussion of loosely *versus* tightly coupled systems see Howard Addrich, 'Visionaries and villains: The politics of designing interorganizational relations', *Organization and Administrative Sciences*, Vol. 8, 1977, pp. 23–40, and Karl E. Weick, 'Educational organizations as loosely coupled systems', *Administrative Science Quarterly*, Vol. 21, 1976, pp. 1–19.
37. See Hofer, 1980, op. cit.
38. See Bibeault, 1983, op. cit.
39. See Hambrick and Schecter, 1983, op. cit.
40. See L.G. Martin, 'What happened at NCR after the boss declared martial law', *Fortune*, Vol. 92, 1975, pp. 100–104, 178, 181.
41. See M.M. Gordon, *The Iacocca management technique* (New York: Bantam, 1987).
42. See R. Heller, 'How money saved BLMC', *Management Today*, August 1972, pp. 42–51; 'An industrial invalid revives', *Time*, 6 February 1984, p. 46.
43. See Ian MacGregor, 'Recovery at British Steel', *Journal of General Management*, Vol. 7, No. 3, 1982, pp. 5–16; David Chambers, 'Consumer orientation and the drive for quality', paper presented at Roundtable on 'Public Enterprise Management: Strategies for Success', New Delhi, 6–11 March 1988.
44. For an exposition of principal components analysis see J. Van de Geer, *Multivariate analysis for the social sciences* (San Francisco: Freeman, 1971).
45. See Slatter, 1984, op. cit., p. 121.
46. See Bibeault, 1982, op. cit., p. 145.
47. For the 20 Indian case studies, see C.K. Prahlad and R.S. Thomas, 'Turnaround strategy: Lessons from HPF's experience', *Vikalpa*, Vol. 2, No. 2, 1977, pp. 99–111; Pradip N. Khandwalla, 1981 and 1989, op. cit.: V. Padaki and V. Shanbhag (eds.), *Industrial sickness: The challenge in Indian textiles* (Ahmedabad: ATIRA, 1984).
48. See Schendel, Patton, and Riggs, 1976, op. cit
49. See Hegde, 1982, op. cit.

50. See William H. Starbuck, Arent Greve, and Bo L.T. Hedberg, 'Responding to crisis', ch. 5, in C.F. Smart and W.T. Stanbury (eds.), *Studies in crisis management* (Toronto: Institute for Research on Public Policy, 1978).
51. See Bibeault, 1982, op. cit., pp. 93–95, 145–48.
52. See Slatter, 1984, op. cit., p. 121.
53. See Bibeault, 1982, op. cit., p. 370.
54. See Slatter, 1984, op. cit., p. 121.
55. See Schendel, Patton, and Riggs, 1976, op. cit.
56. See Hegde, 1982, op. cit.
57. See Slatter, 1984, op. cit., p. 121.

3. SURGICAL TURNAROUNDS

In the eighties, several remarkable managers became the toasts of corporate America. Jack Welch reportedly dragged General Electric kicking and screaming towards a twenty-first century world of hyper tech.[1] Roger Smith pulled mighty General Motors out of a 'pothole' of a $760 million loss in 1980 to a profit of $4 billion in the mid-eighties.[2] Lee Iacocca engineered an even more spectacular turnaround at Chrysler Corporation.[3] David Roderick of US Steel (now USX), in his quest for getting into the black, transformed the largest US steel maker into a profitable steel and oil company.[4]

On the other side of the Atlantic too arose stalwart turnaround managers. Ian McGregor contributed mightily to restoring profitability to beleaguered British Steel.[5] Jolly John Harvey–Jones brought cheer to the shareholders of Imperial Chemical Industries.[6] Olivetti began to charge ahead under the firm hand of Carlo de Benedetti.[7]

But there was a monstrous catch to all of these turnarounds. Jack Welch came to be known as Neutron Jack: 'When Neutron Jack hits a GE plant 'town, they say, the people disappear, but the building still stands'.[8] He got very skilled at cleansing GE of 'deadwood'. In the process some 100,000, of a workforce of 400,000 lost their jobs. In 1980 GM had about three-quarters of a million persons on its payroll; by the late eighties some two-thirds of this grand army had gone. Half the staff of Chrysler disappeared under Iacocca. Roderick of USX waved away a third of US Steel's production capacity and over half of its staff. Ian McGregor inaugurated a purge at British Steel: gone was half the company's production capacity and 80 per cent of its workforce. Harvey-Jones reduced the British workforce of Imperial Chemical Industries from 90,000 to 59,000. Carlo de Benedetti dispensed with nearly 25 per cent of Olivetti's staff and his 'dismissal and retirement programme created such a void that nearly a hundred competent senior managers were engaged to fill the gaps that had been created in the organisation'.[9]

Table 3.1 lists the human costs of several such turnarounds.

Table 3.1

The Human Costs of Surgical Turnarounds

	Country	Human Cost of Turnaround
A. Accounting and Business Machines, Office Equipment		
1.* Olivetti[10] ($4,000 m. sales in 1984, 47,000 employees)	Italy	Staff reduced from 61,000 in 1978 to 47,000 in 1984.
B. Automobiles, Two-wheelers etc.		
1.* Chrysler Corporation[11] ($20,000 m. sales in mid-eighties)	USA	Staff cut from 160,000 in 1979 to 80,000 by 1982.
2.* Fiat[12] (Produced 1.4 m. cars in 1983)	Italy	54,000 persons laid off, 40% of 1979 workforce.
3.* General Motors[13] ($100,000 m. sales in mid-eighties)	USA	367,000 out of 750,000 laid off by 1984; a further third by 1987.
4.* Jaguar[14] (£750 m. sales in mid-eighties)	UK	Reduction of manpower by 30%.
C. Chemicals, Fertilizers, and Pharmaceuticals		
1.* ICI[15] (World's fifth largest chemical company, with sales in mid-eighties of $ 13,000 m.)	UK	World-wide workforce reduction by 20% in Britain, staff cut from 90,000 to 58,600.
2.* Searle[16] ($900 m. sales in early eighties)	USA	Slashed corporate staff from 800 to 350.
D. Computers, Electronics, Telecommunications		
1.* ICL[17] (£1,000 m. sales in mid-eighties)	UK	Closed five plants. Laid off 10,000 (one-third of staff).
2.* Italtel[18] (Lire 1,200 b. sales in mid-eighties)	Italy	Laid off 8,500 persons, 29% of 1980 workforce.
3. Osborne Computers[19] (sold 120,000 computers a year at peak in early eighties)	USA	Original staff of 1,000 in 1981–82 cut down to 35 by 1985.
4.* Ultraelectronic Holdings[20] (£11 m. sales mid-seventies)	UK	Laid off one-third of 1972 staff.
E. Conglomerates		
1.* EID Parry[21] (Rs. 1,500 m. sales in late eighties)	India	Staff reduced by 40%.
2. Henley Group[22] ($7,000 m. in assets, $3,000 m. sales in late eighties)	USA	Laid off 2,000 persons.

Table 3.1 (Contd.)

	Country	Human Cost of Turnaround
3. IRI[23] (470,000 employees in 1986; 47,000 b. lire sales)	Italy	60,000 persons lost their jobs between 1982 and 1986.
F. Household Goods		
1. Black and Decker[24] ($1,800 m. annual sales in mid-eighties)	USA	Closed seven plants, fired 2,000 employees.
2. Epe Plywood[25] (N 7 m. sales in the late eighties)	Nigeria	Reduction of staff from 1,000 to less than 400.
3. Toro[26] ($350 m. sales in early eighties)	USA	Fired 125 managers. Cut workforce in half to 1,800.
G. Packaging, Containers		
1* Metal Box[27] (£1,300 m. sales in mid-eighties)	UK	Closure of four out of 14 'open top' factories. Reduction in staff from 34,000 at the end of seventies to 20,000 in 1984.
2. Rockware[28] (4,500 employees in 1983)	UK	More than halved the staff from 9,600 in 1979 to 4,500 in 1983.
H. Plant, Machinery, Equipment, Engineering Products		
1* Jaipur Metals[29] (Rs. 120 m. sales in mid-eighties)	India	Retrenched 500 employees.
2* Redman Heenan[30] (£34 m. sales in late seventies)	UK	Closed a factory and laid off 600 persons. Additional staff laid off in factories and at head office.
3* Staveley Industries[31] (£100 m. sales in mid-seventies)	UK	Closed down eight machine tool divisions and other units; reduction in staff of machine tool group from 5,250 to 2,500. Reduction in corporate staff.
I. Steel		
1* British Steel[32] (14 m. tonne capacity in late eighties)	UK	Reduced steel capacity by about 50% and reduced staff from a strength of 265,000 to 52,000.
2* USX[33] ($17,000 m. sales in late eighties)	USA	Over the eighties employment slashed by over half. Shut down several plants.
J. Textiles, Fibres, Apparel		
1* Dawson International[34] (£110 m. sales in early eighties)	UK	Laid off 700 employees; closed some factories; two-thirds of HQ staff fired.

Table 3.1 (Contd.)

	Country	Human Cost of Turnaround
2. ICI Fibres Division[35] (£450 m. sales in early eighties)	UK	Plant shutdown in N. Ireland with a loss of 1,000 jobs. Other lay-offs.
3. Munsingwear[36] ($100 m. sales in early eighties)	USA	Reduced staff by 50%.
4.* Warnaco[37] ($500 m. sales in early eighties)	USA	Cut down corporate headquarters staff by half.

K. Timber and Pulp
Nil

L. Trade and Services

	Country	Human Cost of Turnaround
1.* Burton Group[38] (£140 m. sales in late seventies)	UK	Reduced staff from 21,400 to 11,000. Closed nine out of original 11 plants, closed 232 shops, and closed mail order operations.
2. Gambia Produce Marketing Board[39] (no information on size)	Gambia	Closed non-marketing activities and reduced number of employees.
3.* Getz[40] ($500 m. sales in mid-eighties)	USA	Slashed HQ staff from 92 to 40.
4. Wickes[41] ($3,000 m. sales in early eighties)	USA	Closed several chains. Closed 300 poorly located stores.

M. Transportation

	Country	Human Cost of Turnaround
1. Jamaica Railways[42] (revenues of J $45 m. in mid-eighties)	Jamaica	Reduced staff of 1,500 by 350.

N. Tyres

	Country	Human Cost of Turnaround
1. Firestone[43] ($4,500 m. sales in early eighties)	USA	In 1980 the company shut down seven out of 17 plants in the USA and Canada.

O. Miscellaneous

	Country	Human Cost of Turnaround
1.* Macmillan[44] ($400 m. sales in early eighties)	USA	Management team slashed by 66% Closed a number of units.

Note: * denotes complete turnaround (those without asterisk are break-even turn-arounds).

The architects of such turnarounds have often been gilded by the media. Iacocca was touted as a presidential candidate. Jack Welch got the pride of place in a recent book on American turnarounds that drew lessons for management from the deeds of similar stalwarts.[45] De Benedetti topped a poll of 8,000 Italian executives as manager-of-the-year in 1984 for the second time in five years and Fortune listed him as one (the only Italian) of the eleven best managers in Western Europe. The business magazines that sing paeans for such managers seldom stop to count the cost: steep reductions in the standard of living of thousands of families, demoralisation of men and women cast aside like waste paper, the burden on society of providing unemployment compensation, retraining costs, loss of skills and expertise for the corporations laying off staff and managers, loss of commitment in the ones spared, steep reductions sometimes in national manufacturing capacities (as in steel in Britain and the US) that contribute to balance of trade deficits, and beyond that, the deification of a culture of casual violence against humans for purely commercial purposes. If these costs were toted up, the black ink of the greatest of these surgical turnarounds could well turn into a streaming red wound.

This is not to say that people should never be laid off *en masse*—if all else fails, as a last resort they can be, after negotiations with their representatives, and with compensation that cushions them against a calamitous decline in income—but not as the handiest bang-bang tool for cutting costs. There is also a question of fairness. How right is it for managers to deprive people of livelihood for such sins of prior managers as bad growth strategies, financial wrongdoing, overmanning, excessive timidity or reckless diversification?

Let us take a closer look at the design of harsh turnarounds with the help of 22 complete turnarounds that were achieved with surgical methods involving mass lay-offs of more that 10 per cent of the workforce of the corporation or of a significant unit of the corporation. Like the sample of 42 complete turnarounds (see Chapter 2 for an analysis), its sub-sample of 22 surgical turnarounds exhibits considerable variety in corporate size, type of industry, and country of affiliation (Table 3.1 indicates complete surgical turnarounds with an asterisk).

Foundational Elements of Surgical Turnarounds

Table 3.2 indicates the percentage of (complete) surgical turnarounds

Table 3.2

Percentages of Cases Engaging in Different Turnaround Actions

Sample : 22 Surgical Complete Turnarounds

	Percentage Engaging in Action
1. Significant retrenchment	100
2. Diversification, product-line rationalisation, expansion etc.	99
3. Change in top management	91
4. Marketing related actions	73
5. Cost-reduction measures other than retrenchment	64
6. Management control-enhancing actions	59
7. Restructuring (decentralisation, fixing accountability, structural changes etc.)	59
8. Divestiture and liquidation of fixed assets and long-term liabilities	55
9. Innovation, new product development etc.	55
10. Borrowing, raising equity finance etc.	45
11. Disciplining	45
12. Fresh induction of managers, technical staff etc.	45
13. Plant modernisation etc. for greater efficiency, quality, productivity	45
14. Management communicating with staff, lower managers etc.	32
15. Incentives, motivation, grievance redressal	32
16. Better organisational integration, participative management, emphasis on core values	27
17. Credibility-building actions of management	27
18. Garnering stakeholders' support	27
19. Public articulation by management of mission, goals etc.	27
20. Attempts to increase efficiency, quality, productivity other than through plant modernisation etc. and training	23
21. Liquidation of current assets and liabilities	23
22. Example-setting by top managers	23
23. Formal diagnostic activities	23
24. Increased training of managers and staff	18
25. Professionalisation of manufacturing management, personnel management, planning etc.	14
26. Miscellaneous actions	14
27. Initiation of managerial meetings, problem-solving task-forces	9

that was reportedly resorted to each of the 27 turnaround actions. If we take a 60 per cent score as a benchmark for basic turnaround elements, five actions seem foundational for harsh turnarounds: significant retrenchment; diversification, product rationalisation, expansion, and related actions; change in top management; marketing related actions, and miscellaneous cost-reduction measures. The emphasis is clearly on chopping, trimming, and regrouping, with some marketing aggressiveness thrown in. There is little here to cheer the believers in 'Theory Y' management.[46] Indeed, it is the bottom of the Table (items with scores of 30 per cent or less) that emphasises participative management, human resource development, management by mission, diagnostic activity, networking, confidence-building, team-work, institution-building, and similar measures.

Strategic Elements of Harsh Turnarounds

Strategic elements are those that trigger several other turnaround actions and therefore can interestingly differentiate the basic design of the turnaround. Turnaround elements that are relatively more correlated with other turnaround elements are considered strategic. Table 3.3 shows the substantial correlates of each of the 27 elements. The cut-off chosen for considering a correlation as 'substantial' was 0.42 (this would be statistically significant at the 95 per cent level of confidence if the variables in question were normally distributed, which they were not).

Judged by the number of substantial correlations, the most strategic turnaround element seemed to be incentives, motivation, and grievance redressal, with seven substantial correlates. Thus, what distinctive shape a surgical turnaround takes is likely to depend in part on whether the management sees staff motivation as key or not (only in a minority of surgical turnarounds, however, it seemed to be a recourse). Raising capital was a close second. This was followed by mission-articulation, and networking with stakeholders for support. Beyond these there were two others with four substantial correlations apiece, namely, restructuring, and attempts to increase efficiency other than through plant modernisation and training. Thus, motivation, management by mission, networking, and decentralising, some elements of what broadly may be termed 'Theory Y' management, may be interesting options even in surgical turnarounds.

Table 3.3

Substantial Correlations of Each Turnaround Element in Surgical Turnarounds

Sample : 22 'Surgical' Complete Turnarounds

1. *Incentives, motivation, grievance redressal*: Attempts to increase efficiency, quality productivity other than through plant modernisation etc. and training (0.79) plant modernisation etc. for greater efficiency, productivity, quality (0.55), garnering stakeholders' support (0.46), public articulation by management of corporate mission, goals etc. (0.46), initiation of managerial meetings, problem-solving task-forces etc. (0.46), increased training of managers and staff (0.44), restructuring (decentralisation, fixing accountability, structural changes) (−0.44).

2. *Borrowing, raising equity finance etc.*: Credibility-building actions of management (0.67), marketing related actions (0.56), restructuring (decentralisation, fixing accountability, structural changes etc.) (−0.55), garnering stakeholders' support (0.47), public articulation by management of corporate mission, goals etc. (0.47), miscellaneous actions (0.44).

3. *Public articulation by management of corporate mission, goals etc.*: Management communicating with staff, lower managers etc. (0.68), credibility-building actions of management (0.54), garnering stakeholders' support (0.54), borrowings, raising equity finance etc. (0.47), incentives, motivation, grievance redressal (0.46).

4. *Garnering stakeholders' support*: Credibility-building actions of management (0.54), public articulation by management of corporate mission, goals etc. (0.54), borrowings, raising equity finance etc. (0.47), management communicating with staff, lower managers (0.46), incentives, motivation, grievance redressal (0.46).

5. *Restructuring (decentralisation, fixing accountability, structural changes, etc.)*: Borrowings, raising equity finance etc. (−0.55), miscellaneous actions (−0.48), incentives, motivation, grievance redressal (−0.44), attempts to increase efficiency, quality, productivity other than through plant modernisation etc. and training (−0.43).

6. *Attempts to increase efficiency, quality, productivity other than through plant modernisation etc. and training*: Incentives, motivation, grievance redressal (0.79), liquidation of current assets and liabilities (0.48), restructuring (decentralisation, fixing accountability, structural changes) (−0.43), miscellaneous actions (0.42).

7. *Credibility-building actions of management*: Borrowings, raising equity finance etc. (0.67), garnering stakeholders' support (0.54), public articulation by management of corporate mission, goals etc. (0.54).

8. *Increased training of managers and staff*: Plant modernisation etc. for greater efficiency, quality, productivity (0.52), management communicating with staff, lower managers (0.44), incentives, motivation, grievance redressal (0.44).

9. *Management communicating with staff, lower managers etc.*: Public articulation by management of corporate mission, goals etc. (0.68), garnering stakeholders' support (0.46), increased training of managers and staff (0.44).

10. *Plant modernisation etc. for greater efficiency, quality, productivity*: Incentives, motivation, grievance redressal (0.55), increased training of managers and staff (0.52).

11. *Marketing related actions*: Borrowings, raising equity finance etc. (0.56), better organisational integration, participative management, emphasis on core values (−0.54).

12. *Liquidation of current assets and liabilities*: Attempts to increase efficiency, quality, productivity other than through plant modernisation etc. and training (0.48), professionalisation of manufacturing management, personnel management, planning etc. (0.42).

13. *Better organisational integration, participative management, emphasis on core values*: Marketing related actions (−0.54), cost-reduction measures other than retrenchment (0.46).

14. *Miscellaneous actions*: Restructuring (decentralisation, fixing accountability, structural changes etc.) (−0.48), borrowings, raising equity finance etc. (0.44).

15. *Significant retrenchment*: Professionalisation of manufacturing management, personnel management, planning etc. (−0.55).

16. *Cost reduction measures other than retrenchment*: Better organisational integration, participative management, emphasis on core values (0.46).

17. *Divestiture and liquidation of fixed assets and long-term liabilities*: Plant modernisation etc. for greater efficiency, quality, productivity (−0.45).

18. *Initiation of managerial meetings, problem-solving task forces*: Incentives, motivation, grievance redressal (0.46).

19. *Professionalisation of manufacturing management, personnel management, planning etc.*: Significant retrenchment (−0.55).

20. *Changes in top management*: Nil.

21. *Managment control-enhancing actions*: Nil.

22. *Diversification, product-line rationalisation, expansion etc.*: Nil.

23. *Formal diagnostic activities*: Nil.

24. *Example-setting by top managers*: Nil.

25. *Disciplining*: Nil.

26. *Fresh induction of managers, technical staff etc.*: Nil.

27. *Innovation, new product development etc.*: Nil.

Note: Only product moment correlations of 0.42 and above have been reported. These are shown in brackets.

Table 3.4 summarises the foundational and strategic elements of surgical turnarounds.

Table 3.4

Foundational and Strategic Elements of Surgical Turnarounds

Sample: 22 'Surgical' Complete Turnarounds

Foundational Turnaround Elements
1. Significant retrenchment
2. Diversification, product-line rationalisation, expansion etc.
3. Changes in top management
4. Marketing related actions
5. Cost-reduction measures other than retrenchment

Strategic Turnaround Elements
1. Incentives, motivation, grievance redressal
2. Borrowings, raising equity finance etc.
3. Public articulation by management of corporate mission, goals etc.
4. Garnering stakeholders' support
5. Restructuring (decentralisation, fixing accountability, structural changes etc.).
6. Attempts to increase efficiency, quality, productivity other than through plant modernisation etc. and training.

Alternative Designs of Surgical Turnarounds

Eleven factors (with eigen values exceeding 1) were identified through a principal components factor analysis of the 27 variables for the sample of harsh complete turnarounds. These explained 87 per cent of the variability in the 27 variables. Table 3.5 shows the main factors (that is, those factors with eigen values exceeding 2) and the turnaround elements with a minimum loading of 0.5 on each factor. The first factor explained over a fifth of the explained variance, and nearly 40 per cent of the variability accounted for by the main factors. What is more, as many as 10 variables loaded more than 0.5 on it (compared to 4 or less for the other factors), including all the strategic elements. None of these ten elements was foundational. It, therefore, may encapsulate a significant choice in the design of surgical turnarounds.

Table 3.5

*Main Principal Components Factors and Turnaround Elements
Loading Heavily on them*

Sample: 22 'Surgical' Complete Turnarounds

	Heavily Loading Turnaround Elements	**Loading**
Factor 1	1. Incentives, motivation, grievance redressal	0.83
(accounted	2. Borrowings, raising equity finance etc.	0.72
for 22% of	3. Public articulation by management of corporate	
the variance	mission, goals etc.	0.69
explained by	4. Management communicating with staff, lower	
all 11 factors)	managers etc.	0.62
	5. Attempts to increase efficiency, quality,	
	productivity other than through plant	
	modernisation etc., and training	0.62
	6. Garnering stakeholders' support	0.60
	7. Restructuring (decentralisation, fixing	
	accountability, structural changes etc.)	−0.57
	8. Credibility-building actions of management	0.52
	9. Increased training of managers and staff	0.51
	10. Miscellaneous actions	0.50
Factor 2	1. Better organisational integration, participative	
(accounted	management, emphasis on core values	0.73
for 14% of	2. Liquidation of current assets and liabilities	0.70
explained	3. Professionalisation of manufacturing manage-	
variance)	ment, personnel management, planning etc.	0.54
	4. Cost-reduction mechanisms other than	
	retrenchment	0.53
Factor 3	1. Plant modernisation etc. for greater efficiency,	
(accounted	quality, productivity	0.57
for 13% of	2. Initiation of managerial meetings, problem-	
explained	solving task-forces	0.52
variance)	3. Professionalisation of manufacturing manage-	
	ment, personnel management, planning etc.	−0.51
Factor 4	Example-setting by top managers	0.67
(accounted		
for 9% of		
explained		
variance)		

Note: Only loading of 0.5 and over of factors with eigen values exceeding 2 have
been reported.

Factor 1 is rich in elements involving motivation, personnel development, productivity—enhancing actions, communication, mission-articulation, credibility-building, and networking. The implication is that managements adopting a surgical turnaround strategy can either counter-balance it with an inspirational or motivational productivity oriented mode of 'people management', or go the whole hog of 'Theory X' management by not bothering about the 'people management' angle at all. A couple of examples of turnarounds may clarify the choice.

At Henley Group, US, Mike Dingman, a college dropout turned investment banker, put together a motley group of 35 poorly performing companies.[47]. Then he laid about firing people in loss-making units, the object being to restore black ink as quickly as possible and then dispose off the units at a hefty profit. Some 2,000 persons were fired in preliminary purges, over 10 per cent of the total staff. He also ruthlessly slashed wages—at one plant the cut was 50 per cent. Strikers were threatened with dismissal. Spending on maintenance was also reduced. Some plants were closed. Dingman offered stock options to senior managers, gave greater operating authority to them and created more profit centres. The company lost $426 million in 1986 and was expected to report a loss also in 1987, but the subsidiaries were expected to earn $314 million in 1987.

The turnaround of IRI, the Italian public enterprise, reportedly the world's largest, and another conglomerate, is an example of an enlightened surgical effort.[48] IRI did reduce its staff by 60,000, about 12 per cent of its total strength. But this was done after a generous retrenchment compensation package was negotiated with the unions. An agreement was also reached to lower the retirement age. The management established continuous communication with the unions concerning the reorganisation of the IRI group and for evolving appropriate industrial policies for sectoral holding companies under the IRI umbrella. The manufacturing and service activities were restructured into ten sectoral holding companies. Dr. Romano Prodi, an economist who turned around IRI, attracted top class managers from the Italian industry by getting the government to agree to a steep increase of 35 per cent in the salaries of managers. Seventy per cent of top managers at the IRI headquarters and 50 per cent of the senior managers of major constituent companies were replaced by younger, more commercially oriented managers. Prodi went out of his way to protect them from politicians. IRI increased investment in the hi-tech sector and scaled down investment in sunset industries. It also mounted a vigorous effort to export to the USA and the rest of Europe. Twenty-three subsidiaries were sold off to the private sector. This released funds for debt reduction. IRI also offered shares of its constituent companies to the public for subscription. There was a much stronger emphasis on profitability, efficiency, market-orientation, and accountability to investors. There was an increase in R and D expenditure and greater emphasis on developing products in partnership with foreign companies. IRI, which lost on an average 2800 billion lire per year during 1980–85, earned 3000 billion lire in 1986 on sales of 47000 billion lire.

To identify more fully the two types of surgical turnarounds, the 22 complete surgical turnarounds were subjected to a cluster analysis (seeking a 2-cluster solution). The first cluster consisted of 14 turn-arounds and the second, of the balance eight. Table 3.6 gives the scores for the two groups. Both groups resorted to retrenchment and other cost-reduction mechanisms, top management changes, diversification and product-line repositioning, more effective marketing, and greater management control over operations. But they differed significantly (as shown by a test of difference in proportions) in their recourse to six turnaround elements, notably the attempt to motivate as well as discipline staff (item 1 and 6), attempts to increase productivity, including plant modernisation (items 2 and 3), restructuring for greater decentralisation and accountability (item 4), and getting more capital (item 5). Except for more frequent recourse to restructuring in the first group, the second group seemed to use the remaining five elements more frequently. On the basis of the data, the first group could be called the Surgical Reconstructive Turnaround (because of emphasis on product-line repositioning, restructuring, and similar actions, while the second could be called Surgical Productivity/Innovation Oriented Turn-around (because of the emphasis on greater productivity through incentives, discipline, cost-cutting, modernisation, and such like as well as on innovation, besides the usual emphasis on diversification and product-line rationalisation, marketing, and so on). Let us take a closer look at examples of each type.

The turnaround of the American drug and health care company Searle by Donald Rumsfeld (a former US defense secretary) seemed

Table 3.6

Two Types of Surgical Turnarounds Identified from Cluster Analysis

Sample: 22 'Surgical' Complete Turnarounds

	Surgical Reconstructive (14 companies)	Surgical Productivity/ Innovation Oriented (8 companies)	Difference
1. Incentives, motivation, grievance redressal	0%	87%	Significant
2. Plant modernisation etc. for greater efficiency, quality, productivity	14%	87%	Significant
3. Attempts to increase efficiency, quality, productivity other than through plant modernisation etc. and training	0%	62%	Significant
4. Restructuring (Decentralisation, fixing accountability, structural changes etc.)	79%	25%	Significant
5. Borrowings, raising equity finance etc.	29%	75%	Significant
6. Disciplining	29%	75%	Significant
7. Cost-reduction actions other than retrenchment	50%	87%	
8. Credibility-building actions of management	14%	50%	
9. Garnering stakeholders' support	14%	50%	
10. Public articulation by management of corporate mission, goals etc.	14%	50%	
11. Innovation, new product development etc.	43%	75%	
12. Increased training of managers and staff	7%	37%	
13. Management communicating with staff, lower managers etc.	21%	50%	

Table 3.6 (Contd.)

	Surgical Reconstructive (14 companies)	Surgical Productivity/ Innovation Oriented (8 companies)	Difference
14. Divestiture and liquidation of fixed assets and long-term liabilities	64%	37%	
15. Initiation of managerial meetings, problem-solving task forces	0%	25%	
16. Marketing related actions	64%	87%	
17. Liquidation of current assets and liabilities	14%	37%	
18 Professionalisation of manufacturing management, personnel management, planning etc.	21%	0%	
19. Miscellaneous actions	7%	25%	
20. Formal diagnostic activities	29%	12%	
21. Fresh induction of managers, technical staff etc.	43%	50%	
22. Changes in top management	93%	87%	
23. Management control-enhancing actions	29%	25%	
24. Better organisational integration, participative management, emphasis on core values	29%	25%	
25. Example-setting by top managers	21%	25%	
26. Significant retrenchment	100%	100%	
27. Diversification, product-line rationalisation, expansion etc.	100%	100%	

Note: Only those differences that are statistically significant at the 95% level of confidence have been indicated as 'significant'.

to be an example of a surgical turnaround uncomplicated by 'people management' concerns.[49] Rumsfeld slashed corporate staff from

800 to 350 and sold off marginal businesses with annual sales of $430 million. He emphasised discipline. He significantly beefed up R and D, new product introductions, and project management. He pushed hard the franchising of Searle products, expanded retail outlets, and invested in licenses, joint ventures, and small acquisitions. The company that lost $30 million in 1977 on sales of $850 million was earning $100 million on sales of $950 million in 1981.

Subbiah's turnaround of E.I.D. Parry, an Indian conglomerate, was a second example of a fairly Theory X harsh turnaround.[50] He 'persuaded' 40 per cent of the staff and five top managers to leave, disciplined militant unions and indisciplined workers, clamped down on managers' travel costs, and closed some businesses. Through better funds management the burden of interest was brought down. Tight controls were imposed on inventories and the use of funds, and monthly operating results were required to be compiled within two weeks of the month-end in lieu of the earlier two and a half months. Some of the obsolete plants that were guzzling fuel were replaced to cut down fuel costs. Several sales agencies were terminated and unprofitable product-lines were hived off. Several new products were launched. Subbiah introduced the concept of strategic business units, dismantled centralised systems, and pushed for decentralisation. He brought in a large number of new senior managers. He attempted to build an egalitarian culture through such devices as uniforms for all employees and one canteen for all. From a situation of no dividends for 10 prior years, a dividend was declared in 1985–86. The profits in 1985–86 totalled Rs 23 million on sales of Rs 1500 million and the expectations were that sales would go up by 10 per cent and the profits by 15 per cent the next year.

A third example was from Britain. Angus Murray took over as managing director of the Redman Heenan group in 1971.[51] In quick time surplus head office staff was disposed off, a factory was closed down, involving a loss of 600 jobs, several product-lines were dropped and further staff laid off, and a business was relocated. Group-wide financial control systems were installed. Bank loans were rescheduled, there was a strong push to collect debts, inventory levels were significantly reduced, overheads were slashed and restive creditors paid off. Murray arranged for the sale of three subsidiaries after engaging part-time specialists to locate loss makers in the group. There was an emphasis on developing and marketing environment systems. The Redman Heenan group was reorganised into six divisions. A central executive committee of division heads and top officers was formed to coordinate operations, and initially this met weekly. The board was reorganised: several old directors were replaced by younger professionals. Product development and market development were emphasised. The loss-making company broke even in 1972. By 1974 the sales had reached £22 million (compared to 1970 sales of £19 million), and the profits were £0.6 million.

Let us now look at some surgical *and* human resource management oriented complete turnarounds. Jaipur Metals, a sick Indian company taken over by the government of the Indian state of Rajasthan, offers an interesting example of a blend of harshness and staff motivation.[52] I.S. Kavadia, the new chief executive, a government servant on deputation, fired 500 workers (of a total strength of 1,750). He also laid off another 600 workers for a month in retaliation for labour unrest, and some officers were also asked to leave. He acted tough with the unions by presenting a charter of management demands to them. He got unions and workers to agree to longer hours of work for less pay, and he reduced overtime. So far this was a classic harsh turnaround. But then he offered the shares of the company to the employees in lieu of bonus, and 20 per cent of the profits were also converted into shares for them. He took representatives of the workers onto the company's board. He instituted a weekly plant level committee of workers and management and this committee in fact fired some workers whose performance was below the agreed norms. A suggestion scheme was introduced and a grievance committee set up. It was agreed to vary wages with productivity, and production norms were raised through an agreement with the unions. Large sums of money were spent on modernisation and diversification. Kavadia started weekly inter-departmental meetings of managers. The losses of Rs 9 million per year in the early eighties were converted into annual profits of Rs 30 million five years later.

Jaguar of Britain, a subsidiary of British Leyland, offers still another example of the blend of harshness and people-management orientation.[53] In the early eighties Jaguar, under John Egan, reduced its manpower by 30 per cent. However, this was done mostly through voluntary retirements and golden handshakes. Besides, quality circles were started on the shopfloor and the responsibility for training employees in quality improvement was transferred from inspectors to supervisors. The suggestion scheme was strengthened and yielded 8,000 suggestions in 1983. Automation was stepped up and robotisation with Japanese collaboration was introduced. Investment was greatly stepped up in new technologies. Since bought-outs were a problem area, a programme of supplier-education and involvement was introduced to cut down the supply of defective components, and, as a deterrent, penalty clauses were introduced in contracts. Consultants were brought in to study production systems in a couple of plants, and a comparative study was done of Jaguar and its competitors *vis a vis* quality and quality management. Problem areas were identified and a number of defects identified in Jaguar cars were rectified. Customer complaints were forcefully brought to the attention of workers and managers. A strong internal communication drive was launched to educate workers and managers about the company's problems. Videos, meetings, monthly bulletins, and a weekly plant-performance brief were pressed into service. Existing products were further differentiated and a facility for custom-moulding vehicles with special features created. New products were introduced. Dealers were contacted to learn more about customer complaints and also get ideas for product changes. Inadequate sales outlets were weeded out (sales outlets were halved) but bonus was given to dealers giving excellent customer service. A West German marketing subsidiary was set up and a search initiated for new markets all over the world. New directors of finance and personnel were recruited. Egan sought a distinctive identity for Jaguar and complete operating autonomy from British Leyland, the holding company. The company that averaged a £40 million loss in 1980 and 1981 broke even in 1982, earned £50 million in 1983 and £90 million in 1985, on a 1983 turnover of £470 million and a 1985 turnover of £750 million (compared to the 1980 and 1981 sales of below £200 million).

The turnaround of Chrysler, the US car producer, by Lee Iacocca represents another harsh turnaround leavened by adroit stakeholder mobilisation.[54] Iacocca cut total employment down from 160,000 to 80,000. He slashed overhead costs by $1 billion. A third of Chrysler's 60 plants were closed or consolidated. A thousand dealers were dispensed with. But he did not stop at just removing the deadwood. He cut down car-repair costs by placing Chrysler retirees in vendors' plants to improve production practices. The parts list was reduced from 75,000 to 45,000 items in order to pursue standardisation. He also aggressively sought better terms from vendors and workers, negotiated lower interest rates with lenders, and bought parts from cheaper vendors. He harped on a stronger marketing orientation, and heavier advertising and publicity (Iacocca personally marketed new models) to convince sceptial car buyers about the viability and durability of Chrysler models. He got Chrysler to concentrate on cheaper, stripped-down versions of sub-compact cars, but at the same time also to strive for a larger number of models. He also managed stakeholder relations very skillfully. He got the support of the US government, bankers, labour and shareholders for the turnaround, and the UAW (the union) to agree to the joint launching of a quality programme and to the removal of restrictive work practices. He paid off $1.3 billion in short-term debt but at the same time negotiated a federal government guarantee for bank loans, won $1 billion in concessions and loans from the UAW, and arranged a swap of $1.1 billion preferred stock for equity. He inspired staff and opened up channels of communication with managers and staff. He built up a strong top management team by bringing in a number of outsiders, especially from Ford Motor Company. He introduced a culture of faster decision-making. He also launched a vigorous $6.6 billion five-year programme of new product development. From accumulated losses of $3.5 billion in 1981 the company went on to earn $5.6 billion during 1983–86. Its 1985 profits were $1.6 billion on sales of $21 billion.

Concluding Comments

Cost-cutting is an attractive tool for all managements in trouble. Retrenchment of 'surplus' staff is a commonplace option in cost-cutting. But cost-cutting through retrenchment is not an isolated device. In harsh turnarounds it is a catalytic element of a syndrome that includes attempts at pruning loss-making or wasteful operations, more aggressive marketing, and rationalising and upgrading the product-line. It may be a manifestation of the archetypal trimming impulse in managers, which, unchecked, can, however, culminate into viciousness. In the latter form it is not very different from the bloody purges despots and dictators often have resorted to. True, people are not killed in harsh turnarounds. But the images are there: they are 'fired', 'axed', 'got rid off'.

The blackness of harsh turnarounds can, however, be alleviated by a determined attempt to see the remaining stakeholders as resources, mobilise their support, develop their capabilities further, motivate them for greater productivity, and so on. This option is, indeed, fairly commonly exercised, and seems to yield good results. Indeed, the cases indicate that this option, labelled Surgical Productivity/Innovation Oriented Turnaround, tends to yield better results than the purely surgical one (labelled Surgical Reconstructive Turnaround).

But the question remains: Can the human and social cost of turnarounds be reduced? Can there be turnarounds without tears? The next chapter seeks an answer.

Notes and References

1. See Mark Potts and Peter Behr, *The leading edge: CEOs who turned their companies around—what they did and how they did it* (New Delhi: Tata McGraw-Hill, 1987, ch. 1).
2. See O.P. Kharbanda and E.A. Stallworthy, *Company rescue: How to manage a business turnaround* (London: Heinemann, 1987, pp. 115–28).
3. See *Business Week*, 'The next act at Chrysler', 3 November 1986, pp. 48–52. See also *Business Week*, 'Can Chrysler keep its comeback act rolling?' 14 February 1983, pp. 58–62, and Maynard M. Gordon, *The Iacocca management technique* (New York: Bantam, 1987).
4. See *Business Week*, 'Big Steel is humming again', 8 August 1988, pp. 50–51; O.P. Kharbanda and E.A. Stallworthy, 1987, op. cit., pp. 51–61.
5. See Ian MacGregor, 'Recovery at British Steel', *Journal of General Management*, Vol. 7, No. 3, 1982, pp. 5–16. See also David Chambers 'Consumer orientation and the drive for quality', paper presented at the Roundtable on 'Public Enterprise Management: Strategies for Success', held at New Delhi, 6–11 March 1988, under the auspices of the Commonwealth Secretariat, London, and Indian Institute of Management, Ahmedabad.
6. See *Business Week*, 'Behind the stunning comeback at Britain's ICI', 3 June 1985, pp. 48–49; Rebecca Nelson, 'ICI', pp. 83–91, in Rebecca Nelson and David Clutterback (eds.), *Turnaround: How twenty well-known companies came back from the brink* (London: W.H. Allen, 1988).
7. See Kharbanda and Stallworthy, 1987, op. cit., pp. 142–53.
8. See Potts and Behr, 1987, op. cit., p. 1.

9. See Kharbanda and Stallworthy, 1987, op. cit., p. 145.

10. See Kharbanda and Stallworthy, 1987, op. cit., pp. 142–53.

11. See *Business Week*, 'The next act at Chrysler', 3 November 1986, pp. 48–52. See also *Business Week*, 'Can Chrysler keep its comeback act rolling?' 14 February 1983, pp. 58–62, and Gordon, 1987, op. cit.

12. See Fabrizio Galimberti, 'Getting FIAT back on the road', *Long Range Planning*, Vol. 19, No. 1, 1986, pp. 25–30. See also Cesare Romiti, 'Fiat', pp. 151–63, in Nelson and Clutterback, 1988, op. cit.

13. See Kharbanda and Stallworthy, 1987, op. cit., pp. 115–28.

14. See David Chambers, 'Consumer orientation and the drive for quality', 1988, op. cit.

15. See *Business Week*, 'Behind the stunning comeback at Britain's ICI', 3 June 1985, pp. 48–49; Rebecca Nelson, 'ICI', pp. 83-91, in Nelson and Clutterback, 1988, op. cit.

16. See *Business Week*, 'Searle: Rallying a drug company with an injection of new vitality', 8 February 1982, pp. 50 and 52.

17. See D.C.L. Morwood, 'ICL: Crisis and swift recovery', *Long Range Planning*, Vol. 18, No. 2, 1985, pp. 10–21. See also Simon Caulkin, 'ICL's Lazarus act', *Management Today*, January 1987, pp. 56–63.

18. See Marisa Bellisario, 'The turnaround at Italtel', *Long Range Planning*, Vol. 18, No. 1, 1985, pp. 21–24.

19. See *Business Week*, 'Three computer makers and chapter 11: Trying to write a happy ending', 4 March 1985, pp. 60–61.

20. See Stuart Slatter, *Corporate recovery: Successful turnaround strategies and their implementation.* (Harmondsworth, Middlesex: Penguin, 1984, pp. 288–95).

21. See Palakunnithu G. Mathai, 'Parry: Overhaul', *India Today*, 15 June 1987, pp. 116–17.

22. See *Business Week*, 'Mike Dingman tunes'em up, and turns'em around, spins'em off', 5 October 1987, pp. 58–60 and 62.

23. See Dilip Thakore, 'How the world's largest public sector company has been turned around', *Business World*, 22 June-5 July 1987, pp. 34–47. See also K.K. Roy, 'Italy's non-oil public sector: Prodi(gious) turnaround', *Economic Times*, 19 June 1987, p. 5; Romano Prodi, 'Instituto per la Ricostruzione Industrial (IRI)', pp. 93–101, in Nelson and Clutterback, 1988, op. cit.

24. See *Business Week*, 'How Black & Decker got back in the black', July 1987, pp. 70–71.

25. See F.J. Aboderin, 'EPE Plywood situation', paper presented at the Roundtable on 'Public Enterprise Management: Strategies for Success' held at New Delhi, 6–11 March 1988, under the auspices of the Commonwealth Secretariat, London and Indian Institute of Management, Ahmedabad.

26. See *Business Week*, 'Coming to life after warm weather wilted the big plans', 10 October 1983, p. 52.

27. See Geoffrey Foster, 'The remaking of Metal Box', *Management Today*, January 1985, pp. 13–21.

28. See Anita van de Vliet, 'Why Rockware was recycled', *Management Today*, September 1985, pp. 62–69.

29. See Sreekant Khandekar, 'JMEL: Dramatic turnaround', *India Today*, 15 December 1985, pp. 103–4. See also Surya Mookherjee, 'Industrial sickness and revival: A study of select organizations', paper presented at the 'National Seminar on Industrial Sickness in India', held at Gandhi Labour Institute, 3–4 June 1989, Ahmedabad, India.

30. See Stuart Slatter, 1984, op. cit., pp. 279–87.

31. See Stuart Slatter, 1984, op. cit., pp. 271–79.

32. See Ian MacGregor, 1982, op. cit., and David Chambers, 1988, op. cit.

33. See *Business Week*, 'Big Steel is humming again', 8 August 1988, pp. 50–51; Kharbanda and Stallworthy, 1987, op. cit., pp. 55–61.

34. See Nicholas Newman, 'Dawson's well-knit whoosh', *Management Today*, March 1981, pp. 74–82, 165 and 168.

35. See Debra Isaac, 'ICI's new yarn', *Management Today*, February 1984, pp. 66–73.

36. See *Business Week*, 'Munsingwear: Stitching together a comeback', 28 May 1984, p. 60.

37. See *Business Week*, 'Warnaco: Prospering by slimming and donning big name labels', 18 October 1982, p. 64.

38. See Stuart Slatter, 1984, op. cit., pp. 302–12.

39. See Kabbe M.A Jallow, 'The Gambia Produce Marketing Board—A case study', paper presented at the Roundtable on 'Public Enterprise Management: Strategies for Success', New Delhi, 6–11 March 1988, held under the auspices of the Commonwealth Secretariat, London, and Indian Institute of Management, Ahmedabad.

40. See *Business Week*, 'The No. 1 Yankee trader gets its ship back on course', 25 March 1985, p. 60–61.

41. See *Business Week*, 'Wickes: Creditors question Sanford Sigoloff's crash cure', 21 November 1983, pp. 58–59.

42. See Dudley Sackaloo, 'Case study on Jamaica Railway Corporation', presented at the First Pan Commonwealth Roundtable on 'Public Enterprise Management: Strategies for Success', held at Nicosia, Cyprus, 1–5 June 1987.

43. See *Business Week*, 'Survival in the basic industries: A shrunken Firestone picks its turf in tires', 26 April 1982, pp. 46–50 and 52.

44. See *Business Week*, 'Macmillan: Back to the schoolhouse to sustain a text book turnaround', 28 November 1983, pp. 67–68.

45. See Mark Potts and Peter Behr, 1987, op. cit.

46. Douglas McGregor propounded two famed contrasting management theories: Theory X based on distrust and external control of employees, and Theory Y, based on trust and faith in self-control by employees if treated as responsible persons. See Douglas McGregor, *The human side of enterprise* (New York: McGraw-Hill, 1960).

47. See *Business Week*, 'Mike Dingman tunes'em up, and turns'em around, spins'em off', 5 October 1987, pp. 58–60 and 62.

48. See Dilip Thakore, 1987, op. cit. and K.K. Roy, 1987, op. cit.

49. See *Business Week*, 'Searle: Rallying a drug company with an injection on new vitality', 8 February 1982, pp. 50 and 52.

50. See Palakunnithu G. Mathai, 1987, op. cit.

51. See Stuart Slatter, 1984, op. cit., pp. 279–87.
52. See Sreekant Khandekar, 1985, op. cit., and Surya Mookherjee, 1989, op. cit.
53. See David Chambers, 1988, op. cit.
54. See *Business Week*, 'The next act at Chrysler', 3 November 1986, pp. 48–52. See also *Business Week*, 'Can Chrysler keep its comeback act rolling?' 14 February 1983, pp. 58–62, and Gordon, 1987, op. cit.

4. TURNAROUND WITHOUT TEARS

One approach to turnaround emphasises shedding "deadwood" and "fat". This translates into large scale lay-offs and the closing or disposal of loss making facilities. For those who believe in this approach it may be difficult to conceive of an alternative approach that does not utilise surgical means to any appreciable extent. However, an alternative does exist. Indeed, it is an alternative that may be far more palatable in those societies where, because of massive unemployment or underemployment, mass firings by organisations is socially not acceptable or is very costly to the state. It is also an attractive alternative in those cultures, such as Japan's, where lifetime employment is the norm, and in those systems, such as governmental systems. where hiring and firing methods are not a norm. Even in societies, such as America's, that live by the sword in employment matters, it would surely be better to resuscitate a sick organisation without resorting to surgery than to revive it by inflicting vast costs on large numbers of individuals.

But is it possible to have non-surgical turnarounds, especially in near hopeless case situations? Let us take a look at the turnaround efforts of two "twins".

A Tale of Two Behemoths

British Steel and the Steel Authority of India Limited (SAIL) were, at the time of their respective sicknesses, near-twins. Both were government-owned. had very similar product lines, and were vast organisations with a staff of a quarter million each. Both were sick because of overmanning, indifferent management, run-down plant. obsolete technology, and high costs. Both were dominant in the steel industry in their respective countries, with British Steel being a near monopoly in Britain and SAIL having a 50 per cent, or higher, market share in India. And yet there was a great difference in the way the two were turned around. When the dust of the battle against sickness had settled, British Steel had but a fifth of its original staff and only a half of its production capacity. SAIL increased production by 40 per cent, was aggressively planning to increase capacity, and had not fired a single soul for cost saving purposes (some 3,000 did leave, however, on their own volition under a voluntary retirement scheme). How were these two contrasting turnarounds accomplished?

The late seventies and the early eighties were years of haemorrhage for British Steel.[1] During 1979–80 to 1984–85 the company lost an average of £366 million a year. High energy costs, decline in world and British demand for steel, rising tariff barriers and a strong sterling that made it difficult to export steel, labour trouble in feeder industries, work stoppages, rapid wage increases (80 per cent between 1975 and 1980 in Britain versus 27 per cent in West Germany and nil in Japan), and lower productivity than that in West Germany, France, and Japan contributed to the massive bleeding. Sir Charles Villiers formulated a turnaround strategy of plant closures, retrenchment, and modernisation. Ian MacGregor, a Scottish metallurgist who had made his career in US industry replaced Villiers in July 1980 as chairman and went about implementing the turnaround strategy with gusto. After persuading the government and the employees, the workforce was reduced from close to a quarter million to 52,000 and production capacity was slashed from a peak of 28 million tons to 14 million tons. Through modernisation, energy consumption per ton of steel was reduced by 28 per cent and scrap was also reduced. The various businesses of the company were rationalised for better performance control. The company moved vigorously into continuous casting technology so that the percentage of output through this technology rose from 5 per cent in 1974 to over 50 per cent in 1984. This resulted in a dramatic increase in productivity of around 10 per cent to 15 per cent per year. The price of steel was not increased in tandem with escalations in costs so that in effect the real price of steel fell by 25 per cent. This stimulated its demand. The company took up the production of two piece steel for the canning industry and also the manufacture of thinner gauge steel. There was divestment of labour-intensive downstream activities. Further, government funding was obtained and the government agreed to write off £3,500 million in debt. MacGregor lobbied with the government to reduce energy prices. He also publicised British Steel's heroic action.

On the organisational front the product-based divisions were organised into profit centres. Bonus for the staff and the chairman's salary were tied to improvement in the company's performance. British Steel moved from national bargaining to localised, plant level bargaining, MacGregor practiced an open communications style of management. He issued a rescue plan towards the end of 1980 and got it accepted by the employees. He insisted on redeploying workers and on getting rid of narrow job descriptions. He also introduced multi-skill training for workers. At the managerial levels he called frequent meetings with different groups of managers. MacGregor also tried to increase the awareness of market realities in his staff. To drive home the new commercial orientation of the company MacGregor shifted British Steel's "Olympian" headquarters to more modest quarters.

British Steel broke even in 1985–86, and reported a profit of £206 million in 1986–87. However, these profits may be partially illusory because of the interest saved on the £3500 million debt written off by the British government.

The Steel Authority of India (SAIL) was bedevilled on many fronts in the eighties.[2] There had been a neglect of its steel plants for 15 years with the result that the machinery was run down. There had also been constant time and cost overruns of projects. As a consequence, costs had gone haywire. Frequent top management changes and a tendency to take decisions in the ministry rather than at the company level played havoc with the morale of the managers. A permissive work culture had arisen. By international standards, and even by the standards of steel producers in India, productivity was low. During 1980–1984 the company had lost Rs 2760 million.

Mr V Krishnamurthy, a seasoned public sector manager and a sometime senior government servant, took over as chairman in mid-1985. He had no previous experience in steel. Since the company was making losses, his managers and the officials of the ministry were in favour of a price rise. Mr Krishnamurthy successfully opposed it, on the ground that Indian steel, which once was the cheapest, had become the costliest in the world, and a further increase would damage Indian manufacturers. He argued that profits could be earned by increasing productivity and efficiency. He embarked on one of the greatest diagnostic and communications exercises in corporate history. Over a period of five months or so he wandered through plants, met ministry officials, managers, union representatives and around 25,000 employees either singly or in groups. He sought feedback on the problems facing the company. Out of this exercise came a document called Priorities for Action. Krishnamurthy called a series of two-day seminars of senior managers in batches of 80–85 persons at the corporate headquarters to discuss these priorities. He and members of the SAIL Board were present at these workshops which covered all 500 or so of the senior managers. The participants went back and conducted similar workshops in their plants. A large number of ideas and options were generated, and goals, issues, and plans clarified.

Krishnamurthy also got Priorities for Action mailed to all 250,000 employees of SAIL. These were discussed in groups at the plants. From this vast churning emerged the turnaround strategy for SAIL: modernisation, larger internal resource generation to finance modernisation, upgradation of operations to international levels of cost and quality, building of a productive corporate culture to upgrade operations, and the building of such a culture through better human resource management and development. The crucial element was seen as better people management, and accordingly, the emphasis was on team work, two-way communication, participative management, training and development, discipline, efficiency, and debureaucratisation.

A number of steps were taken. Meetings were held with trade unions to tackle indiscipline, and with customers to understand their needs. Fresh recruitment was curtailed. A voluntary retirement scheme was launched. Against union opposition some 7,000 workers were redeployed. Overtime payments were drastically reduced, from Rs 440 million in 1984–85 to Rs 25 million in 1986–87. Wasteful practices were sought to be eliminated. New technologies, such as LD-concast, were introduced for increasing productivity. A determined effort was made to save on fuel costs, and over a three year period the consumption of coke was reduced by 9 per cent. A captive power plant was set up to improve power supply.

Participative management was beefed up. A large number of briefing groups were set up to brief employees about policy issues.

Shift meetings at plants were also encouraged. A number of bipartite forums were created for effective management of employee relations through the participation of workers. Improvements were made in the grievance and welfare systems. The suggestion scheme was modified. Incentive schemes were revised to increase their motivational value. At the same time the management took a tough stance against indiscipline, absenteeism, and wildcat strikes.

A number of systemic changes were made. Decentralisation was pushed hard. The number of levels below the plant general manager was reduced from eight to five. Budgetary, financial, and production controls were recast to support decentralisation and restructuring. Since project management had been a weakness, a vice-chairman was appointed exclusively to look after project implementation and monitoring. SAIL became much more market and customer oriented than before.

Training and human resource development were stepped up. For workers, the emphasis shifted to multi-skill, multi-employment training. Nearly 19,000 employees in 1986–87 and 37,000 in 1987–88 underwent training. Eight hundred officers in the personnel and training departments of various plants attended some eight one-day workshops to discuss perspectives for human resource management in SAIL. Better integration of training and development was sought and training effectiveness reassessed. Managerial training was stepped up. While some 10,000 executives were trained in 1986–87, the number was raised by 40 per cent the next year. A new training campus was set up to train senior managers and a thousand were given training in 1987–88. An executive director was appointed to oversee the training, and a training advisory board was appointed, headed by the chairman himself. A human resource development perspective plan was prepared after extensive discussions to bring about attitudinal changes, facilitate modernisation and expansion, increase efficiency, and give proper orientation to new employees. A manpower planning system was adopted.

Capital expenditure was stepped up. Some Rs 5,000 million was spent in 1987–88. A seven year capital spending plan of Rs 150,000 million was chalked out to ensure plant modernisation and product diversification, including programme to exploit by-product chemicals commercially.

To improve liaison with the government, the corporate head

office was shifted to New Delhi. SAIL entered into a memorandum of understanding with the government under which the respective obligations and commitments of the two parties were spelled out. Despite absorbing cost increases of 8 per cent to 10 per cent per year not matched wholly by price increases, SAIL showed a profit of Rs 1 billion in 1986–87 and a profit of Rs 3 billion in 1988–89. Its output registered a 40 per cent rise during 1986–89 on a declining workforce to show productivity gains of 10 per cent per year. There were no firings and lay-offs for cost reduction purposes. In four years a doddering lady was transformed into a potential Olympics sprinter.

The two turnarounds do have many features in common: modernisation, decentralisation, better management control, attempts at reducing costs, systems building, greater market orientation, diversification, incentives, public relations, open communications, worker discipline, participative managerial decision making. But the differences are no less striking: top management devising a turnaround strategy and then selling it to the staff and other stakeholders versus evolving a turnaround strategy through the widest possible participation and a matchless communications exercise; massive retrenchment and capacity reduction as the centrepieces of turnaround versus no retrenchment and rapid expansion of production as significant elements; modest efforts at retraining workers versus a massive and comprehensive attempt at training and human resource development for both workers and managers; some two-way communication and some worker participation in management versus two-way communication and staff participation in management as an all pervading management practice. It is tempting to wonder whether the costs of British Steel's turnaround—massive lay-offs, drastic reduction in capacity, steep fall in market share—could not have been avoided had a Krishnamurthy rather than a MacGregor been at the helm.

Lest it be thought that SAIL's turnaround-without-tears was an anomaly, Table 4.1 lists 30 break-even and complete turnarounds without significant retrenchment from around the globe from many of the same industries and countries in which surgical turnarounds were reported (see Table 3.1 of Chapter 3). In most of these there was virtually no retrenchment; in the rest it was 10 per cent or less of the total staff.

Table 4.1

Non-surgical Turnarounds from Round the World

	Country	Size
A. Accounting and Business Machines, Office Equipment		
* Docutel[3]	USA	$70 m. sales
(automatic teller machines)		
* Sweda International[4]	USA	$300 m. sales
(cash registers)		
B. Automobiles, Two-wheelers etc.		
* Enfield[5]	India	Rs. 300 m. sales
(two-wheelers, agro-engines)		
* Standard Motors[6]	India	Rs. 240 m. sales
(cars, light commercial vehicles)		
* Toyo Kogyo[7]	Japan	$5,000 m. sales
(cars and trucks)		
* Volkswagen[8]		DM 54,000
(car maker)	Germany	m. sales
C. Chemicals, Fertilisers, and Pharmaceuticals		
Celanese Corporation[9]	USA	$3,500 m. sales
(petro-chemicals, synthetic fibres, plastics)		
Fertilizers and Chemicals Travancore[10]	India	Rs. 2,000 m. sales
(chemicals and fertilisers)		
* Southern Petro-chemicals and Industries[11]	India	Rs. 5,000 m. sales
(fertilisers, chemicals, electronics)		
* Travancore Cochin Chemicals[12]	India	Rs. 150 m. sales
(miscellaneous chemicals)		
D. Computers, Electronics, Telecommunications		
* Ferranti[13]	UK	£190 m. sales
(electronics, computers)		
Wang Labs[14]	USA	$3,000 m. sales
(computers, peripherals, computer software)		
E. Conglomerates		
Nil		
F. Household Goods		
* Sylvania and Laxman[15]	India	Rs. 200 m. sales
(lamps and related products)		
G. Packaging, Containers		
Tinplate[16]	India	Rs. 600 m. sales,
(tinplated containers)		5,000 employees

Table 4.1 (Contd.)

		Country	Size
H.	**Plant, Machinery, Equipment, Engineering Products**		
*	Bharat Heavy Electricals[17]	India	$450 m. sales
	(power plants and allied equipment)		45,000 employees
*	Bharat Heavy Plate and Vessels[18]	India	Rs. 600 m. sales
	(sophisticated heavy engineering products like pressure vessels and heat exchangers)		4,000 employees
*	Lucas[19]	UK	£1,500 m. sales
	(engineering autoparts, aerospace parts, electrical machines)		
	Mining and Allied Machinery Corporation[20]	India	Rs. 800 m. sales
	(mining and bulk material handling equipment, conveyors, coal beneficiation plants etc.)		7,700 employees
*	RFD Group[21]	UK	£19 m. sales
	(life saving equipment)		
	Richardson and Cruddas[22]	India	Rs. 200 m. sales,
	(structurals, different sorts of machineries)		4,000 employees
I.	**Steel**		
*	Steel Authority of India (SAIL)[23]	India	Rs. 60,000 m. sales, 250,000 employees
	(steel and steel products)		
J.	**Textiles, Fibres, Apparel**		
	Nil		
K.	**Timber and Pulp**		
*	Can Cel[24]	Canada	C$160 m. sales
	(timber and pulp)		
*	State Timber Corporation[25]	Sri Lanka	SL Rs. 350 m.
	(timber and pulp)		
L.	**Trade and Services**		
	Nil		
M.	**Transportation**		
	Eastern Airlines[26]	USA	$4,000 m. revenues, 38,000 employees
	(air line)		
	Air India[27]	India	Rs. 12,000 m. revenues, 20,000 employees
	(air line)		
*	Zambia Railways[28]	Zambia	K.400 m. revenues
	(railway)		
N.	**Tyres**		
*	Apollo[29]	India	Rs. 1,500 m. sales
	(tyres for cars and trucks)		

Table 4.1 (Contd.)

	Country	Size
O. Miscellaneous		
* Del E. Webb[30]	USA	$360 m. sales
(leisure, real estate, construction)		
NBC Radio Division[31]	USA	$40 m. revenues
(radio broadcasting)		
Pullman[32]	USA	$200 m. sales
(rail-car maker)		

* Complete turnaround (those not marked by an asterisk were break-even turnarounds)

Foundational Elements of Non-surgical Turnarounds

Table 4.2 shows the extent to which the 27 turnaround elements were utilised in the non-surgical complete turnarounds. Nearly a dozen elements (versus five for the sample of surgical turnarounds—see Table 3.2 of Chapter 3) were utilised by at least 60 per cent of the non-surgical turnarounds. Non-surgical turnarounds were evidently far more multi-dimensional than surgical turnarounds, and to that extent more complex. The two types did have some elements in common, notably diversification, product-line rationalisation, expansion, change in top management, marketing related actions, and cost reduction measures other than retrenchment. But the differences too, were striking. Besides the difference *vis-a-vis* retrenchment, there were sharp differences *vis-à-vis* plant modernisation and related actions (score of 75 per cent for non-surgical turnarounds versus 45 per cent for surgical turnarounds), better organisational integration, participative management, emphasis on core values (65 per cent versus 27 per cent), garnering stakeholders' support (65 per cent versus 27 per cent), formal diagnostic activities (60 per cent versus 23 per cent), and motivating staff (60 per cent versus 32 per cent). Thus, non-surgical turnarounds tended to invest more in finding out the ills of the organisation and opportunities for betterment, in mobilising various stakeholders for the turnaround, in participatively uniting the organisation and motivating the staff to work for the common cause, and in removing manufacturing or technological blocks to profitable operations.

Table 4.2

Percentages of Cases Engaging in Different Turnaround Actions

Sample: 20 Non-surgical Complete Turnarounds

		Percentage Engaging in Action
1.	Diversification, product-line rationalisation, expansion etc.	100
2.	Change in top management	95
3.	Marketing related actions	90
4.	Restructuring (decentralisation, fixing accountability, structural changes etc.)	80
5.	Plant modernisation etc. for greater efficiency, quality, productivity	75
6.	Cost-reduction measures other than retrenchment	65
7.	Better organisational integration, participative management, emphasis on core values	65
8.	Garnering stakeholders' support	65
9.	Innovation, new product development etc.	60
10.	Incentives, motivation, grievance redressal	60
11.	Formal diagnostic activities	60
12.	Management control-enhancing actions	55
13.	Attempt to increase efficiency, quality, productivity, other than through plant modernisation etc. and training	50
14.	Management communicating with staff, lower managers etc.	45
15.	Professionalisation of manufacturing management, personnel management, planning etc.	45
16.	Initiation of managerial meetings, problem-solving task-forces	45
17.	Disciplining	40
18.	Public articulation by management of corporate mission, goals etc.	40
19.	Divestiture and liquidation of fixed assets and long-term liabilities	35
20.	Borrowings, raising equity finance etc.	35
21.	Increased training of managers and staff	35
22.	Fresh induction of managers, technical staff etc.	30
23.	Credibility-building actions of management	30
24.	Liquidation of current assets and liabilities	30
25.	Example-setting by top managers	20
26.	Miscellaneous actions	15
27.	Significant retrenchment	0

Strategic Elements of Non-surgical Turnarounds

Table 4.3 shows the substantial correlates of each turnaround element and identifies the ones that were relatively more widely correlated, and therefore of strategic importance in designing alternative non-surgical turnarounds. The cut-off used for deciding whether a correlation was substantial or not was 0.42, the level at which a correlation between two normally distributed variables would be significant at the 95 per cent confidence level.

About a dozen elements had at least four substantial correlations and therefore could be considered strategic (there were only six similarly strategic elements among surgical turnarounds). In a sense, so many strategic or trigger elements simplifies the turnaround job, for pressing even a few strategic buttons would, because of the chain reactions unleashed, activate a turnaround. Thus, while the basic structure of a humane turnaround seems to be quite multi-dimensional and complex, pressing the right buttons may considerably simplify the job of turning around, without significant retrenchment, a sick organisation. The top three strategic elements were staff incentives, roping in stakeholders, and restructuring (mostly decentralising with accountability). These were followed by credibility building by management, plant modernisation, team problem solving by managers, and attempts at greater internal cohesion for meeting the common challenge. The least strategic were attempts at greater control of operations, professionalisation, diagnosis, and innovation.

Table 4.3

Substantial Correlations of Each Turnaround Element in Non-surgical Turnarounds

Sample: 20 Non-surgical Complete Turnarounds

1. *Incentives, motivation, grievance redressal*: Restructuring (decentralisation, fixing accountability, structural changes etc. (0.61), formal diagnostic activities (0.58), professionalisation of manufacturing management, personnel management, planning etc. (0.53), credibility-building actions of management (0.53), management control-enhancing actions (0.49), plant modernisation etc. for greater efficiency, quality, productivity (0.47), garnering stakeholders' support (0.47), divestiture and liquidation of fixed assets and long-term liabilities (−0.47).

Table 4.3 (Contd.)

2. *Garnering stakeholders' support*: Management control-enhancing actions (0.60), better organisational integration, participative management, emphasis on core values (0.56), credibility-building actions of management (0.48), formal diagnostic activities (0.47), incentives, motivation, grievance redressal (0.47), initiation of managerial meetings, problem-solving task-forces (0.45), professionalisation of manufacturing management, personnel management, planning etc. (0.45).

3. *Restructuring (decentralisation, fixing accountability, structural changes etc.)*: Formal diagnostic activities (0.61), incentives, motivation, grievance redressal (0.61), plant modernisation etc. for greater efficiency, quality, productivity (0.58), management control-enhancing actions (0.55), significant retrenchment (−0.46), initiation of managerial meetings, problem-solving task-forces (0.45), professionalisation of manufacturing management, personnel management, planning etc. (0.45).

4. *Credibility-building actions of management*: Public articulation by management of corporate mission, goals etc. (0.80), incentives, motivation, grievance redressal (0.53), professionalisation of manufacturing management, personnel management, planning etc. (0.50), better organisational integration, participative management, emphasis on core values (0.48), garnering stakeholders' support (0.48), divestiture and liquidation of fixed assets and long-term liabilities (−0.48).

5. *Plant modernisation etc. for greater efficiency, quality, productivity*: Management control-enhancing actions (0.64), restructuring (decentralisation, fixing accountability, structural changes etc.) (0.58), diversification, product rationalisation, expansion, etc. (0.58), better integration, participative management, emphasis on core values (0.54), incentives, motivation, grievance redressal (0.47), formal diagnostic activities (0.47).

6. *Initiation of managerial meetings, problem-solving task-forces*: Better integration, participative management, emphasis on core values (0.66), increased training of managers and staff (0.59), innovation, new product development etc. (−0.48), restructuring (decentralisation, fixing accountability, structural changes etc.) (0.45), garnering stakeholders' support (0.45), miscellaneous actions (0.45).

7. *Better organisational integration, participative management, emphasis on core values*: Initiation of managerial meetings, problem-solving task-forces (0.66), garnering stakeholders' support (0.56), plant modernisation etc. for greater efficiency, quality, productivity (0.54), credibility-building actions of management (0.48), formal diagnostic activities (0.47), professionalisation of manufacturing management, personnel management, planning etc. (0.45).

8. *Management control-enhancing actions*: Plant modernisation etc. for greater efficiency, quality, productivity (0.64), garnering stakeholders' support (0.60), restructuring (decentralisation, fixing accountability, structural changes etc.) (0.55), attempts to increase efficiency, quality, productivity other than through plant modernisation etc. and training (0.50), incentives, motivation, grievance redressal (0.49).

Table 4.3 (Contd.)

9. *Professionalisation of manufacturing management, personnel management, planning etc.*: Incentives, motivation, grievance redressal (0.53), credibility-building actions of management (0.50), garnering stakeholders' support (0.45), restructuring (decentralisation, fixing accountability, structural changes etc.) (0.45), better organisational integration, participative management, emphasis on core values (0.45).

10. *Formal diagnostic activities*: Restructuring (decentralisation, fixing accountability, structural changes etc.) (0.61), incentives, motivation, grievance redressal (0.58), plant modernisation etc. for greater efficiency, quality, productivity (0.47), better integration, participative management, emphasis on core values (0.47).

11. *Innovation, new product development etc.*: Cost reduction measures other than retrenchment (−0.60), liquidation of current assets and liabilities (0.53), initiation of managerial meetings, problem-solving task-forces (−0.49), increased training of managers and staff (−0.47).

12. *Increased training of managers and staff*: Initiation of managerial meetings, problem-solving task-forces (0.59), public articulation by management of mission, goals, etc. (0.47), innovation, new product development etc. (−0.47).

13. *Divestiture and liquidation of fixed assets and long-term liabilities*: Credibility-building actions of management (−0.48), incentives, motivation, grievance redressal (−0.47), marketing related actions (−0.45).

14. *Significant retrenchment*: Diversification, product-line rationalisation, expansion, etc. (−0.69), restructuring (decentralisation, fixing accountability, structural changes etc.) (−0.46).

15. *Cost-reduction measures other than retrenchment*: Innovation, new product development etc. (−0.59), management communicating with staff, lower managers etc. (0.45).

16. *Attempts to increase efficiency, quality, productivity other than through plant modernisation etc. and training*: Management control-enhancing actions (0.50), fresh induction of managers, technical staff etc. (0.44).

17. *Marketing related actions*: Divestiture and liquidation of fixed assets and long-term liabilities (−0.45), borrowings, raising equity etc. (−0.45).

18. *Diversification, product-line rationalisation, expansion etc.*: Significant retrenchment (−0.69), plant modernisation etc. for greater efficiency, quality, productivity (0.58).

19. *Management communicating with staff, lower managers etc.*: Disciplining (0.49), cost-reduction actions other than retrenchment (0.45).

20. *Public articulation by management of corporate mission, goals etc.*: Credibility-building actions of management (0.80), increased training of managers and staff (0.47).

21. *Liquidation of current assets and liabilities*: Innovation, new product development etc. (0.53).

Table 4.3 (contd.)

---

22. *Borrowings, raising equity finance etc.*: Marketing related actions (−0.45).

23. *Disciplining*: Management communicating with staff, lower managers etc. (0.49).

24. *Fresh induction of managers, technical staff etc.*: Attempts to increase efficiency, quality, productivity other than through plant modernisation etc. and training (0.44).

25. *Miscellaneous actions*: Initiation of managerial meetings, problem-solving task-forces (0.45).

26. *Changes in top management*: Nil

27. *Example-setting by top managers*: Nil

Note: Only product moment correlations of 0.44 and above have been reported. These are shown in brackets.

The surgical and the non-surgical varieties shared a few strategic elements in common, notably staff incentives and motivation, garnering stakeholders' support, and restructuring. These three, when pressed into service, may provide a distinctive colour to both types of turnarounds. But there were some differences, too. Management by mission, raising of capital, and non-automation and non-training based attempts at improving productivity and its related functions were strategic elements for surgical turnarounds but not for non-surgical turnarounds. Building management systems for greater operations control and effectiveness, formal diagnostic activities, innovation, modernisation of plant, and above all, attempts at creating confidence in management, collective problem solving, and building teamwork were options that were strategic in non-surgical turnarounds but not in surgical turnarounds.

Table 4.4 lists the foundational and strategic elements of non-surgical turnarounds.

Table 4.4

Foundational and Strategic Elements of Non-surgical Turnarounds

Sample: 20 Non-surgical Complete Turnarounds

Foundational Turnaround Elements

1. Diversification, product-line rationalisation, expansion etc.
2. Change in top management
3. Marketing related actions
4. Restructuring (decentralisation, fixing accountability, structural changes etc.)

Table 4.4 (Contd.)

5. Plant modernisation etc. for greater efficiency, quality, productivity
6. Cost-reduction measures other than retrenchment
7. Better organisational integration, participative management, emphasis on core values
8. Garnering stakeholders' support
9. Innovation, new product development etc.
10. Incentives, motivation, grievance redressal
11. Formal diagnostic activities

Strategic Turnaround Elements
1. Incentives, motivation, grievance redressal
2. Garnering stakeholders' support
3. Restructuring (decentralisation, fixing accountability, structural changes etc.)
4. Credibility-building actions of management
5. Plant modernisation etc. for greater efficiency, quality, productivity
6. Initiation of managerial meetings, problem-solving task-forces
7. Better organisational integration, participative management, emphasis on core values
8. Management control-enhancing actions
9. Professionalisation of manufacturing management, personnel management, planning etc.
10. Formal diagnostic activities
11. Innovation, new product development etc.

Choices in Non-surgical Turnarounds

A principal components factor analysis of the data on non-surgical turnarounds yielded nine factors with eigen values exceeding 1. These accounted for 87 per cent of the total variability in the 27 variables. Table 4.5 shows the more important of these factors (that is, those with eigen values exceeding 2), and the turnaround elements that loaded at least 0.5 on them.

Table 4.5

Main Principal Components Factors and Turnaround Elements Loading Heavily on them

Sample: 20 Non-surgical Complete Turnarounds

	Heavily Loading Turnaround Elements	**Loading**
Factor 1 (accounted for 26% of the variance explained by all 9 factors)	1. Restructuring (decentralisation, fixing accountability, structural changes etc.)	76

Table 4.5 (Contd.)

	Heavily Loading Turnaround Elements	Loading
	2. Incentives, motivation, grievance redressal	.75
	3. Better organisational integration, participative management, emphasis on core values	.71
	4. Garnering stakeholders' support	.69
	5. Formal diagnostic activities	.68
	6. Initiation of managerial meetings, problem-solving task-forces	.67
	7. Professionalisation of manufacturing management, personnel management planning etc.	.66
	8. Plant modernisation etc. for greater efficiency, quality, productivity	.63
	9. Credibility-building actions of management	.62
	10. Management control-enhancing actions	.59
	11. Increased training of managers and staff	.55
Factor 2 (accounted for 15% of total explained variance)	1. Fresh induction of managers, technical staff etc.	.82
	2. Divestiture and liquidation of fixed assets and long-term liabilities	.73
	3. Credibility-building actions of management	−.61
	4. Public articulation by management of corporate mission, goals etc.	−.52
Factor 3 (accounted for 12% of total explained variance)	1. Innovation, new product development etc.	.66
	2. Liquidation of current assets and liabilities	.62
	3. Increased training of managers and staff	−.55
	4. Cost-reduction actions other than retrenchment	−.52
Factor 4 (accounted for 11% of total explained variance)	1. Management communicating with staff, lower managers etc.	.74
	2. Diversification, product-line rationalisation, expansion etc.	−.73
	3. Significant retrenchment	.68
	4. Cost-reduction actions other than retrenchment	.62
Factor 5 (accounted for 10% of total explained variance)	1. Changes in top management	.65
	2. Marketing related actions	−.51
	3. Borrowings, raising equity finance etc.	.50

Note: Only loadings of 0.5 and over of factors with eigen values exceeding 2 have been reported.

The first factor, accounting for over 25 per cent of the variability explained by all the factors (and over a third of the variability explained by the important factors) is of principal interest, allowing for the loading of as many as 11 elements. These elements fell into three main categories. The first consisted of people management elements: credibility-building, better integration, participative management, emphasis on core values, networking with stakeholders, incentives and motivation, and greater training and human resource development. The second category comprised systems elements: structural change, formal management control mechanisms, professionalisation of management functions like manufacturing, personnel and planning, and modernisation of plant. The third category was of problem-solving mechanisms: diagnostic effort and collective problem solving through meetings and task-forces. Therefore, the basic choice suggested by the factor was a turnaround strategy of mobilising the stakeholders for the turnaround, considerable collective troubleshooting, and systems development, versus one that underplays or ignores these dimensions.

A cluster analysis (seeking a two cluster solution) of the 20 (complete) non-surgical turnarounds revealed the companies that exercised the choice. Table 4.6 gives the scores of the first type, consisting of nine turnarounds, and also the scores of the second type, consisting of 11 turnarounds. The score profiles suggest that the first type could be labelled the Non-surgical Innovation Oriented Turnaround (emphasis on innovation and new product development, besides emphasis on such elements as diversification and product rationalisation, changes in the top management, marketing, and cost reduction, that are common to all turnarounds) and the second could be called the Non-surgical Transformational Turnaround (emphasis on networking with stakeholders, professional management systems development, diagnosis, team problem solving, participation, motivation and such like, besides emphasis on such elements as modernisation, restructuring, marketing effectiveness, diversification, top management changes, cost cutting and related activities that are common to all turnarounds). Both were characterised by top management change, aggressive marketing, and repositioning of product-line. But they differed (statistically significantly, using the difference in proportions test) on nine turnaround elements. The main differences related to more frequent diagnosis and problem solving (items 4 and 8), effective people management (items 1, 2 and 5), and development of management systems and operating systems (items 3, 7 and 10) in the Nonsurgical Transformational turnaround. Let us see some illustrative cases from each type. .

Table 4.6

Two Types of Non-surgical Turnarounds

Sample: 20 Non-surgical Complete Turnarounds

	Non-surgical Innovation Oriented (9 cases)	Non-surgical Transform- ational (11 cases)	Difference
1. Garnering stakeholders' support	22	100	Significant
2. Incentives, motivation, grievance redressal	22	91	Significant
3. Management control-enhancing actions	22	82	Significant
4. Formal diagnostic activities	22	82	Significant
5. Better organisational integration, participative management, emphasis on core values	33	91	Significant
6. Credibility-building actions of management	0	55	Significant
7. Professionalisation of manufacturing management, personnel management, planning etc.	11	64	Significant
8. Initiation of managerial meetings, problem-solving task-forces	22	64	Significant
9. Attempts to increase efficiency, quality, productivity other than through plant modernisation etc. and training	33	73	Significant
10. Plant modernisation etc. for greater efficiency, quality, productivity	56	91	

Table 4.6 (Contd.)

	Non-surgical Innovation Oriented (9 cases)	Non-surgical Transform- ational (11 cases)	Difference
11. Restructuring (decentralis- ation, fixing accountability, structural changes etc.	56	91	
12. Innovation, new product development etc.	78	45	
13. Divestiture and liquidation of fixed assets and long-term liabilities	56	27	
14. Miscellaneous actions	0	27	
15. Increased training of managers and staff	22	45	
16. Public articulation by management of corporate mission, goals etc.	22	45	
17. Fresh induction of managers, technical staff etc.	22	45	
18. Marketing related actions	78	100	
19. Management communicating with staff, lower managers etc.	33	55	
20. Disciplining	33	55	
21. Example setting by top managers	11	27	
22. Liquidation of current assets and liabilities	22	36	
23. Borrowings, raising equity finance etc.	44	36	
24. Changes in top management	89	100	
25. Diversification, product line rationalisation, expansion etc.	100	91	
26. Cost reduction mechanisms other than retrenchment	67	73	
27. Significant retrenchment	0	0	

Note: Only those differences are called 'significant' that were so at the 95% level of confidence.

The turnarounds of Del E. Webb, an American corporation in the leisure, real estate and construction business,[33] Docutel Corporation, a US company producing and marketing automatic teller machines for banks,[34] Toyo Kogyo, a large Japanese car producer,[35] and Volkswagen, a West German car maker, [36] were of the Non-surgical Innovation Oriented type. The turnarounds of RFD Group, UK one of the world's leading designers of life-saving equipment and products,[37] State Timber Corporation of Sri Lanka, a government owned company extracting, processing, and selling timber,[38] Can Cel, a company taken over by the government of British Columbia, a Canadian province, and operating saw and pulp mills,[39] and Enfield India, an Indian company producing two-wheelers and agro-engines,[40] were of the Non-surgical Transformational type.

Non-surgical Innovation Oriented Turnarounds

Del E. Webb, the leisure and real estate company, had mounting losses until 1981, due in part to debt incurred from some ill-advised expansion. Robert K. Swanson came in as chairman in 1981. He replaced four out of five divisional presidents and brought in a new financial officer. He sold off a number of resort operations for $170 million to slash the long-term debt of the company. He negotiated acquisitions into new lines of business, expanded commercial real estate business, spent money on sprucing up some hotel-casinos, opened new offices, and downgraded priority to construction and development of retirement communities. Del E. Webb broke even in 1982 and earned $6 million on sales of $360 million in 1983. The earnings were expected to go up substantially in 1984.

Docutel, an American producer of automatic teller machines, lost $8.5 million in 1977 on sales of $25 million, in part because of tardy incorporation of technological innovations in its products. In 1980 there was a change in management, with B.J. Meredith taking over as chairman and Saterson coming in as president. The new management bought a knitwear company to set off tax losses, developed a low-cost retrofit unit for the aging machines of customers, got TRW to perform the maintenance work, emphasised the marketing of product-cum-service packages, and raised fresh capital of $17 million. It acquired Olivetti's financial systems operations in exchange for a 23 per cent share of Docutel, and entered into a joint venture with Olivetti for the Italian company to market Docutel's new automatic teller machine. It also developed a new modular machine. It engaged in vigorous selling and attempts at increasing its market share to 35 per cent by tripling the sales force, with the president himself doing some personal selling, by seeking institutional buyers for the services related to the company's automatic teller machines, and by redesigning products to lower costs and prices. The 1980 earnings went up to $7 million and earnings doubled in the first half of 1981 while sales climbed by 35 per cent.

Toyo Kogyo, the Japanese car maker, fell sick in the mid-seventies due to low productivity, over-dependence on overseas markets, a wrong choice of engine for its car (Mazda), a crushing debt burden, and a poor domestic marketing set-up. Sumitomo Bank spearheaded the recovery by deputing its officers to the company. The new management discontinued the gas-guzzling Wankel rotary engine. It emphasised good relations with the staff and unions. Over the years members of the staff lost by attrition were not replaced, thus reducing the workforce from 37,000 to 28,000. A large number of persons were reassigned from production to sales. The overseas sales force was reorganised and a strategy was implemented for locating niches that could be dominated with unique products in place of the previous one of competing across-the-board with much bigger rivals. Toyo Kogyo linked up with Ford Motor Company for mutually supporting each other's products in Japanese and overseas markets. The Japanese dealerships were strengthened with better personnel and services. Several speciality cars were developed, such as sports cars, cars for the elderly and for women, multi-purpose vehicles, among others. An improved rotary engine was designed that yielded better mileage. The company raised its productivity from 19 vehicles per employee in 1975 to 45 in 1981. It raised its market share in Japan. Its 1981 profits and sales were 27 per cent and 13 per cent higher than those in 1980, and it earned $91 million on sales of $5,300 million in 1981.

Volkswagen, the West German car producer, began a downhill slide in 1980 which culminated in losses in 1982 and 1983. Carl Hahn who, in the sixties, ran Volkswagen's US subsidiary, was brought back in 1982, first to head the ailing US subsidiary and then to take over the chairmanship of the parent organisation. Volkswagen's woes were the poorly functioning plant at West-moreland, US problems in the South American subsidiaries due to hyper inflation, credit control and recession, and the metal workers' strikes in Germany. There was also a general slump in car sales after 1978. Finally, the acquisition, in 1978, of Triumph-Adler, an office equipment company that continued to make losses, was another drain. Hahn re-emphasised good engineering and quality in the US market and cut out the frills in Rabbit, the car marketed there. He changed the name of Golf (the name by which the car was called internationally and in Germany), and sold higher priced Audis made in Germany in the US market. A fully automated, robot based assembly line, Halle 54, was designed in Germany with the involvement of the workers in its planning and design. Halle 54 cut down by 20 per cent the time required to build a car. A new version of Golf was launched with a new high-efficiency engine as well as an all-wheel drive facility. Volkswagen sold off Triumph-Adler to Olivetti, signed collaboration agreements with manufacturers in China and Japan, and entered into a partnership with Spain's Seat in order to market Volkswagen cars in Spain under Spanish names.

Non-surgical Transformational Turnarounds

RFD Group, a British manufacturer of life saving products, made a loss of £300,000 in 1974 on sales of £8 million. The reasons appeared to be a poor management information and control system, inefficient manufacturing operations, poor management, and labour intran-sigence. In 1973 Mr Boxall had come in as the managing director of RFD-GQ, a part of the RFD Group that accounted for 60 per cent of the latter's sales, and in 1975 Mr Craig, who had earlier been a consultant to the company became the managing director of the RFD Group. RFD-GQ was divisionalised into four profit centres. Financial controls were introduced. Immediate price increases were made. Major customers were visited personally by top managers for renegotiation of prices. Since there was a large back-log of unfilled orders, the sales effort was reduced. Mr Boxall, in open communication with the employees, kept them informed of developments *via* speeches and factory meetings. An open style of management was practiced. Efforts were made at internal public relations. The management convinced workers that their products were world leaders and essential to saving lives. There was greater participation in management and stronger results orientation. Initiative and effective communications were emphasised. A small consulting firm was called in by the Board to review operations and make recommendations. Attempts were made to improve manufacturing efficiency—the manufacture of standardised products was locationally separated from the production of custom-tailored products. A packing factory was closed and a factory in Newcastle and one in Australia were sold. Subsidiaries were encouraged to do strategic thinking, especially to diversify in order to reduce dependence on a single customer (the ministry of defence). New products were introduced, such as oil booms and safety netting. An image of high quality products was projected. Turnaround efforts were communicated to customers, suppliers, and bankers. Though there were no mass lay-offs, about 70 persons were made redundant in the process of turning around the company. The company made a profit of £1.4 million on sales of £11.6 million in 1975. In 1976, profits and sales increased to £ 2.1 million and £14.7 million respectively.

State Timber Corporation of Sri Lanka (STC) was set up by the government of Sri Lanka in 1968. It made losses in 1977 and 1978. It faced supply constraints because of the government's policy of preventing deforestation. Also, faulty pricing gave rise to excessive demand, rationing, black market activities, including the siphoning off of timber by contractors for the black market. This was reinforced by the low rates paid to contractors. The management was centralised and industrial relations were poor. The top management numbered several civil servants and there was management discontinuity because of frequent transfers of chief executives. STC was shifted from the ministry of agriculture to the ministry of lands headed by a dynamic young minister. Kenneth Abheywickrame, a professional manager from a multinational, took a considerable salary cut to come in as chief executive officer in March 1979 to bring order to the mess. Very quickly a new Board was appointed with only one civil servant, the rest being professionals. The new CEO hiked rates paid to sub-contractors for extracting and saw-milling timber and raised prices. He raised output rapidly by mechanising the extraction of timber where felling was permitted due to a cyclone or flooding of forest lands. He imported timber to bridge the demand-supply gap, opened two new regional offices and 30 new depots, organised permit-free sales and bargain sales of slow moving items, had a logo designed for the company and appointed an advertising agency for sales promotion. By way of diversification, small scale production of wall panels, charcoal, window frames and other items was started in 1980 for later scaling up. A costly ultra-modern office complex was acquired in Colombo.

The CEO set about vigorously to rebuild the organisation and its systems. A comprehensive management information system was installed. Monthly meetings of management were instituted to discuss corporate and regional performance. The head office was reorganised and the functional areas strengthened. Several new departments were set up, for planning, personnel, and engineering among others. Four new regional administrations were set up, and the organisation was decentralised. Production targets for regions were formalised beginning in 1980. Large sums were spent on modernisation and plant replacement. Later, a formal corporate plan document was prepared in 1981 and the objective was formally stated of transforming the corporation from a primary producer to a manufacturing organisation.

The CEO was active also in the people management area. While he did not raise his own salary in 1980 he raised the salary of others by 35 per cent and also instituted other benefits. He instituted a policy of not taking any of his own relatives into the organisation. There was a strong emphasis on the training of staff and managers. He insisted on dealing impartially with the unions and on consulting them *vis-à-vis* personnel issues. He introduced new welfare programmes. He manned many of the 130 jobs that were created by the reorganisation with people promoted from within STC. He personally picked up promising youngsters for managerial responsibilities during his visits to felling sites. There was also greater emphasis on professional qualifications in staff recruitment.

The CEO also networked actively. He launched a reforestation drive to placate the forest department and set up a forestry committee. He gave donations to political groups and for political activities but resisted political influence on important decisions. He also provided technical and financial help to the parent ministry—cars were provided and ten persons on STC's payroll worked in the ministry.

The performance of STC improved dramatically. Sales went up from Rs 40 million in 1978 to Rs 109 million in 1979 and Rs 300 million in 1980, while from a loss of Rs 4 million in 1978 profits rose to Rs 15 million in 1979 and Rs 46 million in 1980.

Can Cel (Canadian Cellulose Company Limited) was originally a loss making subsidiary of the Celanese Corporation, a US multi-national. Can Cel operated saw and pulp mills in British Columbia. It was taken over by the socialist government of the province in 1972. The company had turned into a loss making unit because of remote location, demoralisation in management because Celanese had lost interest in it and was trying to sell it, high staff turnover, an American management unfamiliar with a British Columbia industrial scene, restrictions on expansion due to subsidiary status, and other such reasons. Ronald M Gross, a professional manager, came in as chief executive in June 1973. He got an independent Board, free of politicians and civil servants.

The top management set about actively to diagnose the company's problems. A number of studies were initiated to work out strategies for resolving the identified issues. The top leadership conveyed to the staff and managers its confidence in the company's longevity. A number of task forces were formed to work out specific corporate strategies in different functional areas such as marketing, finance, manufacturing operations, among others. Emphasis was put on developing a long term relationship with customers, and top managers got busy contacting major customers. The price of kraft paper was raised, and the marketing of bleached kraft paper was stressed. An attempt was made to reduce dependence on particular country markets and customers. The customer base was diversified by exporting to 24 countries. The CEO strongly emphasised the profit motive and the earning of at least a 15 per cent return on investment. The company embarked in 1975 on an ambitious but phased investment and plant conversion programme as well as a programme to clean up the pollution caused by its plants. For this the company borrowed funds in 1976.

The management embarked on a systems development drive. Long term planning was initiated. A system was evolved of decentralised operations of plants, but with centralised long term planning, policy making, and monitoring. Professionals were brought in to deal with the company's problems of pollution control, rise in the prices of raw materials, government forest regulations, cyclical decline in pulp prices, an over-valued Canadian dollar, social responsibility concerns, and others.

The management increased managerial training. It provided rental accommodation to employees and launched a housing project for employees. When 300 persons (of 3,000) had to be laid off due to plant modernisation, the company spent $2 million helping them get jobs, move and resettle, and nearly half were found alternative jobs.

The management also networked aggressively. Executives played an active role in the industry association to gain the trust of the private sector. A highly visible public relations campaign was launched to tell the Can Cel story to the public.

During 1968–1972, the company averaged sales of $95 million a year with an average loss of $14 million. After the government take-over in 1972, the company's performance improved to average annual sales of $165 million during 1973–76, with average annual profits of $29 million.

Enfield India, an Indian manufacturer of two-wheelers and agro-engines, was established in 1955. It was a family managed public limited company. It fell sick in 1977. The fall in demand for two-wheelers following a steep rise in petrol prices contributed to this sickness, as did a conservative pricing policy, a traditional family style of management, rising costs, increasing competition, infrastructural problems, and such like. In April 1977, Mr Viswanathan, a son of the founder replaced an elder son as chief executive. Soon a financial relief package involving fresh loans and a rescheduling of debt was negotiated with the government, the banks, and the term lending financial institutions, following a positive assessment of future prospects by a consultant. Daily, weekly, and monthly performance targets and operations controls were instituted. The Board was reconstituted and professionals inducted. A lockout was declared at a factory plagued by industrial relations problems. A turnaround strategy was worked out involving the payment of outstandings to creditors, reopening the closed factory, and an increase in productivity. Obsolete inventory worth Rs 25 million was written off. Several regional sales offices were opened. Prices were hiked. Sales of the profitable two-wheelers were stepped up. In negotiations with labour unions productivity norms were emphasised, but the attempt was also made to develop a positive relationship. Considerable effort was made to strengthen research and development, develop a wider range of two-wheeler models (including a deluxe model), and to upgrade existing models with innovations. Plant modernisation, expansion, and diversification were planned.

Besides instituting comprehensive operating controls, the management turned each division and department into a profit or responsibility centre with greater delegation of authority. Seven new division heads, all professionals, were brought in. Monthly meetings of the management were held to review company performance. A new marketing division was created to strengthen marketing, conduct market research, and gather market feedback. A policy of manufacturing and product flexibility was instituted. Corporate planning was strengthened.

The chief executive tried to build up team spirit by taking his managers periodically to brainstorming retreats. He persuaded his managers to take a pay freeze in order to persuade workers to moderate their demands, he himself taking a pay cut. He declared a policy of worker participation in management and open communications. Quality circles were introduced.

The company's losses during 1975–76, 1976–77, and 1977–78 averaged Rs 14 million on average sales of Rs 150 million. The average annual profits during the next four years were Rs 13 million on average sales of Rs 250 million.

Both types of non-surgical turnarounds stressed the essentials of turnarounds—management change, cost cutting, aggressive marketing, product mix realignment, restructuring, and so forth. But Non-surgical Transformation turnarounds were palpably more committed to formal, collective diagnosis of ills and troubleshooting, participative management and investing in people, and development of professional management systems. They were committed not just to quick fixes. They were also committed to institution building, to transforming permanently the way the organisation functioned.

Performance of Surgical versus Non-surgical Turnaround Management

Non-surgical turnarounds are not rare. They have been successfully attempted all over the world, including the USA, although they seem to occur more commonly in other countries. They have occurred in a wide variety of industries, and in small, medium sized, as well as very large organisations. Like surgical turnarounds, they too have a basic core to them. This core, however, seems to be substantially more complex than that of surgical turnarounds, because it comprises of many more turnaround elements. Both surgical and non-surgical turnaround cores have some elements in common, such as change in top management, diversification and/or realignment of product line, more aggressive marketing, and emphasis on reducing costs. But there are some notable differences, besides the question of retrenchment. The non-surgical turnarounds seem to emphasise plant modernisation, and such people management actions as participative management, networking with stakeholders for turnaround, and motivating staff far more commonly. There are major choices in both sorts of turnarounds. Interestingly, a strategic element common to both is the presence or absence of a staff motivational stretegy. Garnering the stakeholders' support for the turnaround and restructuring is among the other strategic elements of non-surgical turnarounds. Major alternatives in non-surgical turnarounds revolve around whether collective diagnostic and problem solving effort, people management and human resource development, and development of professional management systems, are or are not major planks of the turnaround effort.

A point of interest is: which of the two turnarounds, surgical or non-surgical, gets a loss making organisation faster to a break-even situation? The proponents of surgical turnarounds may well prefer this type because it may seem to them to be quicker than the more complex non-surgical turnaround. After all, if one fires a quarter or a third of the staff, overheads will fall sharply. As against this is the potential productive power of motivation and commitment and of investing in people.

For the 65 turnarounds, inclusive of both the 42 complete and 23 break-even ones (see Chapter 1, Table 1.1), an attempt was made to estimate the period between the induction of a new chief executive in a loss making firm and the breaking even of the enterprise. Information was available for making this estimate in 27 of the 30 cases of non-surgical turnarounds (for cases of non-surgical turnarounds see Table 4.1 of this chapter) and 26 out of the 35 surgical turnarounds (for cases of surgical turnarounds see Table 3.1 of Chapter 3). In both kinds of turnarounds the range of time to break-even was large—from zero to four years in the case of non-surgical turnarounds, and zero to eight years in the case of surgical turnarounds (zero means the break-even was reached in the same year the new chief executive took over the unit). However, the average number of years for break-even, following a change of chief executive, was a shade over one year for non-surgical turnarounds versus a shade under two years for surgical turnarounds. In a number of cases of complete turnaround it was possible to estimate the time it took from a change of chief executive to the organisation reaching 'normal' profitability level (say, a net profit-to-sales ratio of at least 4 per cent, or a very substantial increase in profits compared to the break-even year). For 17 'complete' non-surgical turnaround cases the average was just about two years (range being one to five years). For 15 complete surgical turnarounds the average was four years (ranging from one to nine years).[41] Thus, non-surgical turnarounds may generally be substantially *faster* than surgical turnarounds! Empowering stakeholders may be a speedier way of reviving a sick organisation than ruthlessly wielding the axe. The pink slip method may be neither humane nor swift. The massive costs of surgical turnarounds may often be unnecessary.

That is not all. In Chapter 2 a criterion measure of turnaround recovery was discussed (see the section, Validity of Turnaround Elements, and Table 2.3 in Chapter 2). This was the rate at which profitability or earning ability (return on sales) of a sick company rises during turnaround. It was measured by taking the difference between the enterprise's profitability one year after the break-even year and the maximum rate of loss during sickness, and dividing this difference by the number of years from the year of maximum sickness to the year after the break-even year. The average on this criterion variable of turnaround effectiveness was 4.2 per cent for the surgical turnaround group and 7.9 per cent for the non-surgical turnaround group. Thus, the rate of recovery was nearly twice as fast for the non-surgical group and the period of recovery just about half. And, of course, the human costs were vastly smaller as compared to the surgical turnarounds. The data point strongly to the general superiority of non-surgical turnarounds.

But even this is not the whole story. Two alternative surgical turnarounds were identified in Chapter 3 and two alternative non-surgical turnarounds have been identified in this chapter (see Diagram 4.1). The average scores on the rate of gain of profitability were 3.8 per cent, 4.9 per cent, 3.4 per cent, and 11.2 per cent respectively for the Surgical Reconstructive turnarounds, the Surgical Productivity/Innovation Oriented turnarounds, the Non-surgical Innovation Oriented turnarounds, and the Non-surgical Transformational turnarounds. Of the four, therefore, the best performance, by far, was that of the last named turnaround. Thus, while the non-surgical turnaround may generally be preferred over the surgical one on humanitarian grounds, the best results may be obtained if the non-surgical turnaround is engineered by heavy participation of external and internal stakeholders and by strengthening the organisation, especially by professionalising its management systems and its operations. This combination of a participative and a professional management orientation has been found to yield excellent results even in normal operating circumstances.[42]

Diagram 4.1

FOUR TYPES OF TURNAROUND MANAGEMENT

Core of All Turnarounds
(see ch. 2)

* Change in top management
* Diversification, product reshuffling, expansion, etc.
* Better marketing
* Cost reduction
* Restructuring for greater accountability
* Plant/facilities modernisation

Surgical Re-constructive Turnaround *(see ch. 3)*	Surgical Productivity/ Innovation Oriented Turnaround *(see ch. 3)*	Non-surgical Innovation Oriented Turnaround *(ch. 4)*	Non-surgical Transformational Turnaround *(ch. 4)*
* Significant re-trenchment	* Significant re-trenchment	* Innovation, new product development etc.	* Attempts to get stakeholders' support
* Divestiture and liquidation of capital assets and liabilities	* Incentives, motivation, grievance redressal		* For ial diagnostic activities
	* Disciplining of staff		* Use of meetings and task-forces for problem-solving

Diagram 4.1 (Contd.)

* Emphasis on efficiency and productivity	* Incentives, motivation, grievance redressal
* Innovation, new product development etc.	* Emphasis on efficiency and productivity
* Raising of long-term capital	* Emphasis on greater management control
	* Professionalisation of management systems
	* Attempts at greater organisational cohesion through participative decision-making, emphasis on core values etc.

Concluding Comments

In 1960 Douglas McGregor presented two contrasting models of management that he labelled Theory X and Theory Y. Both theories rest on certain assumptions.[43] If one assumes that subordinates are lazy and greedy then an authoritarian and manipulative style of management—Theory X—makes sense If one assumes that subordinates are proactive and want autonomy, responsibility, and interesting work, then a decentralised, participative, human resource development oriented management—Theory Y—makes sense. Faced with staff lethargy and cynicism so common during organisational sickness, Theory X may seem to many to make more sense than Theory Y. The superiority of the non-surgical turnaround, both as to the duration of time for recovery and rate of recovery in profitability, indicates the contrary. The Non-surgical Transformational turnaround is especially close to the spirit of Theory Y. It had by far the best rate of recovery performance.

But it would be premature to conclude that Theory Y alone in single combat has triumphed over Theory X. True, the spirit of Theory Y is stronger in non-surgical turnarounds than in surgical ones, especially in the Non-surgical Transformational turnaround. But it takes a lot more than just Theory Y to create spectacular turnarounds. The core of turnaround—top management change, changes in product portfolio, aggressive marketing and cost cutting, restructuring for greater accountability—have to be there (see Diagram 4.1). There is not much Theory Y (nor Theory X) here, just plain good strategic and operations management. Institution building—emphasis on core values, on developing effective pro-fessionalised systems of functional management—also helps. Cultivating the support of external stakeholders like unions, govern-ment agencies, and financial institutions, too, adds value. Thus, super turnaround management is not just Theory Y management. It is that plus good strategic and operations management, insti-tution building, and lining up the support of stakeholders for turnaround. As case after case illustrates, it is multipronged, hyperactive, interaction intensive, Theory Y transformational leadership that differentiates outstanding from routine turnarounds.

Notes and References

1. See Ian MacGregor, 'Recovery at British Steel', *Journal of General Manage-ment*, Vol. 7, No. 3, 1982, pp. 5–16. See also David Chambers, 'Consumer orientation and the drive for quality', paper presented at the Roundtable on 'Public Enterprise Management: Strategies for Success' held at New Delhi, 6–11 March 1988, under the auspices of the Commonwealth Secretariat, London, and Indian Institute of Management, Ahmedabad.
2. See V. Krishnamurthy, 'SAIL blazes a new trail', *The Economic Times*, 19 November 1987. See also Subrata Roy, 'Spotlight on SAIL', *Business World*, 1–14 March 1986, pp. 43–51; 'SAIL rolling plan for 1989–90', *The Economic Times*, 29 December 1989, p. 1; 'Steel price hike unlikely', *The Economic Times*, 1 March 1989, p. 1; T.N. Ninan, 'SAIL: Dramatic turn-around', *India Today*, 30 April 1986, pp. 106–7; 'SAIL to enter chemicals', *The Economic Times*, 2 April 1987, p. 1; Subrata Roy, 'SAIL: Will it succeed?' *Business India*, 10–23 August 1987, pp. 42–52.
3. See *Business Week*, 'Docutel: Born again and counting on new vigor in automatic tellers', 27 July 1981, pp. 48 and 50.
4. See *Business Week*, 'Sweda: Aggressive marketing produces a spirited turn-around', 31 March 1980, pp. 101–2.

5. See Dharani Pani, 'Enfield: Revving up again,' *Business India*, 5–18 December 1983, pp. 84, 85, 87, 89, 91, and 92; and Pradip N. Khandwalla, *Effective turnaround of sick enterprises (Indian experiences): Text and cases* (London: Commonwealth Secretariat, 1989).
6. See Sushila Ravindranath, 'Standard Motors in high gear', *Business India*, 1–14 August 1983, pp. 64–65, 67, 69 and 70–71.
7. See *Business Week*, 'Toyo Kogyo: A sure loser stages a turnaround', 25 January 1982, pp. 74–76.
8. See O.P. Kharbanda and E.A. Stallworthy, *Company rescue: How to manage a business turnaround* (London: Heinemann, 1987, pp. 219–29).
9. See *Business Week*, 'Celanese: Weaving a new pattern to survive a cyclical economy', 15 August 1983, p. 62.
10. See K.G. Kumar, 'The matter of FACT', *Business India*, 3–16 June 1985, pp. 114, 115, 117, 119 and 120.
11. See Sushila Ravindranath, 'SPIC bounces back', *Business India*, 23 April–5 May 1985, pp. 110, 111. 113, 115, 117, 119 and 120.
12. See Pradip N. Khandwalla, 1989, op. cit.
13. See David Mansfield, 'How Ferranti fought back', *Management Today*, January 1980, pp. 66–70 and 128. See also Stuart Slatter, *Corporate recovery: Successful turnaround strategies and their implementation* (Harmondsworth, Middlesex: Penguin, 1984, pp. 354–66).
14. See *Business Week*, 'Why the doctor's son is getting Wang back on its feet', 25 January 1988, pp. 67–68.
15. See Pradip N. Khandwalla, 1989, op. cit.
16. See Subrata Roy, 'Tinplate: The Tata stake', *Business India*, 11–24 April 1983, pp. 64–66 and 71.
17. See V. Krishnamurthy, 'Management of organizational change: The BHEL experience', *Vikalpa*, Vol. 2, No. 2, 1977, pp. 113–19; Ravi Ramamurti, 'National Machinery Corporation of India', a disguised case on BHEL (Boston: Northeastern University, undated).
18. See Pradip N. Khandwalla, 'Turnaround management in the public sector', *Lok Udyog*, Vol. 17, No. 6, 1983, pp. 25–38.
19. See Anita van de Vliet, 'Where Lucas sees the light', *Management Today*, June 1986, pp. 38–45; Sir Godfrey Messervy, 'Lucas', pp. 195–202, in Rebecca Nelson and David Clutterback (eds.), *Turnaround: How twenty well-known companies came back from the brink* (London: W.H. Allen, 1988).
20. See U.K. Roy, 'Mining and Allied Machinery Corporation—India', paper presented at the Roundtable on 'Public Enterprise Management: Strategies for Success', held at New Delhi, 6–11 March 1988, under the auspices of the Commonwealth Secretariat. London, and Indian Institute of Management, Ahmedabad.
21. See Stuart Slatter, 1984, op. cit., pp. 296–301.
22. See Pradip N. Khandwalla. 1983, op. cit.
23. See V. Krishnamurthy, 1987, op. cit. See also Subrata Roy, 1986, op. cit.; 'SAIL rolling plan for 1989–90', *The Economic Times*, 29 December 1989, p. 1; 'Steel price hike unlikely', *The Economic Times*, 1 March 1989, p. 1; T.N. Ninan. 1986, op. cit.; 'SAIL to enter chemicals', *The Economic Times*, 2 April 1987, p. 1; Subrata Roy, 1987, op. cit.

24. See Robert W. Sexty, 'Canadian Cellulose Company Ltd.: A case study of government rescue and turnaround'. Toronto: The Institute of Public Administration of Canada, 1982.

25. See Ravi Ramamurti, 'State Timber Corporation of Sri Lanka (A) and (B)'. Cases 0–382–018 and 0–382–019. Boston: President and Fellows of Harvard College, 1981.

26. See Business Week, 'Why Frank Borman finally has something to smile about', 29 April 1985, pp. 52–53.

27. See Vasuki and S. Tripathi, 'Air-India: Out of the woods', India Today, 30 June 1989, pp. 114–16; S. Narayan, 'Air-India takes wing', Business World, 21 June-4 July, 1989, pp. 42–43.

28. See Emanuel Hachipunka, 'Zambia Railways Limited', paper presented at the Roundtable on 'Public Enterprise Management: Strategies for Success', New Delhi, 6–11 March 1988, held under the auspices of the Commonwealth Secretariat, London, and Indian Institute of Management, Ahmedabad.

29. See K.G. Kumar, 'Apollo Tyres Ltd: No more skidding', Business India, 18–26 June 1988, pp. 61, 63, 67, and Pradip N. Khandwalla, 1989, op. cit.

30. See Business Week, 'Del E. Webb: Back from the brink and ready to grow', 9 June 1984, p. 87.

31. See Geoffrey Colwin, 'Freddie Silverman's secret success', Fortune, 14 July 1980, pp. 123–24.

32. See Business Week, 'Pullman's not a sleeper anymore', 22 July 1985, pp. 70–71.

33. See Business Week, 'Del E. Webb: Back from the brink and ready to grow', 9 June 1984, p. 87.

34. See Business Week, 'Docutel: Born again and counting on new vigor in automatic tellers', 27 July 1981, pp. 48 and 50.

35. See Business Week, 'Toyo Kogyo: A sure loser stages a turnaround', 25 January 1982, pp. 74–76.

36. O.P. Kharbanda and E.A. Stallworthy, 1987, op. cit.

37. See Stuart Slatter, 1984, op. cit., pp. 296–301.

38. See Ravi Ramamurti, 1981, op. cit.

39. See Robert W. Sexty, 1982, op. cit.

40. See Dharani Pani, 1983, op. cit.

41. Interestingly, the average period of American turnarounds may be four years. See Donald Bibeault, Corporate turnaround: How managers turn losers into winners (New York: McGraw–Hill, 1982, p. 83).

42. See Pradip N. Khandwalla, 'Some top management styles: Their context and performance', Organization and Administrative Sciences, Vol. 7, 1976–77, pp. 21–52, and Pradip N. Khandwalla, The design of organizations (New York: Harcourt Brace, 1977, ch. 11).

43. See Douglas McGregor, The human side of enterprise (New York: McGraw–Hill, 1960).

5. THE CONTEXT OF TURNAROUNDS

In earlier chapters we have looked at choices in turnaround management. There is, first of all, a choice as to whether the turnaround should be surgical or non-surgical. If it is to be surgical, should its harshness be offset by attempts at effective networking and people management or not? If it is not to be surgical, should or should there not be emphasis on a collective diagnosis of ills and trouble-shooting, the building up of appropriate management systems, and effective people-management, human resource development, and networking for support?

What factors influence these choices? There is an influential theory of organisational design and functioning called contingency theory that argues that what goes on in organisations is shaped by the contingencies and constraints to which the organisation is subject.[1] For example, the wider social culture and socio-economic system may influence organisational behaviour and thereby influence the choice of organisational design, at least in the short-run.[2] Thus, management practices that have evolved in a culture oriented to individualism and a free-market economy cannot easily be transplanted wholesale into Soviet or Japanese organisations, and *vice versa*. Similarly, the conditions in the market environment—competition, cyclical ups and downs, technological change—shape the functioning of the organisation and thereby influence the choice of design.[3] Organisations operating in complex, dynamic environments need to utilise many more coordinative or integrative mechanisms than those operating in simpler, stabler environments.[4] Several other variables that shape organisational behaviour have been identified, such as the size of the organisation[5], the nature of its technology,[6] the stage in its life-cycle at which the organisation is operating,[7] and so on.

Social Systems and Turnaround Management

The sample of 42 complete turnarounds offered a fairly straight-forward test of whether societal culture affects turnaround management or not. The sample was divided into two sizeable sub-samples: turnarounds of enterprises in the individualistic, free enterprise Western social systems (North America and Western Europe) and in non-Western social systems (Africa, the Caribbean, South Asia, Japan), usually with stronger elements of nurturance and collectivism.[8] There were 28 Western turnarounds and 14 non-Western turnarounds. Of Western turnarounds 71 per cent were surgical, while of non-Western turnarounds 86 per cent were non-surgical. The association between social system or culture and the type of turnaround is clear, with Western corporations predominantly resorting to surgical means to rescue themselves while non-Western, mostly Third World corporations predominantly avoiding surgery.

Table 5.1 shows the scores for the 27 turnaround elements for these two groups. Notice the significant differences (significant at 95 per cent confidence level, using the test of difference in proportions) in scores for garnering stakeholders' support (25 per cent for Western vs. 86 per cent for non-Western), significant retrenchment (71 per cent vs. 14 per cent), attempts (other than through plant modernisation and training) to increase efficiency and related actions (21 per cent vs. 71 per cent), the use of incentives and other staff motivators (29 per cent vs. 79 per cent), plant modernisation and similar recourse (43 per cent vs. 86 per cent), participative management and emphasis on core values (32 per cent vs. 71 per cent), team effort in problem solving (14 per cent vs. 50 per cent), and professionalisation of management systems (14 per cent vs. 50 per cent). Western turnarounds seem to rely more on the stick while non-Western (mostly Third World) turnarounds seem to rely more on the carrot for turning around sick organisations. Also, Western turnaround managers tend to go it alone, while non-Western ones tend to do a fair bit of networking with various stakeholders like the financial institutions, government, unions, customers, suppliers and others for help in turnaround. Non-Western turnaround managers also tend to use a different array of mechanisms for increasing productivity. The principal method used by the Western turnaround managers appears to be staff rationalisation reinforced on occasion by plant modernisation. On the other hand, non-Western turnaround managers avoid staff rationalisation and instead rely heavily on plant modernisation and such other methods of improving productivity and performance as in-house productivity campaigns, participative, collective diagnosis, change of production manager, use of consultants, professionalisation of management systems, and so on.

Table 5.1

Percentages of Western and Non-Western Turnarounds
Employing Different Turnaround Elements

Sample: 42 Complete Turnarounds

	Percentage for 28 Western Turnarounds	Percentage for 14 Non-Western Turnarounds	Difference
1. Garnering stakeholders' support	25	86	Significant
2. Significant retrenchment	71	14	Significant
3. Attempts to increase efficiency, quality, productivity other than through plant modernisation etc. and training	21	71	Significant
4. Incentives, motivation, grievance redressal	29	79	Significant
5. Plant modernisation etc. for greater efficiency, quality, productivity	43	86	Significant
6. Better organisational integration, participative management, emphasis on core values	32	71	Significant
7. Initiation of managerial meetings, problem-solving task-forces	14	50	Significant
8. Professionalisation of manufacturing management, personnel management, planning etc.	14	50	Significant
9. Divestiture and liquidation of fixed assets and long-term liabilities	57	29	
10. Formal diagnostic activities	29	57	
11. Disciplining	36	64	
12. Management control-enhancing actions	50	71	
13. Borrowings, raising equity finance etc.	50	29	

Table 5.1 (Contd.)

	Percentage for 28 Western Turnarounds	Percentage for 14 Non-Western Turnarounds	Difference
14. Cost-reduction actions other than retrenchment	61	79	
15. Restructuring (decentralisation, fixing accountability, structural changes etc.)	61	79	
16. Increased training of managers and staff	21	36	
17. Liquidation of current assets and liabilities	21	36	
18. Credibility-building actions of management	25	36	
19. Example-setting by top managers	18	29	
20. Innovation, new product development etc.	61	50	
21. Miscellaneous actions	11	21	
22. Marketing related actions	79	86	
23. Diversification, product-line rationalisation, expansion etc.	100	93	
24. Management communicating with staff, lower managers etc.	36	43	
25. Fresh induction of managers, technical staff etc.	39	43	
26. Public articulation by management of corporate mission, goals etc.	32	29	
27. Changes in top management	93	93	

Note: Only those differences significant at the 95% level of confidence have been indicated as 'significant'.

The differences between Western and non-Western turnarounds are relatively minor for many elements. For 14 elements the difference in percentages is 20 points or less. In both social systems change in top management, cost reduction attempts other than retrenchment, aggressive marketing, shuffling of product line, restructuring, and innovation and new product development are frequently used. In both systems there is a relatively infrequent resort to credibility building actions, training, liquidation of current assets and liabilities, management communicating with staff, management articulating a corporate mission, example setting by top managers, and fresh induction of managers and technical staff.

Western turnarounds do seem harsher and more oriented to trimming while non-Western turnarounds tend to be more inter-action intensive, more centred on development. But the similarities are also substantial. In sum, social systems seem to affect turn-around management selectively rather than comprehensively.

Size and Turnaround Management

Size is known to have substantial effects on the structure and functioning of organisations.[9] As the organisation grows bigger, the hierarchy gets longer, operations get standardised and formalised, new departments come into being to discharge key functions in a more specialised way and within these departments roles get more specialised, and there are more controls and rules.

Communications get formalised, distortions emerge in the flow of information from top echelons to lower levels and *vice versa*, inter-departmental conflicts get accentuated, feelings of dissatis-faction arise at lower levels as jobs get mechanical, and so forth. Because of all these, one expects turnarounds to be more difficult in larger organisations than in smaller ones, and therefore handled in a different way.

An attempt was made to identify the relationship between size and turnaround management. The 42 complete turnarounds were classified into those occurring in large organisations and relatively smaller ones. This classification was not easy since the organisations were from all over the globe, and since data were not always avail-able for the two main indicators of size, the annual sales and the number of employees. A rough set of criteria were used: if the organisation had over $500 million annual sales (at 1988 prices and rates of exchange) *or* over 5,000 employees, it was considered large; otherwise, it was considered small.

Sixteen companies were unambiguously small and nineteen clearly large. Seven, whose size status could not be determined with certainty, were deleted from the analysis. Seventy-five per cent of small com-panies had non-surgical turnarounds while 68 per cent of the large ones had surgical turnarounds. Thus, there was a distinct association of the size of the organisation with the type of turnaround, with larger ones resorting more commonly to surgical turnarounds.

Table 5.2 shows the scores of the two groups on 27 turnaround elements. There was, as noted, a difference with respect to the use of significant retrenchment—large organisations indulged in this far more frequently than small ones. This was possibly because large organisations, usually more monopolistic, more decentralised and more bureaucratic than smaller ones, put on a lot of 'fat' during good times. But the harshness or retrenchment seemed partially offset by an attempt to communicate the problems of the organisation to the staff. On the other hand, attempts to motivate the staff and, to a lesser extent, professionalisation of management systems and formal diagnostic work seemed to occur in the turnaround management of smaller organisations more frequently than in that of larger ones. In the vast majority of elements, however, the scores did not differ appreciably. On the whole, size seemed to have a lesser influence on turnaround management than societal culture.

Table 5.2

*Percentages of Small and Large Organisation Turnarounds
Employing Turnaround Elements*

	Sample: 42 Complete Turnarounds		
	Percentage of 16 Small Firms	Percentage of 19 Large Firms	Difference
1. Significant retrenchment	25	74	Significant
2. Incentives, motivation, grievance redressal	69	37	Significant
3. Professionalisation of manufacturing management, personnel management, planning etc.	50	21	
4. Management communicating with staff, lower managers etc.	25	53	
5. Formal diagnostic activities	56	32	
6. Restructuring (decentralisation, fixing accountability, structural changes etc.)	81	58	
7. Divestiture and liquidation of fixed assets and long-term liabilities	31	53	
8. Borrowings, raising equity finance etc.	31	53	
9. Attempts to increase efficiency, quality, productivity other than through plant modernisation etc. and training	50	32	

Table 5.2 (Contd.)

	Percentage of 16 Small Firms	Percentage of 19 Large Firms	Difference
10. Public articulation by management of corporate mission, goals etc.	31	47	
11. Management control-enhancing actions	62	47	
12. Better organisational integration, participative management, emphasis on core values	56	42	
13. Credibility-building actions of management	25	37	
14. Increased training of managers and staff	25	37	
15. Fresh induction of managers, technical staff etc.	25	37	
16. Innovation, new product develop ment etc.	56	68	
17. Example-setting by top managers	25	16	
18. Miscellaneous actions	12	21	
19. Changes in top management	87	95	
20. Cost-reduction actions other than retrenchment	62	68	
21. Liquidation of current assets and liabilities	31	26	
22. Initiation of managerial meetings, problem-solving task-forces	31	26	
23. Marketing related actions	87	84	
24. Garnering stakeholders' support	50	47	
25. Disciplining	44	42	
26. Plant modernisation etc. for greater efficiency, quality, productivity	62	63	
27. Diversification, product-line rationalisation, expansion etc.	100	100	

Note: Only those differences significant at the 95% confidence level have been indicated as 'significant'.

Turnaround in the Public versus Private Sectors

In countries representing nearly 80 per cent of the world's population, government-owned enterprises, more generally called public enterprises, are a dominant economic institution.[10] In all the ex-Communist and in most Third World countries public enterprises have been set up to pursue major national economic missions like rapid industrialisation, import substitution, economic self-reliance, regionally balanced growth, and employment creation. Public enterprises are economically important even in a few Western countries like Britain, Canada, France, Italy and Spain.

In recent years, however, public enterprises have come under attack. Their performance has been spotty,[11] and following the lead of conservative governments in Britain and the US, there has been a cry for their privatisation. The argument is that given public accountability and the wooden hand of government control, commercial public enterprises are bound to fare badly and so should be handed over to private management. The fact, however, is that without a vital public sector many Third World countries could not have set up a strong, self-reliant industrial base. Also, their sickness is exaggerated. In India, for instance, about 60 per cent of the enterprises set up by the Government of India make profits, and of the remaining 40 per cent loss-making enterprises, a large number are terminally sick private enterprises nationalised by the government to protect employment.[12]

An important question is whether sick public enterprises can be revived despite government regulations, political interference, multiple and conflicting mandated objectives, lethargy induced by monopoly power, and such factors.[13] If they can be, then the cry for their privatisation as a remedy for their allegedly inherent fallibility is unwarranted, and study can focus not on changing their ownership but on vitalising their management.

Twenty of 65 turnarounds reported in Table 1.1 of Chapter 1 were of public enterprises. These included a dozen complete turnarounds and eight break-even turnarounds. They were reported from a wide variety of countries. In the West the turnarounds of Jaguar Motors (UK), Italtel (Italy), IRI (Italy), British Steel (UK), and Can Cel (Canada) were engineered. Public enterprises turned around in the Third World included enterprises producing fertilisers and chemicals, furniture, timber, and wood products, plant and equipment, and steel. They also included marketing organisations and enterprises in the air and rail transportation businesses. In the face of so many turnarounds in the public sector, the salvageability of sick enterprises under public management cannot be doubted. The question is not whether sick public enterprises can be revived but rather what sort of management can revive them. Another interesting question is, given the differences in the context in which public and private sector enterprises operate, is there a difference in the way they can be turned around?

Turnaround data on a dozen complete turnarounds in the public sector could be compared with similar data on 30 complete turnarounds in the private sector. Only 33 per cent of the public enterprises underwent surgical turnarounds involving large-scale retrenchment, *versus* 60 per cent in the private sector. Within the general category of surgical turnarounds were two major sub-categories (see Chapter 3), namely, Reconstructive turnarounds and Productivity/Innovation Oriented turnarounds (the latter resorted more frequently to such mechanisms as incentives and motivation, disciplining, plant modernisation and other attempts to increase productivity, innovation, and induction of fresh capital). Among the surgical turnarounds in the public sector, 75 per cent were of the Productivity/Innovation Oriented type, while only 28 per cent of the surgical turnarounds in the private sector were of this type. Within the category of non-surgical turnarounds, two sub-categories were noted in Chapter 4, namely the Innovation Oriented type and the Transformational type (the latter resorted more frequently to formal diagnostic efforts, team effort at problem-solving, effective networking and people-management, and development of management and operating systems). Here the differences were equally sharp: 87 per cent of the non-surgically turned around public enterprises resorted to the Transformational mode, *versus* only 25 per cent of the private enterprises. To see the differences more sharply, Table 5.3 shows the scores of 12 public *versus* 30 private sector complete turnarounds on the 27 turnaround elements.

The differences in the way turnarounds were secured in the two sectors are pronounced. For 13 of the 27 elements the differences (using a difference in proportions test) were statistically significant. There was a much stronger human resource development, diagnostic and team effort at problem-solving, participative management, and motivational and inspirational tilt in the public sector turnarounds; equally, there was a much stronger emphasis in the private sector turnarounds on divestiture, innovation, and fresh managerial blood. Private enterprises also resorted to retrenchment more frequently, but the difference was not statistically significant.

Table 5.3

Public versus Private Sector Scores of Turnaround Elements

Sample: 42 Complete Turnarounds

	Public Sector (12 companies)	Private Sector (30 companies)	Difference
1. Increased training of managers and staff	67%	10%	Significant
2. Initiation of managerial meetings, problem-solving task-forces	67%	10%	Significant
3. Incentives, motivation, grievance redressal	83%	30%	Significant
4. Formal diagnostic activities	75%	23%	Significant
5. Public articulation by management of corporate mission, goals etc.	67%	17%	Significant
6. Divestiture and liquidation of fixed assets and long-term liabilities	17%	60%	Significant
7. Garnering stakeholders' support	75%	33%	Significant
8. Credibility-building actions of management	58%	17%	Significant
9. Plant modernisation etc. for greater efficiency, quality, productivity	83%	47%	Significant
10. Innovation, new product development etc.	33%	67%	Significant
11. Fresh induction of managers, technical staff etc.	17%	50%	Significant
12. Professionalisation of manufacturing management, personnel management, planning etc.	50%	17%	Significant
13. Better organisational integration, participative management, emphasis on core values	67%	37%	Significant
14. Management communicating with staff, lower managers etc.	58%	30%	
15. Significant retrenchment	33%	60%	
16. Liquidation of current assets and liabilities	8%	33%	
17. Restructuring (decentralisation, fixing accountability, structural changes etc.)	83%	60%	

Table 5.3 (Contd.)

	Public Sector (12 companies)	Private Sector (30 companies)	Difference
18. Attempts to increase efficiency, quality, productivity other than through plant modernisation etc. and training	50%	33%	
19. Example-setting by top managers	33%	17%	
20. Marketing related actions	92%	77%	
21. Miscellaneous actions	25%	10%	
22. Cost-reduction actions other than retrenchment	75%	63%	
23. Disciplining	50%	43%	
24. Diversification, product-line rationalisation, expansion etc.	100%	97%	
25. Changes in top management	92%	93%	
26. Management control-enhancing actions	58%	57%	
27. Borrowings, raising equity finance, etc.	42%	43%	

Note: Only those differences that are statistically significant at the 95% level of confidence have been indicated as 'significant'.

The reasons for these differences may lie in ownership and the purpose for which enterprises are set up. Public enterprises operate in the glare of public visibility and they are set up to pursue strategic national, rather than short-term commercial, objectives. Hire-and-fire methods not only attract bad publicity and political comment, they are not even legally very feasible in Third World countries where, because of chronically high unemployment and absence of social security, the courts frown upon large-scale lay-offs. Perforce, therefore, the management has to resort to motivating and mobilising the staff and other stakeholders for the turnaround. In the process, of course, the costs of turnaround tend to get minimised.

Depth and Duration of Sickness and Turnaround Management

It stands to reason that the depth of corporate sickness influences the turnaround strategy. Charles Hofer suggested that if the sick organisation is operating close to its break-even point (marginal loss situation) the appropriate turnaround strategy should be anchored in cost-cutting. On the other hand, if operations are far below break-even point (high loss situation), an asset reduction strategy would be appropriate.[14] A revenue increasing strategy, Hofer argued, should be employed if the loss situation is not quite so drastic as to warrant asset reduction, and a combination strategy, if the loss situation is only a little worse than the one requiring a cost-cutting strategy. Donald Hambrick and Steven Schecter proposed that capacity utilisation (a surrogate for break-even point) would affect the choice of turnaround strategy, with firms operating at low capacity utilisation (high loss) opting for an asset reduction or divestiture strategy and firms operating at relatively high capacity utilisation (relatively marginal losses) choosing a cost cutting strategy (slashing of overheads, marketing expense, administrative expense, R and D and other 'discretionary' expenses).[15] From their study of 53 successful American turnarounds they identified (through cluster analysis) several types of turnaround strategies. What they called the asset/cost surgery type (divestiture-cum-cost cutting) used by six firms was employed in a low capacity utilisation (that is, high loss operations) situation, while what they labelled as selective product/market pruning (opting for high price and quality niches, lowering of marketing and inventory expenses, liquidation of receivables, increase in value added per employee, and similar measures) used by 19 firms was practised mainly in the high capacity utilisation (that is, marginal loss) situation. Thus, depth of sickness, as measured by extent of loss, may shape turnaround strategy.

In order to see how depth of sickness affects subsequent turnaround action, the sample of 42 complete turnarounds was divided into two sub-samples. The first sub-sample comprised 18 companies whose maximum loss-to-sales ratio during sickness was at least 10 per cent (deep sickness condition). The second was that of 22 companies whose maximum loss/sales ratio was below 9 per cent (marginal sickness condition). The average maximum loss ratio for the companies in deep sickness was an incredible 26 per cent; the average for the marginally sick companies was only 4 per cent.

Thirty-nine per cent of the deeply sick companies had surgical turnarounds *versus* 64 per cent of the marginally sick companies.

Table 5.4

Depth of Sickness and Turnaround Management

Sample: 42 Complete Turnarounds

	Percentage of 22 Marginally Sick Companies	Percentage of 18 Deep Sickness Companies	Difference
1. Incentives, motivation, grievance redressal	23	72	Significant
2. Formal diagnostic activities	18	67	Significant
3. Garnering stakeholders' support	27	72	Significant
4. Attempts to increase efficiency, quality, productivity other than through plant modernisation etc. and training	18	61	Significant
5. Increased training of managers and staff	14	44	Significant
6. Initiation of managerial meetings, problem-solving task-forces	14	44	Significant
7. Better organisational integration, participative management, emphasis on core values	32	61	
8. Plant modernisation etc. for greater efficiency, quality productivity	45	72	
9. Significant retrenchment	64	39	
10. Professionalisation of manufacturing management, personnel management, planning etc.	14	39	
11. Example-setting by top managers	9	33	
12. Borrowings, raising equity finance etc.	32	56	
13. Divestiture and liquidation of fixed assets and long-term liabilities	55	33	
14. Management control-enhancing actions	45	67	
15. Public articulation by management of corporate mission, goals etc.	23	44	

Table 5.4 (contd.)

	Percentage of 22 Marginally Sick Companies	Percentage of 18 Deep Sickness Companies	Difference
16. Credibility-building actions of management	23	39	
17. Disciplining	36	50	
18. Restructuring (decentralisation, fixing accountability, structural changes etc.)	59	72	
19. Miscellaneous actions	9	22	
20. Marketing related actions	77	89	
21. Management communicating with staff, lower managers etc.	32	44	
22. Liquidation of current assets and liabilities	23	33	
23. Diversification, product-line rationalisation, expansion etc.	100	94	
24. Changes in top management	95	89	
25. Cost-reduction actions other than retrenchment	64	67	
26. Innovation, new product development etc.	59	56	
27. Fresh induction of managers, technical staff etc.	36	39	

Note: Only those differences significant at the 95% confidence level have been indicated as 'significant'. The worst loss of marginally sick companies during sickness was below 9% on sales; of the deep sickness companies, 10% on sales or higher.

Clearly, therefore, deep sickness need not lead to extensive retrenchment. Table 5.4 shows the scores of the two groups of companies on the 27 turnaround elements. Companies in deep sickness had significantly more frequent recourse to such productivity enhancing actions as incentives and other attempts at motivating the staff, training, and at raising productivity, such as, a new chief of production or an in-house productivity campaign. There was also more of formal diagnosis and team effort at problem-solving, and greater networking with stakeholders. Although not reaching significant levels, the other differences pointed to greater recourse by the deeply sick group to professionalisation of management, participative management, and plant modernisation. In 12 elements this group scored 60 per cent or more, *versus* five elements for the marginally sick group. Thus, deeply sick companies tended to resort to a more comprehensive, as well as a more interaction intensive diagnosis, and productivity-centred turnaround. The marginally sick companies tended to resort more to short-term, 'quick fix' actions like retrenchment and divestiture. Both succeeded in their turnaround efforts; but the costs of turnaround may have been much higher for the quick-fix types and the depth of recovery much smaller.

Apart from depth, the duration of sickness may also affect turnaround action. Prolonged sickness may, upon change of management, legitimise radical and comprehensive overhaul of operations and management practices. In order to examine the effect of the duration of sickness on turnaround management, two contrasting sub-samples were assembled from the 42 complete turnarounds. The first was of companies with only one year of loss before break-even, and the other with at least three years of losses before break-even. The first group, of relatively transient sickness, consisted of 11 cases; the second, of prolonged sickness, consisted of 15 cases. Of the transient sickness group, 73 per cent had surgical turnarounds; of the prolonged sickness group only 40 per cent had surgical turnarounds. As with depth of sickness, long duration sickness apparently softens the harshness of turnaround action. Table 5.5 shows the scores of the two groups on 27 turnaround elements. Only on one item (disciplining) is the difference statistically significant. Nevertheless, there is a tendency for the group with prolonged sickness to engage more frequently in networking with stakeholders, in team effort at problem-solving, attempts at motivating staff, increased training, participative management, diagnostic activity, and related actions. On the other hand, the group with transient sickness tends to resort somewhat more frequently to retrenchment. There is also a modest tendency for the turnarounds from prolonged sickness to be more comprehensive than the ones from transient sickness—the scores of 60 per cent or more for 10 elements in the former *versus* the same percentage for 7 in the latter.

As noted earlier, asset-cost surgery, involving divestiture, retrenchment, and other cost-cutting, is supposed by some American turnaround scholars to be appropriate in a deep, and possibly prolonged, sickness situation. The data in this study indicate the opposite. Globally, the worse the sickness, the greater seems to be

Table 5.5

Duration of Sickness and Employment of Various Turnaround Elements

	Sickness Lasting One Year (% of 11 cases)	Sickness Lasting over 2 Years (% of 15 cases)	Difference
1. Disciplining	27	67	Significant
2. Garnering stakeholders' support	27	60	
3. Significant retrenchment	73	40	
4. Initiation of managerial meetings, problem-solving task-forces	9	40	
5. Incentives, motivation, grievance redressal	36	67	
6. Increased training of managers and staff	18	47	
7. Formal diagnostic activities	27	53	
8. Better organisational integration, participative management, emphasis on core values	27	53	
9. Credibility-building actions of management	18	40	
10. Example-setting by top managers	18	40	
11. Changes in top management	100	80	
12. Marketing related actions	73	93	
13. Management communicating with staff, lower managers etc.	27	47	
14. Innovation, new product development etc.	73	53	
15. Professionalisation of manu-facturing management, personnel management, planning etc.	9	27	
16. Borrowings, raising equity finance etc.	36	53	
17. Management control-enhancing actions	45	60	
18. Plant modernisation etc. for greater efficiency, quality, productivity	55	67	
19. Divestiture and liquidation of fixed assets and long-term liabilities	45	33	

Table 5.5 (contd.)

	Sickness Lasting One Year (% of 11 cases)	Sickness Lasting over 2 Years (% of 15 cases)	Difference
20. Miscellaneous actions	9	20	
21. Cost-reduction actions other than retrenchment	64	73	
22. Public articulation by management of corporate mission, goals etc.	36	27	
23. Diversification, product-line rationalisation, expansion etc.	100	93	
24. Liquidation of current assets and liabilities	27	33	
25. Attempts to increase efficiency, quality, productivity other than through plant modernisation etc. and training	36	40	
26. Fresh induction of managers, technical staff etc.	36	33	
27. Restructuring (decentralisation, fixing accountability, structural changes etc.)	73	73	

Note: Only those differences significantly different at the 95% level of confidence have been shown as 'significant'.

the tendency to resort to interactive, humane, constructive, participatory turnarounds; the lesser the sickness the greater seems to be the tendency to resort to harsh, asset-cost surgery types of turnarounds.

Causes of Sickness

Just as there cannot be one cure for different illnesses, there may not be one turnaround mode for different sorts of corporate sickness. A number of writers have tried to identify major types of corporate sickness and some have also suggested effective turnaround responses to these.[16]

A variety of conceptual approaches have been employed to

study organisational sickness. One early approach tried to identify various vicious cycles that afflicted bureaucratic forms of organisation.[17] The management's insatiable need for control precipitates one vicious cycle—of the imposition of rules and/or close supervision, alienation and demotivation of the staff, deterioration in organisational performance, further tightening of the screws to cope with 'laziness' and 'indiscipline', and the repetition of the vicious cycle. Another vicious cycle is triggered by the opposite impulse—to delegate authority to lower levels in order to lighten the burden at the top. This in turn, it was argued, leads to sub-optimisation and inter-departmental squabbles, to management recruiting technical experts to remedy the situation to whom further authority has to be delegated, and the repeating of the vicious cycle. Thus over-control as well as under-control leads to a tail-spin.

A quite different view of sickness is provided by the population ecology perspective.[18] This perspective applies to organisations Darwinian notions of the survival of the fittest in a hostile, competitive world, limited adaptability of organisms, and their attempt to survive by seeking out relatively safe, congenial environmental niches. If the environment were to change significantly, as any other organism, the organisation would become vulnerable because of its limited adaptability. Thus sickness or decline is seen as failure to adapt to hostile shifts in the macro environment such as structural changes in the industry, changes in government policies affecting the industry, major technological changes, and so on, or in the micro environment, such as changes in the specific markets in which the organisation operates, or in its particular terms of trade.[19]

These two factors—the vicious cycle and the population ecology perspectives—complement one another. The first points to internal causes of sickness while the second points to external causes of sickness. A number of scholars have identified a large number of specific external and internal causes.[20] Such external causes have been identified as increased competitive pressure, recession or decline in demand, industry-wide bad industrial relations, adverse price movements in inputs and finance markets, adverse changes in government policies or practices, excess capacity in industry through new entrants, government or political interference and constraints, hostile behaviour of financial institutions, poor law and order, transport, power, water, and similar infrastructural bottlenecks, among others. A large number of internal causes have also been identified. These include deficient general and functional management, bad technological, locational, strategic, and other choices, internal intrigues and discord, poor work ethic, corrupt management, growth mania, excessive conservatism, a bureaucratic management, excessive authoritarianism, poor control or coordination, bad personnel and industrial relations management, under-capitalisation, and so on.

A scan of the already identified external and internal causes of sickness as well as the causes indicated in the 65 cases of complete and break-even turnarounds led to the identification of 20 categories of sickness causes (see Table 5.6). Compiling this list, like the list of turnaround elements, was a trial and error process, the object being to encompass the diversity of both the published causes of sickness and those disclosed in the 65 cases, but keeping the number of categories down to manageable proportions. A binary system of scoring was employed: 1, if a sickness-cause category was present in the case, and 0 if it was absent. Various possible biases of reporting or not reporting causes of sickness were dealt with in a way similar to dealing with such biases in reporting or not reporting turnaround actions (see Chapter 2). Two persons independently scored each case for sickness categories. There was agreement on over 90 per cent of the scores. In the few instances in which disagreement could not be resolved, the author used his judgement after close textual reading. The 20 categories listing cause of sickness turned out to be reasonably independent. Principal components analysis yielded as many as eight factors with eigenvalues of 1 and over. The total variance explained by these eight factors was 65 per cent, but there was no dominant factor. The first factor explained only 12 per cent of the variance.

The frequency of occurrence of sickness categories is indicated in Table 5.6. The three most frequently reported external sickness causes were an adverse market environment, an adverse control environment, and shortages or high costs of inputs. Incompetent or weak management, poor marketing management, and poor operations management were the three most frequent internal causes of sickness. Poor personnel and industrial relations management was also a cause of sickness in a significant number of cases.

Seldom is there only a single cause of sickness. For the 65 turn-around cases, there were on an average a shade over four causes,

Table 5.6

Frequency of External and Internal Causes

Sample : 65 Turnaround Cases

	Percentage of 65 cases

External Context of Sickness

1. *Adverse governmental or controlling authority behaviour*—government restrictions, policy changes, political instability, political interference, imposition of too many or conflicting or inappropriate objectives on the organisation, not providing adequate leadership to the organisation and in time, taxation, exchange rate fluctuations, over-valuation of domestic currency or its under-valuation, steep inflation etc.   34
2. *Adverse market environment*—competition, stagnation, recession, industry decline, too fast a rate of technological change, too much market turbulence etc.   57
3. *Industrial unrest* affecting industry as a whole or in the supplier or customer industries.   6
4. *Insufficient or excessively costly inputs* such as finance, raw materials, power, water, transportation facilities etc.   31
5. *Miscellaneous other external* (including natural calamities).   9

Internal Causes of Sickness

6. *Authoritarian management*—management by fiats, centralisation etc.   8
7. *Bad technological and related choices*—wrong technology, wrong plant scale, excess capacity, wrong location.   22
8. *Bureaucratic management and inappropriate organisational structure*—too much hierarchy, rule-bound administrative rigidity, sanctity to precedents etc.; structure without proper accountability; structure that creates coordination difficulties.   9
9. *Conservatism*—complacency, risk aversion, timidity, lack of innovation, insufficient R and D, traditionalism, obsession with established products and technologies, rigidity in strategic management, slowness in responding to technological change.   18
10. *Ill-advised growth*—mistaken expansion/diversification, poor acquisitions or inability to manage acquisitions, diversification, expansion etc.   22
11. *Inappropriate staff work culture*—general lethargy, sloppiness, intrigues and squabbles, staff inefficiency etc.   6
12. *Incompetent or weak management*—inability to cope, rampant managerial inefficiency and lack of management control, poor coordination, lack of any sort of professionalism, weak board, management discontinuity not traceable to controlling authority, weak, confused or demoralised management, inability to manage new technologies etc.   42
13. *Obsessive management*—obsession with technological leadership, growth mania, market leadership etc.   6

Table 5.6 (contd.)

	Percentage of 65 cases
14. *Poor financial management*—high cost financing, mismanagement of funds, poor evaluation of funding requirements, poor portfolio management.	20
15. *Poor management of external stakeholders*—like the public, government, suppliers, customers, bankers, etc.; poor image.	6
16. *Poor marketing management*—inappropriate pricing, wrong marketing strategy, practices, poor product mix.	38
17. *Poor operations management*—poor planning of operations, poor plant maintenance, poor renovation, poor inventory control, poor quality control, low productivity, poor purchasing of inputs etc.	35
18. *Poor personnel and industrial relations management*—overmanning, nepotism, lack of HRD, poor industrial relations.	29
19. *Poor project management*—time and cost delays and escalations.	9
20. *Discord at the top.*	8

with an average of 1.3 external and 2.9 internal causes. The average number of causes was 4.3 for the non-surgical turnarounds *versus* 4.0 for the surgical turnarounds. Nor did the average number of external or internal causes for the two groups differ significantly (1.4 external causes and 2.9 internal causes for the non-surgical group *versus* 1.2 and 2.8 respectively for the surgical group). Thus, the number of causes or the distribution between internal and external causes did not seem to decide whether the turnaround response was surgical or non-surgical.

In order to see which cause may activate which category of turnaround action, the 20 causes were correlated with the 27 turnaround elements for the sample of 42 complete turnarounds (the 23 break-even turnarounds were not considered because of the possibility that some of the turnaround actions may be taken *after* a break-even is achieved. Table 5.7 shows substantial turnaround correlates (all correlations of 0.30 and above were considered substantial; 0.30 would be significant at the 95 per cent confidence level if the variables were normally distributed).

Only one cause—adverse market environment (most commonly intensified competition or recession)—had a large number (eight) of substantial turnaround correlates. When an adverse market environment precipitates sickness, such actions as managerial meetings and task forces, attempts at motivating employees with

Table 5.7

Substantial Correlations of Sickness Causes with Turnaround Elements

Sample : 42 Complete Turnarounds

Correlated Turnaround Elements

External Causes of Sickness

1. *Adverse governmental or controlling authority behaviour:* Garnering stakeholders' support (-0.32).
2. *Adverse market environment:* Initiation of managerial meetings, problem-solving task-forces (0.38); better organisational integration, participative management, emphasis on core values (0.36); incentives, motivation, grievance redressal (0.36); miscellaneous actions (0.34); significant retrenchment (-0.31); attempts to increase efficiency, quality, productivity other than through plant modernisation etc. and training (0.31); example-setting by top managers (0.31); cost-reduction actions other than retrenchment (0.30).
3. *Industrial unrest:* Nil
4. *Insufficient or excessively costly inputs:* Attempts to increase efficiency, quality, productivity other than through plant modernisation etc. and training (-0.36); innovation, new product development, etc. (-0.30).
'5. *Miscellaneous other external causes* (including natural calamities): Nil

Internal Causes of Sickness

6. *Authoritarian management:* Nil
7. *Bad technological and related choices:* Nil
8. *Bureaucratic management or inappropriate organisational structure:* Credibility-building actions of management (0.34).
9. *Conservatism:* Management control-enhancing actions (-0.56).
10. *Ill-advised growth:* Initiation of managerial meetings, problem-solving task-forces (0.49); plant modernisation etc for greater efficiency, quality, productivity (0.31).
11. *Inappropriate staff work-culture:* Nil
12. *Incompetent or weak management:* Professionalisation of manufacturing management, personnel management, planning, etc. (0.35).
13. *Obsessive management:* Increased training of managers and staff (0.38); diversification, product-line rationalisation, expansion, etc. (-0.37); attempts to increase efficiency, quality, productivity other than through plant modernisation etc. and training (0.30).
14. *Poor financial management:* Nil
15. *Poor management of external stakeholders:* Nil
16. *Poor marketing management:* Increased training of managers and staff (0.31).
17. *Poor operations management:* Nil
18. *Poor personnel and industrial relations management:* Nil
19. *Poor project management:* Divestiture and liquidation of fixed assets and long-term liabilities (0.36); significant retrenchment (0.31).
20. *Discord at the top:* Nil

incentives or otherwise, participative management and emphasis on core values, productivity campaigns, example setting by top executives, and cost reduction attempts tend to get activated. The negative correlation between an adverse market environment and retrenchment is noteworthy. Globally, therefore, causes of sickness like intensified competition or an industry decline tend to generate institution building, participatory, interaction intensive, efficiency oriented, but non-surgical efforts for successful turnarounds. The findings may surprise some people who think that harsh measures and authoritarian leadership are needed to combat intensified competition or an industry decline. But Western research on the organisational response to intensified competition suggests that besides such strategic actions like competitive pricing and promotion, innovation, and diversification and vertical integration, the management tends to become more cohesive, focus more sharply on organisational goals, become more sensitive to external forces, make decisions in a more professionalised and participative manner, plan more comprehensively, findings that are compatible with the present findings on turnaround response to an adverse market environment.[21]

Other than an adverse market environment, and possibly other than obsessive management (which had three correlates), the rest of the 18 causes did not have too many significant turnaround correlates. That does not mean that these 18 do not precipitate turnaround efforts, simply that the design of the turnaround effort may not be significantly influenced by them. It would seem that the nature and values of a social system, the size of the organisation, the nature of its ownership, the depth and duration of sickness and similar factors may shape turnaround response more than most of the identified causes of sickness, the one exception being an adverse market environment.

Concluding Comments

In this chapter an attempt has been made to examine various contingencies that may shape turnarounds: norms of the wider social system or culture, size of the organisation, whether it is publicly owned or privately, the depth and duration of sickness, and the various causes of sickness. Had the sample of turnarounds been much larger, more careful tests could have been made of how these contingencies affect turnaround management. For example, in examining the effect of various factors like the social system or size or ownership, matched sub-samples of turnarounds could have been identified in companies similar in all but the one contingency the effect of which on turnaround management was under examination. Alternately, with a large enough sample, multivariate statistical techniques like regression analysis could have been resorted to in order to isolate the *ceteris paribus* effects of each contingency. But with a sample size of only 42, only simple analysis could be undertaken. It provides only preliminary understanding of the contextual factors shaping turnarounds. Having thrown in this caveat, let us proceed to discuss the broad picture revealed by the analysis.

In this book, two major concerns so far have been the costs of turnaround (principally stemming from retrenchment) and alternatives for minimising these. In this chapter several contextual conditions have been examined which have a bearing on both concerns.

As far as turnaround costs are concerned (in terms of retrenchment and plant closures), the preliminary analysis reported in this chapter suggests that these tend to be higher in large, private sector. corporations that have encountered a temporary and modest dip in viability, especially those that operate in Western-style socio-economic systems with tremendous pressure to restore black ink soonest. Many reasons may be operating here, some cultural (aggressive individualism, a mercenary world view), some economic (intense pressures faced by firms operating in mature, globalised markets and a free enterprise system), some stemming from large organisational size (difficulty in communicating with myriad stakeholders and of persuading them to support a turnaround), some legal (the feasibility of laying off large numbers of employees without hindrance by the courts). Clearly the fascinating phenomenon of organisational violence against the organisation's own members begs careful multi-disciplinary study.

The other issue concerns alternatives to this sort of organisational violence. The analysis reported in this chapter suggests that humane, management systems turnarounds that are development oriented, interaction-intensive, people management oriented, are more likely in long suffering organisations with a strong public or social purpose, especially those operating in relatively nurturant, collectivist cultures. The proclivity to engage in these sorts of turnarounds may be reinforced if the organisation is of manageable size and is facing a turbulent market environment. As a suggestion, to minimise turnaround costs, large, sick Western corporations may like to decentralise turnaround to divisions, and instal at the top of these divisions innovative managers who can cope with size, turbulence, and sickness participatively and interactively. This would be in lieu of the slash-and-burn turnaround managers commonly installed at the head of sick large corporations in the West (especially in the USA).[22]

The findings also have interesting implications for a good deal of management and organisation theory. First of all, the contingency theory is reinforced. but only partially. Several factors do seem to shape turnarounds, some quite profoundly. However, size, which is one of the most important contingency theory variables, seems to have very limited impact on turnaround management. Secondly, the population ecology perspective may be savaged. For one thing, external causes of sickness (with the exception of an adverse market environment) do not seem to be significant shapers of turnaround. For another, deeply sick organisations (presumably their sickness stems from operating in highly unfavourable niches) seem to be more prone to change and adaptability during turnaround than marginally sick ones (presumably these operate in modestly unfavourable niches). Also, turnaround response to adverse market turbulence seems to be greater resilience, not less, thus negativing the cardinal assumption of the population ecologists that organisations have limited adaptability. The more influential of the literature on strategic management has over-emphasised the seeking of niches, portfolio management, other market oriented or externally directed actions, and under-emphasised people management as a major strategic option. The data call for a rectification of this lopsided view of strategic management.[23]

Notes and References

1. For a review of some significant contributions to contingency theory, see John Child and Alfred Kieser, 'Development of organizations over time', pp. 28–64,

in Paul C. Nystrom and William H. Starbuck, *Handbook of organizational design*, Vol. 1 (London: Oxford University Press, 1981). Also see Jeffrey Pfeffer, *Organizations and organization theory* (Boston: Pitman, 1982, pp. 148–61).

2. For an examination of how societal cultures may affect the behaviour of organisations see G. Hofstede, *Culture's consequences: International differences in work-related values* (Beverly Hills, Cal.: Sage, 1980). For corporate cultures, see T.E. Deal and A.A. Kennedy, *Corporate cultures: The rites and rituals of corporate life* (Reading, Mass.: Addison-Wesley, 1982). For the way societal and organisational cultures interact, see Pradip N. Khandwalla (ed.), *Social development: A new role for the organizational sciences* (New Delhi: Sage, 1988, part III).

3. See Andrew H. Van de Ven and William F. Joyce (eds.), *Perspectives on organization design and behavior* (New York: John Wiley, 1981, chapters 7 and 8); Pradip N. Khandwalla, 'Properties of competing organizations', pp. 409–32, in Paul C. Nystrom and William H. Starbuck, 1981, op. cit., Vol. 1.

4. See James D. Thompson, *Organizations in action* (New York: McGraw–Hill, 1967); Paul R. Lawrence and Jay W. Lorsch, *Organization and environment* (Boston: Harvard, 1967); A.H. Van de Ven, A.L. Delbecq, and R. Koenig, 'Determinants of coordination modes within organizations', *American Sociological Review*, April 1976, pp. 332–38.

5. See Derek S. Pugh, David S. Hickson, Christopher R. Hinings, and Christopher Turner, 'The context of organization structures', *Administrative Science Quarterly*, Vol. 14, 1969, pp. 91–114; John Child and Roger Mansfield, 'Technology, size and organization structure', *Sociology*, Vol. 6, 1972, pp. 369–93.

6. See Donald Gerwin, 'Relationship between structure and technology', pp. 3–38, in Nystrom and Starbuck, 1981, op. cit., Vol. 2.

7. See J. Kimberly and R.H. Miles, *The organizational life cycle* (San Francisco: Jossey-Bass, 1980).

8. See Hofstede, 1980, op. cit., who found the Third World, especially Oriental cultures, higher on femininity and collectivism, compared to Western cultures, particularly the American culture. For a review of Western, particularly American individualism, see Robert N. Bellah, Richard Madsen, William M. Sullivan, Ann Swidler, and Steven M. Tipton, *Habits of the heart* (Los Angeles, California: University of California Press, 1985).

9. See Pfeffer, 1982, op. cit., pp. 148–51.

10. See Howard Thomas and K.L.K. Rao (eds.), *Multinational corporations and state-owned enterprises: A new challenge in international business* (Greenwich, Conn.: Jai Press, 1986).

11. See V. Sri Ram, N. Sharma, and K.K.P. Nair, *Performance of public sector undertakings* (New Delhi: Economic and Scientific Research Foundation, 1976); A.M. Choksi, 'State intervention in the industrialisation of developing countries: selected issues', World Bank staff working paper no. 341, 1979; and Liaquat Ahmed, 'A functional review of public enterprises in bank reports', Washington, D.C.: The World Bank, 1978.

12. See *Public enterprises survey* annual volumes brought out by Bureau of Public Enterprises, Ministry of Finance, Government of India.

13. See Pradip N. Khandwalla, 'Performance determinants of public enterprises: Significance and implications for multinationalisation', pp. 195–220, in Thomas

and Rao, 1986, op. cit.; Pradip N. Khandwalla, *Effective management of public enterprises* (Washington, D.C.: The World Bank, 1987).

14. See Charles W. Hofer, 'Turnaround strategies', *The Journal of Business Strategy*, Vol. 1, No. 1, 1980, pp. 19–31.

15. See Donald C. Hambrick and Steven M. Schecter, 'Turnaround strategies for mature industrial-product business units', *Academy of Management Journal*, Vol. 26, No. 2, 1983, pp. 231–48.

16. See Hofer, 1980, op. cit.; Donald B. Bibeault, *Corporate turnaround: How managers turn losers into winners* (New York: McGraw-Hill, 1982); Stuart Slatter, *Corporate recovery: Successful turnaround strategies and their implementation* (Harmondsworth, Middlesex: Penguin, 1984).

17. See James G. March and Herbert A. Simon, *Organizations* (New York: Wiley, 1958); Michel Crozier, *The bureaucratic phenomenon* (Chicago: The University of Chicago Press, 1964).

18. See Michael T. Hannan and John H. Freeman, 'The population ecology of organization', *American Journal of Sociology*, Vol. 82, 1977, pp. 929–64; Pfeffer, 1982, op. cit., pp. 180–91.

19. See K.S. Cameron, R.I. Sutton, and D.A. Whetten, 'Issues in organizational decline', pp. 3–19, in K.S. Cameron, R.I. Sutton, and D.A. Whetten (eds.), *Readings in organizational decline: Framework, research and prescriptions* (Cambridge, Mass.: Ballinger, 1988).

20. See Bibeault, 1982, op. cit.; Slatter, 1984, op. cit.; Pradip N. Khandwalla, *Effective turnaround of sick enterprises: Text and cases* (London: Commonwealth Foundation, 1989, chapter 2).

21. See Pradip N. Khandwalla, 'Properties of competing organizations', pp. 409–32, in Nystrom and Starbuck, 1981, op. cit., especially p. 427.

22. For some engaging examples, see 'The green berets of corporate management', *Business Week*, 21 September 1987, pp. 52–56; Mark Potts and Peter Behr, *The leading edge* (New Delhi: Tata McGraw-Hill, 1987).

23. See R. Miles and C. Snow, *Organizational strategy, structure, and process* (New York: McGraw-Hill, 1978); Michael E. Porter, *Competitive strategy* (New York: Free Press, 1980). A notable exception is the work of Thomas J. Peters and Robert H. Waterman, *In search of excellence: Lessons from America's best-run companies* (New York: Harper, 1982).

6. TURNAROUND CREATIVITY

Management creativity is generally not as stunning as the great breakthroughs of science or art.[1] But the management innovations of this century, such as scientific management, operations research, job enrichment, quality circles, brainstorming, human relations, organisation development, portfolio management, long-range planning, matrix structure, cost-benefit analysis, social marketing, formal managerial training, have had as profound an influence on the shaping of our civilisation as relativity, quantum physics, the double helix, psychoanalysis, Keynesian economics, or Cubism. Even less glamorous than these major management innovations are the numberless organisation-specific innovations that may not be very original but represent quite ingenious and effective variations on the familiar.

Turning around sick corporations boils down to improving their profitability. Improving profitability boils down to decreasing costs and/or increasing revenues. Decreasing unit costs boils down to cutting costs and/or increasing productivity; and increasing revenues boils down to improved pricing and marketing and a better product-mix. These are the essentials of turnaround management, secured by changing the quality of management, restructuring, plant modernisation, divestiture, professionalising management systems, giving incentives, reducing staff, mobilising the rank-and-file, bringing in more cash, training managers, replacing them, and like actions. There are conventional ways of doing these things, and there are others, smarter, and more ingenious.[2] In earlier chapters we have examined some choices, especially constructive and effective alternatives to organisational blood-letting. Let us push further our quest for turnaround creativity, beginning with two case studies.

Lucas Industries of Britain, a giant manufacturer of autoparts, aerospace parts, and electrical machines, was turned around creatively in the eighties.[3] Lucas had a decline in profitability in the late seventies, culminating in 1981 with a loss of £21 million on sales of over £1 billion. The dwindling car manufacture in Britain and rising imports had hit it hard. Besides, there had been strikes and stoppages affecting major customers. Most important, however, the company had, over its 110 years, grown notoriously inward looking, with a management that had become complacent in the face of changes in the industry. Sir Godfrey Messervy was appointed chairman in 1980 and Tony Gill became the group managing director. One of the first acts of the turnaround was weekend retreats of the 12-man executive, during which the gentlemen "argued, analysed and reflected their way into the small hours". These resulted in a fundamental shift in the Lucas approach. Competitiveness Achievement Plans (CAPs) were formulated, communicated throughout the Lucas empire, embodying operations decentralisation with accountability for performance, a major shift from the earlier centralisation of decision-making at the corporate centre. The centre adopted the role of helping, not dictating.

Each business unit was asked to compare its performance in detail with that of its best international competitor. It was also asked to assess how it was perceived by customers, and to propose plans for improving performance in the shortest possible time. If a viable CAP for the unit was not forthcoming, the unit would be sold or closed. Following this, 40 units were in fact disposed off, although massive purges were avoided. Some heads of units were asked to leave despite long tenure, another sharp departure from tradition.

The CAPs revealed that the major deficiency lay in the manufacturing methods the company employed rather than in technology *per se*. While R and D expenditure was maintained even during the year it sustained a loss, the emphasis was on revamping manufacturing systems.

Lucas manufacturing was designed along the assembly line concept, ideal for mass production. However, demand had been shifting in favour of small volumes and high variety. There were too many supporting staff members, overly complex control systems, and high levels of stock, combined with poor responsiveness to customer needs. Professor John Parnaby was appointed as the production management expert, heading a team of 50 systems and engineering project managers who were to act as consultants to individual companies. Parnaby's study comparing Japanese practices with the British revealed stark differences. For example, the ratio of indirect support staff to direct labour was 0.5 in Japan, while it was 1.2 in

Britain; stock turnover was three to five times faster in Japan; the Japanese lead time from development to manufacturing was half that of Britain's; and Japanese per employee sales were about three times the British. As a consequence, the Japanese costs were 60 per cent to 80 per cent of the British.

Lucas set up over 30 multi-disciplinary task forces and provided them with intensive training in systems engineering to redesign the factories. Earlier, only production engineers would have been involved in this sort of an exercise. Now marketing, finance, design, and personnel managers and trade unionists also participated. The factories were redesigned into self-contained manufacturing cells operated by small teams of employees. Productivity shot up by about 40 per cent, manufacturing lead times were cut by 60 per cent, stock levels were halved, the quality of the final product improved, and the indirect labour component was drastically cut.

Workers were re-educated so as to be able to operate in small teams. The old distinction between workers and staff was virtually erased. Lucas began to spend an unprecedented 3 per cent of turnover (nearly £40 million in 1986) on training, a large jump over past budgets. The emphasis was on multi-skill training. For example, skilled craftsmen picked up the expertise of electricians, plumbers, and machine tool setters. An open learning centre was established to train managers in computing, finance, marketing, and so on.

A search was started to extend the reach of Lucas beyond its British base, and on diminishing the relative importance of the automotive business. Search was on for acquisitions overseas, especially in the U.S.

Nothing that Lucas did was profoundly original. But it aggressively diagnosed its problems, and broke with its traditions in a number of areas. It aggressively innovated, especially in manufacturing management, an area often neglected by giant corporations in a hurry to drop "obsolete" plants and get on to the shiniest and the newest.

Bharat Heavy Electricals Limited (BHEL), a large Indian government-owned manufacturer of power plants and allied engineering equipment, offers another example of turnaround creativity.[4] BHEL was set up in the early seventies by merging two separate public enterprises. One of them was a losing concern while the other was profitable. Mr V Krishnamurthy became the head of the combine. During 1972–73 the two constituents, with a staff of

45,000, had a net loss of $22 million (Rs 176 million apporx) on sales of $200 million (Rs 1.6 billion approx). BHEL was in hot water with the Indian parliament because of losses and customer complaints—BHEL's major customers were government owned state electricity boards. There was a clamour for importing power equipment during India's fifth five-year Plan (1974–79), rather than risk delays and related problems by having it produced in BHEL—a demand that was nurtured by the multinational competitors of BHEL. If this demand had been conceded, BHEL would have received a mortal blow that would have gravely compromised its capacity utilisation.

Krishnamurthy went about creatively dealing with BHEL's credibility problem. He organised an internal study on the reasons for BHEL's low efficiency and delivery delays. Technical experts from BHEL's foreign collaborators were asked to recommend measures to improve productivity. A crisp report on BHEL's plans for improvement was produced for distribution to members of a government task force on industrial machinery that was to decide BHEL's fate. Krishnamurthy, as a member of this task force, went on record with a forceful plea to let BHEL be the major supplier of power equipment during the forthcoming five-year Plan. He personally contacted every member of the task force to make sure that the facts and issues were clearly understood. He invited them to visit BHEL's plants and personally escorted them around.

Simultaneously, Krishnamurthy launched a drive to improve relations with key customers who could influence the government's decision. A new Field Service Division was set up to provide urgent repair and maintenance services to customers. The division stocked critical parts and rushed trouble-shooting groups to customers' plants during breakdowns. Services were made available not only to repair machinery supplied by BHEL, but also imported necessary machinery. Since these services rapidly improved the performance of customers' plants (many of these were in the public sector), goodwill for BHEL soared. Krishnamurthy made it a point to get to personally know the chief executive officers of his customer firms and to brief them about the steps he was taking to revitalise BHEL.

Krishnamurthy lured his competitors (mostly Indian subsidiaries of foreign multinationals) with attractive sub-contracting offers if they would drop their opposition to BHEL. In this he succeeded.

As a result of all these efforts, the idea of importing power equipment in a big way was dropped and BHEL was assured of getting the lion's share of the orders.

Besides the creativity displayed by BHEL in stakeholder management, the company, under Krishnamurthy's leadership, also displayed much ingenuity in people management, institution building, and reorganisation. A high level worker–management negotiation committee was set up. The company promoted 1,000 stagnating workers. Bonuses to workers were promised if the production targets were met. Mr Krishnamurthy practised an open-door policy and continued to meet workers' representatives even when there was no burning issue to be settled. Every quarter the top managers from the headquarters visited the plants and talked to cross-sections of executives and workers. The company launched a big institutional advertisement campaign that highlighted BHEL's contribution to India's industrialisation and its improved performance. At the same time the top managers avoided high visibility for themselves.

Krishnamurthy conceived of a plan for a much-needed rationalisation—the same products were being produced at several plants—with greater product specialisation by each plant. Instead of forcing this plan through, Krishnamurthy elected to implement it only after a public discussion of its merits and demerits. A booklet on the plan was widely circulated within BHEL and also in government circles. While the press and the government strongly welcomed rationalisation, there was resistance from labour and local politicians who feared transfers of men and equipment. The management publicly announced that no equipment or men would be transferred without the consent of the employees and the provincial government. The controversy subsided after a compromise with the unions was struck: no facilities would be moved between plants, although plant layouts could be changed and products could be shifted from one plant to another provided no loss of overall work was involved, and employees could be transferred between locations with their consent.

BHEL embarked on a corporate plan involving diversification. Choosing a foreign collaborator was politically a very sensitive issue—Krishnamurthy personally preferred a Western collaborator to the earlier (but still influential) collaborator from the Soviet bloc. To get over this problem, he requested his minister to appoint an inter-ministerial committee to evaluate alternative collaborators.

The technical evaluation for the committee was done by Krishna-murthy's nominees from BHEL, and Krishnamurthy was able to get the collaboration he wanted.

Krishnamurthy was also able to get some top level personnel changes he wanted (not an easy job in the Indian public sector). He got rid off a powerful top manager near retirement by getting the BHEL board to agree not to give any extensions beyond the retirement age. This gentleman was made a consultant to the company. Five other officers near retirement were shifted from line to staff jobs and promising younger managers were moved up. Since financial rewards in the Indian public sector were extremely limited, Krishnamurthy motivated his men by providing positive feedback, appreciation, and exciting jobs. He also sponsored the high fliers to external training programmes, transferred them from the plants to prestigious jobs at the headquarters, nominated them to new, responsible posts created by the reorganisation, sent them abroad for training at the collaborators' plants, and so on.

The BHEL management decided to break into foreign markets. This would win BHEL friends in a government beset by foreign exchange problems and also even out domestic demand fluctuations in BHEL products. It would force BHEL to upgrade its products, technology, and management. And it would provide challenging opportunities to the younger managers. BHEL aggressively got VIPs from foreign countries to visit its plants, and sought turnkey projects abroad.

BHEL strengthened its R and D effort by setting up a corporate research and design organisation. It also sought to provide a more coordinated customer service through the total systems engineering of power systems and erection and the commissioning of projects on a turnkey basis. An engineering reorganisation was carried out by appointing engineering development managers for each product or product group in order to raise engineering capacity and improve product quality. Engineering development centres were set up to coordinate product developmental efforts. Marketing and sales divisions were set up to enhance customer service and to provide single point contacts for customers. Several technical divisions were also set up. Planning, budgeting, and information systems were streamlined. The basic philosophy adopted was of centralised policy formulation and decentralised execution and administration.

A number of coordination committees were set up to harmonise diverse interests.

BHEL broke even in 1974–75. In 1975–76 sales rose to $450 million (compared to $200 million in 1972–73), and profits climbed to $35 million. The turnaround was complete, without any plant closures, without retrenching a single person. Operating as BHEL did, in a constraining controlled environment with a legacy of a bureaucratic management, BHEL under Krishnamurthy showed unusual resilience and innovativeness in its turnaround ordeal, especially in managing its external and internal stakeholders.

Let us look at the potential for turnaround creativity in four broad areas. These are: people management, operations management, management structure and systems, and strategic management. These areas broadly encompass the 27 turnaround elements described in Chapter 2. For assessing the potential for turnaround creativity we survey actions taken by the managements of turned around companies that seemed innovative within their operating contexts.

People Management

People management is a nearly limitless arena for turnaround creativity.[5] Getting cynical or even hostile internal and external stakeholders to enthusiastically contribute to a turnaround is the essence of creative people management in a turnaround situation. People management in a turnaround has many facets to it: a new top management acquiring credibility with the stakeholders; mobilising the organisation for a turnaround by collective diagnosis, trouble shooting, and decision-making; renewed emphasis on missions and core values; effective communications; motivation, disciplining, example-setting leadership; human resource development; networking with important stakeholders, and related actions. Ingenuity is possible in each of these facets.

Getting Credibility

Most turnarounds are effected by new top managements.[6] The latter must have credibility to make headway in a decline situation in which employees and other stakeholders have grown pessimistic, cynical, or even hostile to any management initiatives. A commonplace way of getting this sort of credibility, at least in the USA, seems to be "...to spread a little blood and guts around the organisation. Many men break psychologically when it comes to firing a lot of people who have been in the corporation for fifteen years, and who have families, etc."[7] The conventional wisdom about the way turnaround managers "take charge" in America is apparently to shock the system: "You must get everyone's attention, and the way you do that is by rationally shocking the system. You've got to make everyone in the organization, from the man who sweeps your floors to your immediate staff, understand that you mean business."[8] Stern pronouncements that the new leader means business, bruising meetings with the staff, finding a few sacrificial lambs or visible scapegoats, a massacre or two, are the ways of getting everyone's attention.

There are, however, creative alternatives to baring fangs. Romano Prodi, who turned around IRI, the world's largest government-owned enterprise, won credibility by getting the government to agree to a 35 per cent increase in managers' salaries.[9] De Benedetti, who turned around Olivetti, earned attention by bringing in his own $17 million into the sick company as an act of faith.[10] At SAIL, India's government-owned giant steel maker, Krishnamurthy earned credibility by arguing the government out of a price increase to cover costs because, he said, SAIL should instead try and increase its woefully low productivity.[11] At British Steel the new management earned credibility by shifting from its "Olympian" headquarters to more modest, businesslike quarters.[12] At Richardson and Cruddas, a government-owned Indian engineering company, Mr Sharangpani, the new CEO, earned credibility by facing up to a strike (and breaking it) rather than giving in quickly to union demands as his predecessors were wont to do.[13] At Bharat Heavy Plates and Vessels, another Indian public enterprise, Mr Mansukhani, the new CEO, earned credibility by working almost continuously for seven days and nights with representatives of a hostile workforce to hammer out a new wage agreement.[14] In an Indian textile mill, the new CEO gained credibility by shutting off the airconditioners in his office during a power crisis at the peak of a very hot summer and diverting the power saved to running a few more looms.[15]

These examples illustrate the range of options in acquiring credibility. Basically, they boil down to doing what may otherwise be commonplace but is uncommon or unexpected in the particular circumstances of a sick organisation. In a sick organisation there can be innumerable opportunities for credibility building because so many systems are malfunctioning, so much incompetence or indifference is on display, so many profitable opportunities are going a-begging. A little brainstorming can uncover dozens of opportunities for demonstrating top management competence and concern. These can range from such mundane actions as getting filthy toilets or factory floors cleaned up, making sure quality control is exercised, better lighting, firing dishonest guards, salesmen, or cashiers, or taking back defective goods earlier dumped on customers, to such dramatic actions as breaking a strike or giving an across-the-board salary increase or getting an international certification for quality.

Mobilising the Organisation for Turnaround

Ordering people around is one thing; getting them turned on for regenerating the organisation is several orders of magnitude more difficult. Articulation of key issues, credible approaches for resolving them, and participative understanding and direction taking are needed for mobilising a differentiated, faction ridden mass of people. A sharply focussed awareness of what is wrong and how it can be righted has to be engineered. How may this be done innovatively in a sick organisation?

Corporate consciousness can be imaginatively changed with the help of consultants. SPIC got a management audit done by the faculty of a management school, and followed this up with plant surveys to get a definition of its ailments.[16] Italtel hired consultants to do a study of its image which led to a wide ranging review of Italtel's products, processes, and structure.[17] GM had a comparative study done comparing itself and a Japanese affiliate which revealed substantial cost differences.[18]

There are other innovative ways to unfreeze paralysed organisations. As we noted earlier, Lucas did it by hiring a noted scholar to present to its managers some stark contrasts between inefficient British and efficient Japanese practices. The Jaguar management arranged dealers to visit Jaguar plants to bring customer complaints forcefully to the attention of the workers and managers so as to shock them into facing the problem of shoddy quality.[19] At Enfield the top management organised retreats for managers to brainstorm on corporate problems and solutions.[20]

The ingenuity in diagnostic work lies not so much in how thorough it is, as in how effectively the information is used to shock an apathetic or distracted staff into a recognition that something must be done. The ills are not unknown; more commonly however, they are not sharply etched on the consciousness of the staff. Outside experts, graphs, charts, slides, films, talks can be pressed into service to drive home the enormity of the collective fall.

Creativity is also needed in getting people to move from the state of shock to a clear perception of the priorities for action. This was done brilliantly at SAIL, by the chairman talking to 25,000-odd persons before formulating priorities for action, discussing these with his top managers at two-day retreats, mailing the formulations to 250,000 staff members for discussion, before finalising a turn-around strategy which had a tremendous backing of the staff.[21] Next comes actual individual and group action. This can be attempted through task forces. Lucas formed over 30 multidisciplinary task forces to help units diagnose their manufacturing problems and begin solving them. Rockware established strategic groups for policy making.[22] Meetings too can help. At BHEL top managers made it a practice to meet cross-sections of workers and managers on every visit to the plant.[23] At British Steel plans of action and strategies were shared with the staff to infuse them with an awareness of the market forces.[24]

Organisational Integration

Another important facet of people management during turnaround is organisational integration, or ways by which the organisation as a whole develops a unity of purpose.[25] This unity, even in a situation of grave peril to the organisation, is seldom automatic. Large modern organisations are far too differentiated by hierarchy, roles, functions and the like to have that unity of purpose so essential for the heroic job of turning them around. This unity of purpose has to be engineered. How can this be done innovatively?

A whole lot of processes need to be activated for achieving unity of purpose: highlighting of the *raison d' etre* of the organisation and emphasis on core values and goals, effective communication with the rank-and-file, decision processes based on consensus. This is another major arena for management creativity. Let us take a look at some creative options that were tried out in turnaround situations.

Organisational goals and missions are powerful organisational integrators.[26] Besides, they can unleash much organisational creativity for concretising them. Their imaginative reformulation can move many hardened hearts. ICL developed a document called "The ICL way". It set out corporate objectives and standards, and these were then communicated to managers throughout ICL.[27] The Air India management visualised the corporation as a first class international carrier not dependent in the main on Indian traffic.[28] Docutel reformulated its mission as selling services to customers rather than selling merely automatic teller machines.[29]

There can be novel ways of institutionalising new values (or newly emphasised values). For example, GM transferred 7,000 employees to EDS, its electronic data processing subsidiary, to pick up the more organic, dynamic EDS culture.[30] De Benedetti at Olivetti started a practice of the top management meeting at 6 a.m. in order to instil his workaholism in his top managers.[31] EID Parry sought to replace a hierarchical culture with an egalitarian culture by having a single canteen and a single uniform for all employees.[32] Lucas tried to replace a smug culture with a competitive one by forcing each unit to develop a plan for closing the gap with its best international competitor and threatening closure or disposal of the unit in case the plan was not forthcoming.[33] MAMC tried to build a collaborative culture through inter-departmental sports and cultural activities and festivities.[34]

A number of devices can be creatively used to bring about a change in values: exposure and information; inter-unit or inter-corporate competitive challenges; indoctrination; persuasion; training; rewards; example-setting by the top man; fresh inductions; job rotation; and, of course, threat. These need to be creatively blended for maximum impact in specific turnaround situations.

Effective Communication

Merely articulating core missions, goals and values is obviously not enough; these have to be communicated to the rank-and-file. Communication is not merely the dissemination of information;

effective communication is two-way communication resulting in a shared understanding and the acceptance of common mission, goals, and values.

The usual way for communicating goals is to make formal announcements through newsletters or at staff meetings. The element missing here is two-way communication. Several turnaround examples shed light on how creative communicating can build commitment to a turnaround.

At Apollo Tyres, the management communications with the staff were earlier in English, the country's corporate *lingua franca*, not in the local language.[35] The new management decided to issue bulletins in Malayalam, the local language. At Travancore Cochin Chemicals, top management communication with workers and managers was greately stepped up through letters, local language bulletins, mettings, "bitching" sessions, and brainstorming sessions.[36] At BHEL, ideas on a major reorganisation were published in a booklet which was widely disseminated both inside and outside the organisation for intensive discussion.[37] Italtel practised intense information transparency: it prepared a strategic plan for recovery which was presented to the shareholders and the government, and discussed at length with the unions; the press and the external audiences were kept informed through press releases, numbering about 100, and nearly 250 interviews with top managers; over 130 speeches were delivered at technical or political meetings and symposia.[38] Jaguar gave extensive internal publicity to its uphill struggle. There was continuous communication with workers and managers about the company's problems. There was sharing of information through the use of videos, meetings, plant performance briefs, monthly management bulletins, and similar media.[39] Structured participative management during turnaround may be an important device for uniting two frequently hostile internal stakeholders, namely managers and workers. At IRI union representatives were continuously engaged with managers in discussing the reorganisation of the company and the industrial policies of IRI's sector holding companies.[40]

Motivating and Disciplining

Staff apathy and recalcitrance characterise many sickness situations. Emphasis on missions, goals, core values, communications, task forces, meetings, and similar means do help. But they need to be supplemented by a strategy of motivating and disciplining employees. Carrots and sticks are the commonplace ways of motivating and disciplining staff. But there can be creative variations here, as well as creative alternatives to carrots and sticks.

Apollo Tyres offered the staff monetary incentives for increasing capacity utilisation.[41] Can Cel started a housing project in its remote location in British Columbia to keep people from leaving because of the difficulty of finding suitable housing.[42] Also, when Can Cel had to lay off some 300 workers, the company spent $2 million to relocate the laid-off workers. About half were found jobs. State Timber Corporation gave its staff a 35 per cent salary hike.[43] Also, the CEO of State Timber Corporation started the practice of picking up promising persons during his visits to timber felling sites and giving them responsible jobs at the head office. At BHPV, a company producing sophisticated custom-tailored equipment, the new CEO abolished overtime and instead started an incentive system for staff that had them clamouring for work, whereas earlier they put in an effort only if they got overtime. He also introduced an Own Your House Scheme, and instituted a monthly esteem prize for the worker with the best productivity in each shop.[44] Travancore Cochin Chemicals started a job enrichment programme for junior and middle-level managers.[45] Volkswagen involved workers in the planning and design of Halle 54, a fully automated assembly line.[46] BHEL promoted *ad hoc* over 1,000 workers who had been stagnating for the past several years, and, in a public sector seniority oriented system, promoted and in other ways rewarded high fliers.[47] At British Steel bonus payment was tied to plant level profitability.[48] At Jaipur Metals, bonus was paid to the employees in the form of company's shares (workers now own 58 per cent of the company's capital).[49] Eastern Airlines gave 25 per cent of its shares and four Board seats to employees.[50] At RFD, employees were encouraged to think that they turned out world class life saving products, and an employee was given a seat on the Concorde inaugural flight to demonstrate the usefulness of the company's equipment.[51]

The usual way to enforce discipline is for the management to act tough. But there can be creative ways of bringing greater discipline to the staff. Apollo Tyres faced the problem of a youthful and undisciplined workforce. The management instituted the policy of hiring only older, married workers to cut down militance.[52]

At Standard Motors a policy of giving preference to relatives of existing, loyal employees was instituted as an alternative means of increasing discipline.[53] At Jaipur Metals the management presented a charter of demands to the union. Some officers were sacked, gate passes to employees for personal work were curtailed, the right to redeploy workers was negotiated with the union, and, most interestingly, the plant level committee with worker and management representation was used to discipline workers.[54] Thus, while punishment, or the threat of punishment, is the commonplace way of disciplining the undisciplined, there can be creative ways of using threats or punishments, and some ways that do not resort to threats or punishment at all.

The setting of a personal example by the top manager can move people as few other mechanisms can. The effect of leading from personal example is not a favoured topic of leadership research (as compared to, for example, task versus employee orientation),[55] but in crisis situations this may often be of extraordinary importance in mobilising a sceptical, demoralised, or dependency prone rank-and-file. There can be many creative ways of leading by personal example. Marketing is one. In BHPV, the new chief executive personally went on a hunt for orders that netted the largest volume of orders in the history of the company.[56] At Chrysler, Iacocca personally marketed on television the company's new car models.[57] But marketing apart, there are many other operating areas where leadership by personal example can be exercised. For instance, at Enfield India, the CEO, an insider, took a pay cut upon taking charge, and thereby induced his senior colleagues also to take a cut in salary.[58] At State Timber Corporation of Sri Lanka, not only did the new CEO take a cut in earnings to join the company, he did not raise his salary when he gave an across-the-board raise to his managers and staff.[59] Also, in a culture of nepotism, he made certain that none of his relatives was recruited during his tenure in office. At Getz, the chief executive travelled abroad extensively in search of business opportunities, infusing a spirit of enterprise in Getz's far flung business units.[60] At Ultra Electronics the chairman personally chased government dues.[61] At British Steel the CEO tied his pay packet to the improvement in the company's performance.[62]

Human Resource Development

During a turnaround, human resource development through

training can be a very important way of changing the competence as well as attitudes of significant internal stakeholders.[63] But training can be conventional or uncommon, or uncommonly emphasised. Both British Steel and SAIL emphasised multi-skill, multi-equipment training for workers in order to equip them to tackle modernisation and also to break down a mechanistic culture of narrow specialisation. SAIL went much further, however. It unleashed a training blitz in which 14,000 executives and 37,000 non-executives were given training in 1987–88. A plan was drawn up to integrate training and development. It reassessed its training effectiveness, set up a new campus for this purpose for senior managers, and appointed an executive director to coordinate all training: A training advisory board was formed, headed by the chairman himself.[64] Managers were encouraged in Travancore Cochin Chemicals to get higher qualifications, and capsule training programmes in different aspects of managerial and organisational effectiveness were set up. Indeed, the chief executive himself took a hand at teaching.[65] Zambia Railways launched a five-year training programme.[66] There is obviously great scope for creativity in the training function, with innovative options in the content, process, depth, location, and coverage of training.

Besides training, there may be other interesting ways of human resource development. Enfield and Jaguar introduced quality circles to increase competency in group effort at problem solving.[67] Travancore Cochin Chemicals raised the minimum qualifications of workmen.[68] BHEL rotated 300 executives between divisions in 1975.[69] Chrysler introduced joint quality programmes in collaboration with the union (UAW).[70] Jaguar transferred responsibility for training in quality maintenance from inspectors to supervisors.[71]

Networking with External Stakeholders

Turnarounds often require forbearance and support of external stakeholders. If the government presses its claims for back taxes, the banks and financial institutions for interest arrears, suppliers for payment, and unions for wage hikes, a sick unit would crash quickly into insolvency. These stakeholders have to be persuaded to postpone their claims, and indeed, to make "sacrifices" so that the unit may recover and become viable. Negotiation and communication skills of a high order are needed in the turnaround manager. Management of external stakeholders is a special and important aspect of people management and requires much ingenuity.

A variety of actions is possible. Ferranti involved government, labour, and shareholders in the reorganisation of its transformer plants in order to prevent a shut down and thus save jobs.[72] SAIL moved its corporate headquarters several hundred miles (from Ranchi to New Delhi) for better liaison with the government.[73] It was also one of the first public enterprises in India to enter into a memorandum of understanding with its parent ministry, promising a pattern of performance and securing in turn explicit promises of support from the government. Can Cel, a nationalised enterprise, mounted a highly visible public relations effort to tell its turnaround story, cleaned up pollution at a plant to improve its image, and had its executives play an active role in the industry association to gain acceptance by an apprehensive private sector.[74] The State Timber Corporation of Sri Lanka gave donations to political groups, but without letting them influence decision-making. It gave technical and financial support and such conveniences as cars to its parent ministry. It also undertook reforestation on a small scale to placate the forestry department.[75] BHEL briefed the heads of its customer firms about BHEL's plans to revamp itself. It set up a field services division for quick servicing of customer complaints. It actively lobbied in the government to scuttle plans to import power equipment. And it took over and revived some sick units as a public relations gesture.[76] British Steel lobbied government for changing energy pricing policies, persuaded its parent ministry to let it reduce capacity drastically, and won the assent of the unions for a major lay-off. It was also able to persuade the government to write off £3,500 million in loans to British Steel.[77] Tinplate persuaded the government to stop the unrestricted import of tinplate into India and also to decontrol its pricing.[78]

There is no standard way to rope in stakeholders. But thinking of them as partners in recovery helps. It makes sense to bare the accounts books to them, share operating constraints or other problem areas, brief them about the immediate steps being taken to stem losses, and seek ideas, guidance, and help. Brainstorming with stakeholders can uncover dozens of innovative ways to speed turnaround. Creativity resides in turning an often adversarial relationship into a richly collaborative one.

Operations Management

More effective management of day-to-day operations is the nuts and bolts of turnaround. It boils down to cutting operating costs, increasing productivity, enlarging sales and/or getting better price realisation. In each of these areas there are a number of choices. Turnaround creativity in operations management consists of going beyond the usual ways of cutting costs, increasing productivity, improving margins or increasing sales, and of using commonplace alternatives in unusual ways that is, however, suited to the organisation's unique situation.

Cost Cutting

The usual ways of cutting costs are an across-the-board budget cut, firing people, and cuts in postponable spending (such as advertising, research and development, training, maintenance, and such like). The turnaround cases showed some interesting variants as well as other options. Toyo Kogyo, for example, reduced its manpower from 37,000 to 28,000 but through attrition, not by firing.[79] It cut excessive production costs by relocating manpower from production to the undermanned sales operations. SAIL cut labour costs by voluntary retirements and by practically eliminating overtime, a bugbear of public enterprises, bringing it down from Rs 440 million in 1984–85 to Rs 25 million in 1986–87.[80] Italtel reduced excessive manpower by arranging to transfer 2,000 employees to sister companies.[81] Dawson cut labour costs by moving (for a while) to a three-day week.[82] Jaipur Metals, a public sector company, was able to do the unthinkable in India: negotiate with its unions a freeze on dearness allowance rates, reduction in overtime, and a deferment of pay increases for a year, besides longer working hours.[83] IRI got rid off a good part of its surplus manpower by lowering the retirement age and by giving golden handshakes to those retiring.[84] Thus these companies avoided, by a variety of means, the trauma of retrenchment.

There are many other ways of cutting costs. Lucas reduced manufacturing costs by radically changing the way the work in the factory was organised.[85] SAIL cut costs by substituting gas for fuel oil, and did an energy audit to save on energy costs.[86] Sylvania and Laxman negotiated with government tax departments drastic reductions in tax liabilities.[87] BHPV persuaded the government to convert its loans to the company into equity and thus saved on interest costs.[88] Travancore Cochin Chemicals entered into five-year contracts with suppliers of materials frequently in short supply.[89] Chrysler cut down car repair costs by placing retired technicians in vendors' plants. It also reduced the parts list from 75,000 to 45,000 by standardisation of the basic car and its constituent systems.[90] Jaguar embarked on a programme of supplier education and involvement to cut down supplies of defective components.[91] This was buttressed by introducing penalty clauses for defective supplies. Air India negotiated with the government to buy fuel in India at the lower international rates, and saved money by rescheduling loans at favourable exchange rates.[92] Munsingwear transferred some work to Caribbean seamstresses at lower wage rates.[93] Black and Decker reorganised 25 manufacturing facilities into nineteen.[94] These examples simply illustrate what a rich range of opportunities there may be to cut costs in any malfunctioning organisation.

Productivity Increase

Incentives, modernisation, and manpower training are the most commonly employed means for increasing productivity. There can be interesting variations on these and also interesting alternatives. Besides, the focus generally is on worker productivity. But productivity may often be low for other groups as well, such as among salesmen, engineers, accountants, and managers. Lucas increased productivity by reorganising factory work into manufacturing cells manned by small, multi-skilled teams.[95] Quality circles were tried out by Enfield.[96] SPIC's problem was that productivity was impaired by an erratic power supply and irregular supply of essential inputs. So SPIC set up a captive power plant and developed a port to handle imports for SPIC.[97] RFD sought to increase productivity by specialising in the production of standardised products and customised products in separate plants.[98] Volkswagen embarked on extensive robotisation that cut the time required to build a car by 20 per cent.[99] Chrysler attempted to increase productivity by trying to get rid of restrictive work practices.[100] ICL tackled sales productivity.[101] Jaguar tried suggestion schemes.[102] GM entered into partnership with several Japanese companies to access their better manufacturing practices and techniques.[103]

Effective Marketing

Marketing is an area of great creative potential. There can be interesting ways of pricing, promoting products, distributing, selling and interesting combinations of these four basics to increase sales and/or margins. Some of the creative potential in marketing can be gauged by looking at examples from cases of turnaround. As a selling point, Docutel got prestigious TRW to handle the maintenance of Docutel's automatic teller machines.[104] Docutel offered a retrofit kit to old customers that would keep them with Docutel. SPIC developed some small ports to speed up the distribution of its fertiliser products.[105] At RFD the CEO personally visited major customers to renegotiate prices upwards.[106] Sylvania and Laxman resorted to such non-conventional distribution channels for its bulbs as van retailing in cities and cigarette shops in rural areas.[107] It also sought to reduce price competition in the industry through action in the industry association. BHEL began to market total energy systems both within and outside India in place of pieces of power equipment.[108] Searle bought a minority stake in a three-store chain to push retail sales.[109] Jaguar gave bonuses to dealers with excellent customer service.[110] NBC Radio brought in creative persons in excessively automated FM stations, and started some pioneering programmes.[111] Richardson and Cruddas doubled scrap sales and sought to capitalise on Indian aid to Nepal and Viet Nam by seeking orders from the aid recipients.[112]

Management Systems and Structure

The area of management systems and structure is less fecund in terms of innovation because that is the one area of management most systematised. Much of what we call professional management consists of such systemic tools and techniques as budgetary control, cost control, inventory control, production planning and scheduling, statistical quality control, decision analysis, breakeven analysis, portfolio management, investment and project appraisal, market segmentation analysis, operations research techniques, forecasting techniques, formal planning, management by objectives, and so on. Most of these come packaged.

Nonetheless few of them are useable without some modification to make them suitable in the organisation's specific circumstances. Management creativity lies in this sort of modification. Let us look at turnaround creativity in this area.

SAIL linked its human resource development plan to its modernisation, expansion, and efficiency enhancement plans.[113] BHPV introduced budgetary control for individual orders and appointed a project coordinator for each.[114] Warnaco advanced the annual budget planning deadline by two months to force managers to make earlier cost projections.[115] Fiat opted for a version of the Japanese Just in Time (JIT) system.[116] EID Parry provided monthly operating results to managers within two weeks of month end rather than the earlier two and a half months.[117] MAMC sought better monitoring and control of its ancillaries.[118] Richardson and Cruddas stimulated managerial succession planning by telling managers that none who failed to provide at least two names (with justifications) of potential successors would be promoted.[119]

Restructuring in large organisations usually boils down to divisionalising a functionally organised company. While this was resorted to frequently by turnaround managements, some interesting other options in restructuring were also tried. Sweda got rid off one whole level of management between the president and the field organisation,[120] and SAIL reduced the number of levels below the plant general manager from eight to five [121] British Steel disentangled some businesses and grouped some homogeneous others into divisions.[122]

Too often, management systems and structures get invested with a sanctity they do not deserve. Too often the changes in systems and structures follow predictable, textbookish lines. As the turnaround examples show, the spirit of experimenting and improvising can be extended even to this area.

Strategic Management

Strategic management is the attempt to conceptualise what business one should be in, draw up plans to get into the desired lines of business, and implement these plans.[123] Strategic management involves the consideration of such alternatives as related *versus* unrelated diversification, growth *via* acquisitions *versus via* plant constructions, expansion in some product lines and contraction or stagnation in some others or even exit or entry strategy (being first to enter a market *versus* being a quick follower), competitive strategy (banking on a niche *versus* on cost advantage), domain strategy (being local or national in one's operations *versus* being international), technology strategy (high tech *versus* lower tech options), financing strategy (high *versus* low leveraging), joint venturing strategy, and so on. Strategic management has been a highly innovative area of corporate management, and a great many academics and consultants have made hay formulating exciting "new" strategic management models. Corporate practice may be a good deal more prosaic and at variance with these models. Indeed most organisations may not consciously have a strategy, although strategic patterns could be discerned in their actions.[124] Let us see some examples of fresh strategic thinking in the case of the turnaround cases.

Toyo Kogyo realised that it could not compete across-the-board with its larger rivals. It therefore opted for a strategy of dominating particular niches with unique products. For example it developed special cars for the aged, for women, for the disabled, and so on.[125] Lucas changed from mass production goods to more niche tailored quality products. It initiated a search for high value-added sophisticated products to be manufactured preferably with joint venture partners.[126] SPIC, a fertiliser producer, expanded its plant maintenance function into a full fledged diversification into maintenance services.[127] BHPV did an ABC analysis of its equipment orders. It found that small orders were highly unprofitable and decided to take orders of only above a certain value.[128] GM acquired hot-shot artificial intelligence, consulting, data processing, electronics, and like companies, not so much to diversify as to get access to expertise that would help it design a highly computerised car of the future.[129]

Some of the turnaround managements also displayed financial innovativeness. Apollo Tyres and Epe Plywood, faced with a funds shortage, garnered deposits from dealers and distributors.[130] Metal Box, in similar straits, sold off its offices for £22 million and leased them back,[131] while Ultra Electronics did likewise with a factory.[132] Pullman bought Peabody with its equity so as to increase Pullman's borrowing capacity.[133] Chrysler bludgeoned reluctant banks, government and unions to fork out cash by threatening insolvency.[134]

Some of these turnaround companies also followed other interesting innovative strategies. Standard Motors, for instance, built up good relations with its ancillaries to speed up the indigenisation of its vehicles.[135] Although R and D expenditures are typically slashed during declines, Lucas did not, and got valuable mileage out of this.[136] Italtel coordinated its R and D effort with leading European rival producers of digital switching equipment.[137] ICL entered into collaborative research with academic institutions as well as other commercial organisations, and acquired a design centre.[138]

Turnaround Creativity and Turnaround Performance

Turnaround creativity may be good organisational fun. But does it yield dividends? Does it reduce the costs of turnaround? To get at least some preliminary answers, the sample of 42 complete turnarounds was divided into two contrasting groups: a group of companies that had, as reported in the cases, demonstrated much innovativeness during turnaround, and another group that had demonstrated much less innovativeness.

To get at these sub-samples, each case was scored on 14 categories of turnaround action rather than the 27 categories of turnaround elements described in Table 2.2 of Chapter 2. The reason was that almost by definition, creative or innovative turnaround actions are relatively rare events, and having too many categories for scoring would have yielded null scores in most categories for most of the cases. Thus, several elements in Table 2.2 of Chapter 2 were combined for scoring turnaround creativity, such as: cost reduction (element 15) and retrenchment (element 13); motivating (element 10), example setting (element 11), and disciplining (element 12); diagnostic activities (element 3) and problem solving meetings (element 4); modernisation (element 16) and other attempts at increasing productivity (element 17); and so on. Some elements in which creativity was not likely, were eliminated, such as changes in top management (element 1), and fresh inductions (element 2). At the end of this sort of combining and eliminating,

14 categories for scoring turnaround creativity emerged: six categories of people management (innovativeness in credibility building, collective effort at problem solving and diagnosis, organisational integration, motivation and disciplining, human resource development, and networking with stakeholders), three categories of operations management (innovativeness in cost reduction, productivity increasing activities, and marketing), three categories of strategic management (innovativeness in diversification and product line shuffling, funds management, and innovation), and two categories of systems management (innovations in management control and other systems and restructuring).

Innovativeness was judged in the context in which the company operated. An action was deemed innovative if it was relatively novel in the context of the company's operations. To set this concept of turnaround creativity (novelty in the company's operations context) in motion, a method by which originality is measured in creativity research was adopted.[139] Novelty in this method is equated with relative infrequency. If, for example, subjects list various uses for an óbject, such as a chair, the use or uses listed is rarely (say in only 10 per cent of the subjects) an original response—provided, of course, that it is also an appropriate response. In judging turnaround creativity, therefore, the attempt was to identify rare (but appropriate) responses within each of the categories of turnaround action. Since what may be rare in one type of culture may not be rare in a very different type of culture, and *vice versa*, and what may be rare in the public sector may not be rare in the private sector (and *vice versa*), the sample of turnarounds was divided into four groups: private sector Western turnarounds, public sector Western turnarounds, private sector non-Western turnarounds, and public sector non-Western turnarounds. For each group, turnaround actions were listed for each of the fourteen action categories. Thereafter, for the two relatively small groups (Western public sector and non-Western public sector) actions taken by no other members of the group were judged to be creative, while for the somewhat larger groups, Western private sector and non-Western private sector, actions taken by not more than one member of the group were judged to be creative. A company scored 1 in a category if it had taken a "creative" action in that category, and zero otherwise. A company's turnaround creativity was the sum of the ones it had received across the fourteen categories.

To derive two fairly clearly differentiated groups, scoring 5 and above (of a maximum possible score of 14) were classified as high on turnaround creativity while those scoring 3 and below were classified as low on turnaround creativity. This way the chance of misallocating a company low on creativity as high and *vice versa* was substantially reduced. Table 6.1 shows the 16 complete turnaround highly creative companies and Table 6.2 the 20 complete turnaround companies low on creativity. The tables show the creativity scores for people management, operations management, strategic management, systems management and the total for all 14 categories. The non-surgical and surgical turnaround companies are separately shown in each table. Given the crudeness of the measure of creativity, the aggregate turnaround creativity score is likely to be more reliable than the scores for any of the four constituent heads.

Table 6.1

High Scorers on Turnaround Creativity

Sample: 16 Complete Turnarounds

	People Management (out of 6)	Operations Management (out of 3)	Strategic Management (out of 3)	Systems Management (out of 2)	Total (out of 14)
Non-surgical Turnarounds					
1. SAIL,* India	5	2	1	2	10
2. Travancore Cochin Chemicals,* India	5	3	0	1	9
3. Lucas, UK	3	2	2	1	8
4. RFD, UK	4	2	1	1	8
5. BHEL,* India	5	1	0	1	7
6. BHPV,* India	2	2	1	1	6
7. Apollo Tyres, India	2	2	1	0	5

Table 6.1 (Contd.)

	People Management (out of 6)	Operations Management (out of 3)	Strategic Management (out of 3)	Systems Management (out of 2)	Total (out of 14)
8. SPIC,* India	1	2	1	1	5
9. Sylvania and Laxman, India	0	3	2	0	5
Surgical Turnarounds					
1. ICL, UK	4	3	1	1	9
2. Jaguar,* UK	3	3	2	0	8
3. British Steel,* UK	5	1	1	1	8
4. Chrysler, US	3	2	1	0	6
5. Italtel,* Italy	3	1	1	0	5
6. GM, US	3	1	1	0	5
7. Olivetti, Italy	3	1	1	0	5

* Government-owned during turnaround.
Note: Those scoring a total of 5 points and above were categorised as high on turnaround creativity.

Table 6.2

Low Scorers on Turnaround Creativity

Sample: 20 Complete Turnarounds

	People Management (out of 6)	Operations Management (out of 3)	Strategic Management (out of 3)	Systems Management (out of 2)	Total (out of 14)
Non-surgical Turnarounds					
1. Del E. Webb, US	0	0	0	0	0
2. Zambia Railways,* Zambia	1	0	0	0	1

Table 6.2 (Contd.)

	People Management (out of 6)	Operations Management (out of 3)	Strategic Management (out of 3)	Systems Management (out of 2)	Total (out of 14)
3. Sweda, US	0	0	0	1	1
4. Toyo Kogyo, Japan	0	1	1	0	2
5. Docutel, US	2	1	0	0	3
6. Enfield, India	2	1	0	0	3
7. State Timber Corporation,* Sri Lanka	2	1	0	0	3

Surgical Turnarounds

	People Management (out of 6)	Operations Management (out of 3)	Strategic Management (out of 3)	Systems Management (out of 2)	Total (out of 14)
1. Warnaco, US	0	0	0	1	1
2. Macmillan, US	1	0	0	0	1
3. Metal Box, UK	0	0	1	0	1
4. USX, US	0	1	0	0	1
5. Burton Group, UK	0	1	0	0	1
6. ICI, UK	1	0	0	1	2
7. Staveley, UK	0	0	1	1	2
8. Redman Heenan, UK	1	0	0	1	2
9. Searle, US	0	1	1	1	3
10. Fiat, Italy	1	1	0	1	3
11. Getz, US	1	1	1	0	3
12. Ultra Electronic, UK	2	0	1	0	3
13. Dawson, UK	1	1	•1	0	3

* Government-owned during turnaround

Note: Those scoring a total of 3 points and below were categorised as low on turnaround creativity.

As the tables show, there is some tendency for surgical turnarounds to be associated with low turnaround creativity and non-surgical turnarounds to be associated with high turnaround creativity. Sixty-five per cent of cases low on creativity were surgical turnarounds while 58 per cent of the cases high on creativity were non-surgical turnarounds. Thus turnaround creativity may mitigate the costs of turnaround. However, the association between creativity and type of turnaround was not statistically significant.

Interestingly, there was a statistically significant (chi-square significant at the 99 per cent level of confidence) association between ownership and turnaround creativity. Fifty per cent of the highly creative turnarounds were government-owned enterprises at the time they were turned around (one or two were later privatised) while 90 per cent of the turnarounds low on creativity were private enterprises. This belies the popular stereotype of wooden public enterprises and dynamically innovative private enterprises.

In order to see whether creativity speeds turnaround, an attempt was made to estimate the rate of improvement in the profitability of the 16 highly creative and the 20 cases low on creativity. The rate of improvement in profitability was calculated by subtracting from the earnings on sales a year after break-even the largest loss on sales during the sickness period, and dividing this difference by the number of years in between. As an example, if a company's maximum loss was 10 per cent on sales in 1980, and the company broke even in 1982, and earned 4 per cent on sales in 1983, then the turnaround would be 4 per cent − (− 10 per cent) = 14 per cent. Divided by 3 (1983–1980), the annual gain in profitability would be 4.7 per cent of sales. Table 6.3 provides the data for the two groups.

Table 6.3

Gain in Turnaround Profitability for
High versus Low Turnaround Creativity Cases

	Average Annual Rate of Gain in Profitability
High Turnaround Creativity Group	
1. 9 non-surgical turnaround cases	9.8
2. 7 surgical turnaround cases	5.9
3. All 16 high creativity cases	8.1

Table 6.3 (contd.)

	Average Annual Rate of Gain in Profitability
Low Turnaround Creativity Group	
1. 7 non-surgical turnaround cases	6.1
2. 13 surgical turnaround cases	3.0
3. All 20 low creativity cases	4.1

As Table 6.3 shows, the average annual rate of gain in profitability for the turnaround group high on creativity was just about double that of the group low on creativity. Furthermore, the nine non-surgical turnaround highly creative companies outperformed the seven non-surgical turnaround companies low on creativity while the seven surgical turnaround highly creative companies outperformed the 13 surgical turnaround companies low on creativity. The worst performance of the four groups was of the surgical group low on creativity, while the best performance was of the non-surgical highly creative group.

A chi-square test of association between the gain rate for profitability and creativity was made, with over 4 per cent (on sales) annual rate of gain constituting the fast gain group and below 4 per cent the slow gain group (16 were in the fast gain group and 18 in the slow gain group). The chi-square was significant at the 95 per cent confidence level. In addition, total turnaround creativity for 40 complete turnaround cases was correlated 0.32 with gain in profitability, a relationship that was statistically significant at the 95 per cent level of confidence (gain in profitability could not be computed for two companies). Thus, there was reasonably strong evidence that management creativity is linked with the rate of improvement in profitability.

On both counts, therefore—of reduction in the human cost of turnaround and of improvement in profitability—turnaround creativity seems to yield dividends.

How may turnaround creativity be increased? A few fairly simple and fairly widely tried management techniques are available, that can substantially increase organisational creativity during turnarounds.

Techniques for Turnaround Creativity

Ordinarily techniques amount to programmed action. Programming and creativity may seem poles apart, and usually are. But there are techniques that foster divergent, innovative thinking and often, therefore, uncover innovative solutions to organisational problems. Such techniques can usefully supplement management exuberance during turnaround. Indeed, they can buttress the culture of asking basic questions, redefining priorities, improvising, experimenting and innovating, that often characterises turnaround situations. These techniques can reduce the costs of turnaround by drawing on the creativity of the many rather than just the few. By throwing up innumerable unsuspected oppportunities for cutting costs, increasing productivity, and returns on sales, they can also obviate the need for harsh action.

Brainstorming

This technique, pioneered by Alex Osborn,[140] is well-known, but often badly practised. The term brainstorming is commonly applied by managers to free-ranging discussion. Brainstorming is not this. Instead it has a lot of structure to it. The group takes its time in understanding and defining the problem. Then it follows a procedure—and there can be many alternatives here—for generating ideas, the principles being that evaluation inhibits ideation and quantity (of ideas) begets quality. Also, hitch-hiking, that is, building on others' ideas, is encouraged (in contrast to the competitive spirit that often prevails in open ended discussion sessions). Unlike meetings where usually only a few dominate, everyone is expected to contribute ideas, and indeed the procedure guarantees this. Long-winded speeches and expression of wishes (rather than crisp "do this" ideas) are banned. Because of the ban on evaluation, people are encouraged to go for wacky ideas. These may or may not be practical, but have the effect of opening up fresh perspectives and demolishing mental sets. Bizarre ideas can precipitate innovative and useful ideas.

The technique is extraordinarily productive. Scores of ideas on cost cutting, improving margins, increasing productivity, reducing wastage, motivating employees, roping in outside stakeholders, improving the corporate image, raising finance, changing the work culture, reorganising a structure, avenues of diversification and product line rationalisation, more effective marketing, more appropriate management systems, and so forth can be generated in a hectic hour.

The problem becomes one of what to do with so many ideas. A sensible procedure needs to be followed of combining ideas, 'cleaning them up' and eliminating redundancies, and then having an expert panel identify a few innovative, high potential ideas. Thereafter, task forces could be formed to develop the selected ideas further, examine their costs and benefits, and recommend action. Some such procedure as the above, maximizes participative divergent thinking, leads to the identification of some exceptional alternatives, and gets people involved in implementation work. The cultural message of brainstorming is that structured democracy is excellent for divergent thinking and participative autocracy is excellent for implementation of selected innovations.[141]

There are several other techniques, too, for creative thinking, such as attribute listing, a questions checklist, and synectics.[142] Attribute listing helps uncover a large number of options to a current unsatisfactory alternative. It basically identifies three or four key (but modifiable) attributes of a product, service, activity, or function, and then three or four high potential alternatives for each attribute. This way, if three attributes are listed, and three alternatives are identified for each attribute, 27 (3 to the power 3) alternative designs of the product, or whatever is under study, can be generated in a matter of minutes. A questions checklist subjects a current option to a barrage of questions—what can be usefully added to it or deleted from it; how its design or sequencing could be altered; how it could be miniaturised, how magnified; in what other ways could it be produced; to what other uses could it be put; in what other ways could it be utilised, and so on. Synectics works by analogising. It seeks various sorts of analogies to a problem situation. It tries to get at creative approaches to the situation by seeking analogies in some other field (as in the attempt to try and understand how whales dive 10,000 feet without being crushed as a means to designing sturdier submersibles). It also uses empathy in a special way by asking the problem solver to imagine himself as the thing being examined and then reporting what he or she sees, feels, thinks, and so on (for example, ask a person to imagine himself to be the metal of a jet plane undergoing fatigue and then report his empathetic experience). Other features of the synectics technique are the evocative question (such as—how can we get the earthquake to tell us where it will strike?), book title (a poetic or paradoxical title for a situation or event such as a price war), fantasies (what would happen if humans could communicate telepathically?), and so on.

SWOT

SWOT stands for strengths, weaknesses, opportunities and threats.[143] SWOT analysis is generally done by asking a group of organisational members to indicate what they see are the strengths and weaknesses of their organisation, the threats faced by the organisation, and opportunities available to the organisation. A useful variation is to ask the respondents for their suggestions— how to increase the strengths further, eliminate the weaknesses, face threats, pursue available opportunities effectively or create fresh opportunities. The respondents can also be asked what changes they would suggest in current goals, strategies, policies, structure, operating values, management systems, technologies, and other such areas, to make the organisation more effective. Another possibility is to ask the respondents to do a SWOT for the organisation as a whole and also for their departments. The usefulness of SWOT is that it accesses very quickly perceptions of organisational members, the functioning of the organisation and suggestions for improving the organisation's effectiveness. In a large organisation having every member as a respondent may be infeasible and provide largely redundant data. It may, therefore, be useful to perform SWOT on a carefully stratified sample. SWOT is particularly useful to a new management trying to get to grips with the problems besetting the organisation and generate some ideas in a hurry about how to act. SWOT is likely to generate much excitement if its results are fed back to the organisation members in the survey feedback tradition.[144] The feedback can generate fresh collective attempt at making sense, proliferation of ideas and action.

Action Research

Action research is a powerful technique for unfreezing paralysed, demoralised organisational sub-systems and get them on to an innovation trajectory.[145] The basic idea is to combine a collective diagnosis with collective action and a testing of hypotheses. Typically, a team (usually of trained behavioural scientists) gets to a problem sub-system of the organisation, interviews people working within it, and calls them to meetings where the findings are presented. Following a joint diagnosis, action plans are collectively generated to improve functioning. These are treated as hypotheses. These action plans are collectively implemented. Thereafter, the team tries to gather data on what was attempted, what actually happened, and the impact on the functioning of the sub-system. These data are fed back to the members of the troubled sub-system for a fresh round of a collective attempt at clarity, making plans, implementing, examining, and the related steps. These rounds go on until the sub-system internalises collective decision-making, innovating, and implementing. Then the team may move to another under-performing sub-system. Action research is a time consuming process but it has worked in many cultures and organisational and other systems.[146] Although it is initially over-dependent on trained behavioural scientists, it is not too difficult to train a few individuals from each sub-system to join the action research team, and indeed, ultimately displace all external experts.

Value Analysis

A group technique that can throw up creative options in operations is value analysis or engineering.[147] The basic idea is to maximise the value of a product, service, process, function, or activity by providing its functions at minimum cost. It attempts this by analysing the various components that contribute value to a product or a service or an activity, such as different manufacturing and marketing processes, different materials and components, or different labours. Thereafter, every component of value is questioned as to how essential it is, whether some cheaper way is available to create the same value, whether the various functions performed by the product or service are necessary or not, and if necessary, whether the same can be achieved in cheaper ways, and so on. These are basic questions that can provoke profound reappraisals of technological and operating processes and lead to much fresh thinking.

Zero-base Budgeting

After a while, most budgeting tends to become extrapolative and mechanical. The sort of careful scrutiny that any planned expenditure needs, tends to get eroded as activities get mechanical and simple percentage add-ons to existing levels of expenditure, income, or activity levels become ingrained in budgetary decisions. Zero-base budgeting is a technique whereby fresh justification is periodically sought for all (or most) budgetary allocations.[148]. The questions asked are: If the organisation had no prior commitments, would it engage in the activity for which a budgetary provision is sought? What is the current justification for activities initiated in the past? These are disturbing questions that managers seldom care to ask in good times but certainly should during a turnaround. Many cost cutting opportunities could be uncovered by persisting with such questions.

Concluding Comments

In earlier chapters we have explored two major alternatives in turning around sick organisations, the surgical versus the non-surgical, with their variants. In this chapter we have described yet another alternative, that of harnessing or not harnessing management creativity in revitalising a sick organisation. The alternatives of surgical *versus* non-surgical and innovative *versus* conventional modes of turnaround are not, of course, unrelated. Choosing the non-surgical path, that is, accepting the constraint of not firing people, may well stimulate a management to search for innovative means of reducing costs, increasing productivity, and increasing margins and sales. To an extent this may be true of choosing the surgical path too; the resulting demoralisation in staff may have to be creatively tackled. Thus, both alternatives are potential stimuli for management creativity. The choice of the innovationist path may generate quick dividends and thus obviate the need for harshness. On the whole, the nexus between humaneness and creativity may be stronger.

The creativity of individuals has received a great deal of research attention.[149] Not so collective creativity, inclusive of the organisational variety.[150] Looking to the vast unmet needs of humanity, especially of its poorer 80 per cent, and severe limitations of resources, collective creativity can play the Santa Claus role in human affairs. It needs to be far more intensively studied. Already beginnings have been made in looking for and at the organisational version of collective creativity.[151] Some useful techniques have also been developed. But much remains to be done.

From the perspective of turning around sick organisations, some evidence has been presented in this chapter that management creativity can reduce the human costs of turnaround and increase the amplitude of recovery. The findings are, of course, quite tentative, and beg more and better research. There are two kinds of management creativity that need study. The first is the variety illustrated in this chapter: fresh approaches in people management, strategic management, operations management, redesigning management systems and structure, and similar issues. The second, a subtler kind, hinted at in the literature on synergy, is of putting together unique and effective combinations or gestalts of commonplace elements of the organisation: goals, policies, strategy, culture, structure, technology, and management systems among others.[152] The latter creativity is the realm of management as high art.

If creativity is indeed a significant means for revitalising sick organisations, then a critical question is how to get thus started. The techniques of creativity are there. But they have been there for quite some time. There is no evidence that they are widely in use in sick organisations attempting to turnaround. The point is: how does an organisation get started on the high road of management innovation? It may get started through fortuitous circumstances. The new chief executive brought in to turnaround the organisation may happen to be an innovative person, thus sending ripples of innovation down the line. But the challenge is in institutionalising the spirit of creativity in the organisation even when it does not have a Land or a Fuller or an Edison at its head.

Two recent approaches may be mentioned here. In a research on 75 Indian corporate organisations, Khandwalla identified what he called the pioneering-innovationist (PI) orientation of top management that some of them had.[153] He then sought to identify the forces that may have triggered this orientation.[154] He found two sets of forces, one external, the other internal, that seemed to nurture PI orientation. The external forces welled from the type of environment in which the organisation operated. An opportunity-rich, dynamic, complex environment tended to energise a PI orientation. The internal forces sprang from certain management choices, such as the desire to contribute to society, the search for high potential but risky ventures, the preference for organic and professionalist management practices, and several policy choices that, in the final analysis, turned out to be the primary generators of PI management. These policies were: management commitment to being a generous employer (so as to attract talent to the organisation); the hiring of innovative staff and provision of substantial autonomy to them (talent utilisation strategy); commitment to offering off-beat, novel products and services (strategy of being unique); opportunistic diversification; and striving for greater operating efficiency even if it displeased the staff (efficiency strategy). Thus, for triggering innovationist turnarounds, it may be useful to conceptualise a talent attraction and utilisation strategy, a strategy of being a unique organisation (which may also be a secondary attractor of talent and commitment), an opportunistic growth strategy, and an efficiency strategy. In other words, if a turnaround manager adopts these strategies, innovations down the line may more or less automatically follow.

Since turnarounds are entrepreneurial situations, a second approach worth considering is the decision rules or heuristics approach used by Manimala in his study of PI *versus* non-PI entrepreneurs.[155] Manimala looked at the case histories of 164 entrepreneurial ventures and identified a large number of decision rules or heuristics used by the entrepreneurs. He then devised an index of innovation consisting of 10 areas of innovation and divided his 164 cases into high innovation, moderate innovation, and low innovation cases. Finally, he compared the decision heuristics used in 52 cases that scored the highest on the index of innovation with the 46 that had the lowest scores. Although several decision heuristics were used by both groups, there were some interesting differences *vis-à-vis* idea search and idea management, management of autonomy, management of competition, growth management, risk management, and networking. For instance, the high PI group tended to use more search channels for innovative ideas, and continued to search for fresh ideas even when good ideas had been located and were being implemented. Also, the idea search was vision and mission driven. At the same time while missions and goals were not lost sight of, the PI group was more flexible regarding the means to attain these. The PI group was more choosy about partners, more proactive towards the external environment, chose to develop expertise internally by coopting experts, and was more oriented to self-reliance in capabilities and resources. In terms of its competitive strategy, the high PI group chose to avoid competition and sought monopolistic niches through new products and markets, it also relied more heavily on differentiating its products by quality, reliability, and better customer servicing. The PI group opted for organic growth, that is, starting small, learning the ropes fast, and then scaling up rapidly. It also emphasised related diversification and vertical integration more. And structurally, it metamorphosed the organisation as the company grew in size, becoming more decentralised, divisionalised, and professionally managed. The PI group took bigger risks but it also sought to reduce them by seeking more information, testing ideas out more, and such like actions. Finally, the PI group networked in distinctive ways. Its managers offered honorary service on public bodies and were more frequently involved in public interest activities, including during community crises. The PI group was more oriented to developing casual contacts, and inducting on the company Boards reputed and influential people. The PI group also extended help more frequently to friendly concerns in trouble. Many of these decision heuristics make sense even in turnaround situations.

Khandwalla's research suggests some of the management strategies that may trigger a pioneering, innovationist management culture in a sick organisation; Manimala's research suggests the kinds of decision heuristics that can institutionalise organisational creativity in turnaround situations. Although as yet formal programmes for training turnaround managers are practically non-existent, these strategies and decision heuristics could well be harnessed for training purposes or for advising turnaround managers.

Notes and References

1. For some recent work on management creativity, see Robert L. Kuhn (ed.), *Handbook for creative and innovative manager* (New York: McGraw–Hill, 1988); Pradip N. Khandwalla, *Fourth eye: Excellence through creativity*, 2nd edition (Allahabad: A.H. Wheeler, 1988, chapters 7, 8, and 9).
2. See The Editors of Fortune, *Working smarter* (New York: Viking, 1982).
3. See Anita van de Vliet, 'Where Lucas sees the light', *Management Today*, June 1986, pp. 38–45; Sir Godfrey Messervy, 'Lucas', pp. 195–202, in Rebecca Nelson and David Clutterback, *Turnaround: How twenty well-known companies came back from the brink* (London: W.H. Allen, 1988).

4. See V. Krishnamurthy, 'Management of organizational change: The BHEL experience', *Vikalpa*, Vol. 2, No. 2, 1977, pp. 113–19; Ravi Ramamurti, 'National Machinery Corporation of India', a disguised case on BHEL (Boston: Northeastern University, undated).

5. See Editors of Fortune, 1982, op. cit.

6. A number of studies have been cited in Chapter 2 under the heading *A Stock Taking* that indicate that turnarounds are usually accomplished by new managements.

7. See Donald B. Bibeault, *Corporate turnaround: How managers turn losers into winners* (New York: McGraw–Hill, 1982, p. 152).

8. See Donald B. Bibeault, 1982, ibid., p. 167.

9. See Dilip Thakore, 'How the world's largest public sector company has been turned around', *Business World*, 22 June–5 July 1987, pp. 34–47. See also K.K. Roy, 'Italy's non-oil public sector: Prodi(gious) turnaround', *Economic Times*, 19 June 1987, p. 5; Romano Prodi, 'Instituto per la Ricostruzione Industriale (IRI)', pp. 93–101, in Nelson and Clutterback, 1988, op. cit.

10. See O.P. Kharbanda and E.A. Stallworthy, *Company rescue: How to manage a business turnaround* (London: Heinemann, 1987, pp. 142–53), and G. Turner, 'Inside Europe's giant companies—Olivetti goes bear hunting', *Long Range Planning*, Vol. 19, 1986, pp. 13–20.

11. See V. Krishnamurthy, 'SAIL blazes a new trail', *The Economic Times*, 19 November 1987. See also Subrata Roy, 'Spotlight on SAIL', *Business World*, 1–14 March 1986, pp. 43–51; 'SAIL rolling plan for 1989–90', *The Economic Times*, 29 December 1989, p. 1; 'Steel price hike unlikely', *The Economic Times*', 1 March 1989, p. 1; T.N. Ninan, 'SAIL: Dramatic turnaround', *India Today*, 30 April 1986, pp. 106–7; 'SAIL to enter chemicals', *The Economic Times*, 2 April 1987, p. 1; Subrata Roy, 'SAIL: Will it succeed?' *Business India*, 10–23 August, 1987, pp. 42–52.

12. See Ian MacGregor, 'Recovery at British Steel', *Journal of General Management*, Vol. 7, No. 3, 1982, pp. 5–16. See also David Chambers 'Consumer orientation and the drive for quality', paper presented at the Roundtable on 'Public Enterprise Management: Strategies for Success', held at New Delhi, 6–11 March 1988, under the auspices of the Commonwealth Secretariat, London, and Indian Institute of Management, Ahmedabad.

13. See Pradip N. Khandwalla, *Excellent management in the public sector: Cases and models* (New Delhi: Vision, 1990, ch. B. 2).

14. See Pradip N. Khandwalla, 1990, ibid., ch. C. 2.

15. See Pradip N. Khandwalla, 'Strategy for turning around complex, sick organizations', *Vikalpa*, Vol. 6, 1981, pp. 143–66.

16. See Sushila Ravindranath, 'SPIC bounces back', *Business India*, 23 April–5 May 1985, pp. 110, 111, 113, 115, 117, 119 and 120.

17. See Marisa Bellisario, 'The turnaround at Italtel', *Long Range Planning*, Vol. 18, No. 1, 1985, pp. 21–24.

18. See Kharbanda and Stallworthy, 1987, op. cit., 115–27; B.O' Reilly, 'Is Perot good for General Motors?', *Fortune*, Vol. 110, No. 6, August 1984, pp. 84–85; G.G. Burck, 'Will success spoil General Motors?', *Fortune*, Vol. 108, August 1983, p. 94.

19. See David Chambers, 'Consumer orientation and the drive for quality', 1988, op. cit.

20. See Dharani Pani, 'Enfield: Revving up again', *Business India*, 5–18 December 1983, pp. 84, 85, 87, 89, 91, and 92, and Pradip N. Khandwalla, *Effective turnaround of sick enterprises (Indian experiences): Text and cases* (London: Commonwealth Secretariat, 1989, pp. 197–207).

21. See note 11 above.

22. See Anita van de Vliet, 'Why Rockware was recycled', *Management Today*, September 1985, pp. 62–69.

23. See note 4 above.

24. See note 12 above.

25. For some classics on organisational integration, see Chester Barnard, *Functions of the executive* (Cambridge, Mass.: Harvard University Press, 1938); Paul Lawrence and Jay Lorsch, *Organization and its environment* (Cambridge, Mass.: Harvard University Press, 1967).

26. See Barnard, 1938, op. cit.; H.A. Simon, 'On the concept of organizational goal', *Administrative Science Quarterly*, Vol. 9, No. 1, 1964, pp. 1–22; Warren Bennis and Burt Nanus, *Leaders: The strategies for taking charge* (New York: Harper and Row, 1985); C.C. Lundberg, 'Zero-in: A technique for developing better mission statement', *Business Horizons*, September 1984, pp. 30–33.

27. See D.C.L. Morwood, 'ICL: Crisis and swift recovery', *Long Range Planning*, Vol. 18, No. 2, 1985, pp. 10–21. See also Simon Caulkin, 'ICL's Lazarus act', *Management Today*, January 1987, pp. 56–63.

28. See Vasuki and S. Tripathi, 'Air-India: Out of the woods', *India Today*, 30 June 1989, pp. 114–16; S. Narayan, 'Air India takes wing', *Business World*, 21 June-4 July 1989, pp. 42–43.

29. See *Business Week*, 'Docutel: Born again and counting on new vigor in automatic tellers', 27 July 1981, pp. 48 and 50.

30. See note 18 above.

31. See note 10 above.

32. See Palakunnithu G. Mathai, 'Parry: Overhaul', *India Today*, 15 June 1987, pp. 116–17.

33. See note 3 above.

34. See U.K. Roy, 'Mining and Allied Machinery Corporation—India', paper presented at the Roundtable on 'Public Enterprise Management: Strategies for Success', held at New Delhi, 6–11 March 1988, under the auspices of the Commonwealth Secretariat, London, and Indian Institute of Management, Ahmedabad.

35. See K.G. Kumar, 'Apollo Tyres Ltd: No more skidding', *Business India*, 18–26 June 1988, pp. 61, 63, 67; Pradip N. Khandwalla, 1989, op. cit., pp. 231–44.

36. See Pradip N. Khandwalla, 1989, op. cit., pp. 183–96.

37. See note 4 above.

38. See note 17 above.

39. See note 19 above.

40. See note 9 above.

41. See note 35 above.

42. See Robert W. Sexty, 'Canadian Cellulose Company Ltd: A case study of government rescue and turnaround'. Toronto: Institute of Public Administration of Canada, 1982.

43. See Ravi Ramamurti, 'State Timber Corporation of Sri Lanka (A) and (B)'. Cases 0–382–018 and 0–382–019. Boston: President and Fellows of Harvard College, 1981.

44. See note 14 above.

45. See note 36 above.

46. See Kharbanda and Stallworthy, 1987, op. cit., pp. 214–29.

47. See note 4 above.

48. See note 12 above.

49. See Sreekand Khandekar, 'JMEL: Dramatic turnaround', *India Today*, 15 December 1985, pp. 103–4; Surya Mookherjee, 'Industrial sickness and revival', paper presented at National Seminar on Industrial Sickness in India at Gandhi Labour Institute, 3–4 June 1989, Ahmedabad, India.

50. See *Business Week*, 'Why Frank Borman finally has something to smile about?', 29 April 1985, pp. 52–53.

51. See Stuart Slatter, *Corporate recovery: Successful turnaround strategies and their implementation* (Harmondsworth, Middlesex: Penguin, 1984, pp. 296–301).

52. See note 35 above.

53. See Sushila Ravindranath, 'Standard Motors in high gear', *Business India*, 1–14 August 1983, pp. 64–65, 67, 69–71.

54. See note 49 above.

55. For a review of over 3,000 studies of leadership, see Ralph M. Stogdill, *Handbook of leadership* (New York: Free Press, 1974).

56. See note 14 above.

57. See Maynard M. Gordon, *The Iacocca management technique* (New York: Bantam, 1987).

58. See note 20 above.

59. See note 43 above.

60. See *Business Week*, 'The No. 1 Yankee trader gets its ship back on course', 25 March 1985, pp. 60–61.

61. See Stuart Slatter, 1984, op. cit., pp. 288–95.

62. See note 12 above.

63. See Rolf Lynton and Udai Pareek, *Training for development* (Homewood, Ill.: Richard D. Irwin, 1967), and Udai Pareek and T.V. Rao, *Designing and managing human resource systems* (New Delhi: Oxford and IBH, 1981).

64. See notes 11 and 12 above.

65. See note 36 above.

66. See Emanuel Hachipunka, 'Zambia Railways Limited', paper presented at the Roundtable on 'Public Enterprise Management: Strategies for Success', New Delhi, 6–11 March 1988, held under the auspices of the Commonwealth Secretariat, London, and Indian Institute of Management, Ahmedabad.

67. See notes 19 and 20 above.

68. See note 36 above.

69. See note 4 above.

70. See note 57 above.

71. See note 19 above.
72. See David Mansfield, 'How Ferranti fought back', *Management Today*, January 1980, pp. 66–70 and 128; Slatter, 1984, op. cit., pp. 354–56.
73. See note 11 above.
74. See note 42 above.
75. See note 43 above.
76. See note 4 above.
77. See note 12 above.
78. See Subrata Roy, 'Tinplate: The Tata stake', *Business India*, 11–24 April 1983, pp. 64–66 and 71.
79. See *Business Week*, 'Toyo Kogyo: A sure loser stages a turnaround', 25 January 1982, pp. 74–76.
80. See note 11 above.
81. See note 17 above.
82. See Nicholas Newman, 'Dawson's well-knit whoosh', *Management Today*, March 1981, pp. 74–82, 165, 168.
83. See note 49 above.
84. See note 9 above.
85. See note 3 above.
86. See note 11 above.
87. See Khandwalla, 1989, op. cit,. pp. 173–82.
88. See Khandwalla, 1990, op. cit., Part C.
89. See note 36 above.
90. See note 57 above.
91. See note 19 above.
92. See note 28 above.
93. See *Business Week*, 'Munsingwear: Stitching together a comeback', 28 May 1984, p. 60.
94. See *Business Week*, 'How Black & Decker got back in the black', July 1987, pp. 70–71.
95. See note 3 above.
96. See note 20 above.
97. See note 16 above.
98. See note 51 above.
99. See note 46 above.
100. See note 57 above.
101. See note 27 above.
102. See note 19 above.
103. See note 18 above.
104. See note 29 above.
105. See note 16 above.
106. See note 51 above.
107. See note 87 above.
108. See note 4 above.
109. See *Business Week*, 'Searle: Rallying a drug company with an injection of new vitality', 8 February 1982, pp. 50 and 52.
110. See note 19 above.

111. See Geoffrey Colwin, 'Freddie Silverman's secret success', *Fortune*, 14 July 1980, pp. 123–24.
112. See note 13 above.
113. See note 11 above.
114. See note 14 above.
115. See *Business Week*, 'Warnaco: Prospering by slimming and donning big name labels', 18 October 1982, p. 64.
116. See Fabrino Galimberti, 'Getting Fiat back on the road', *Long Range Planning*, Vol. 19, No. 1, 1986, pp. 25–30.
117. See note 32 above.
118. See note 34 above.
119. See note 13 above.
120. See *Business Week*, 'Sweda: Aggressive marketing produces a spirited turn-around', 31 March 1980, pp. 101–2.
121. See note 11 above.
122. See note 12 above.
123. See H. Igor Ansoff, *Strategic management* (London: Macmillan, 1979); William F. Glueck and Lawrence R. Jauch, *Business policy and strategic management*, 4th edition (New York: McGraw–Hill, 1984).
124. See Joseph L. Bower, *Managing the resource allocation process: A study of corporate planning and investment* (Homewood, Ill.: Irwin, 1970); Henry Mintzberg and James A. Waters, 'Of strategies, deliberate and emergent', *Strategic Management Journal*, Vol. 6, 1985, pp. 257–72.
125. See note 79 above.
126. See note 3 above.
127. See note 16 above.
128. See note 44 above.
129. See note 18 above.
130. See note 35 for Apollo Tyres; for Epe, see F.J. Aboderin, 'EPE Plywood situation', paper presented at Roundtable on 'Public Enterprise Management: Strategies for Success', at New Delhi, 6–11 March 1988, Commonwealth Secretariat, London, and Indian Institute of Management, Ahmedabad.
131. See Geoffrey Foster, 'The remaking of Metal Box', *Management Today*, January 1985, pp. 13–21.
132. See note 61 above.
133. See *Business Week*, 'Pullman's not a sleeper anymore', 22 July 1985, pp. 70–71.
134. See note 57 above.
135. See note 53 above.
136. See note 3 above.
137. See note 17 above.
138. See note 27 above.
139. See E. Paul Torrance, *The Torrance tests of creative thinking: Norms technical manual* (Lexington, Mass.: Personnel Press, 1974).
140. See Alex F. Osborn, *Applied imagination* (New York: Scribner's, 1953).
141. See Robert B. Duncan, 'The ambidextrous organization: Designing dual structures for innovation', in Ralph H. Kilmann, Louis R. Pondy, and Dennis P. Slevin (eds.), *The management of organization design*, Vol. 1 (New York: Elsevier North Holland, 1976).

142. See R.P. Crawford, *The techniques of creative thinking: How to use your ideas* (New York: Hawthorne, 1964); W.J.J. Gordon, *Synectics: The development of creative capacity* (New York: Harper, 1961); and Osborn, 1953, op. cit., chapters 21–24.
143. See B.L. Maheshwari, *Management by objectives: Concepts, methods, and experiences* (New Delhi: Tata McGraw–Hill, 1980); William F. Glueck and Lawrence R. Jauch, 1984, op. cit., chapters 3 and 4.
144. See D.A. Nadler, *Feedback and organization development* (Reading, Mass.: Addison-Wesley, 1977).
145. See Somnath Chattopadhyay and Udai Pareek (eds.), *Managing organizational change* (New Delhi: Oxford & IBH, 1982); N. Sanford, 'Whatever happened to action research?', *Journal of Social Issues*, Vol. 26, 1970, pp. 3–23.
146. See Nitish R. De, *Alternative designs of human organizations* (New Delhi: Sage, 1984); Robert Golembiewski, 'OD applications in non-affluent settings: Four perspectives on critical action research', pp. 282–318, in Pradip N. Khandwalla (ed.), *Social development: A new role for the organizational sciences* (New Delhi: Sage, 1988).
147. See American Society on Tool and Manufacturing Engineers Publications Committee, *Value engineering in manufacturing: A reference book on the theory, principles, application and administration of value engineering and analysis in industry* (Englewood Cliffs, N.J.: Prentice–Hall, 1967), and Robert H. Clawson, *Value engineering for management* (Princeton, N.J.: Auerback Publishers, 1970).
148. See Peter A. Pyhrr, *Zero-based budgeting: A practical management tool for evaluating expenses* (New York: Wiley, 1973).
149. See for a review, Teresa Amabile, *The social psychology of creativity* (New York: Springer–Verlag, 1983).
150. For a review of some approaches to social, collective creativity, see Khandwalla, 1988, op. cit., ch. 10; H.G. Barnett, *Innovation: The basis of cultural change* (New York: McGraw-Hill, 1953).
151. See Tom Burns and G.M. Stalker, *The management of innovation* (London: Tavistock, 1961); Gary Steiner (ed.), *The creative organization* (Chicago: University of Chicago Press, 1965); Kuhn, 1988, op. cit.; Khandwalla, 1988, op. cit., chapters 8 and 9.
152. See Ansoff, 1979, op. cit.; John Child, 'Organizational design and performance: Contingency theory and beyond', pp. 169–83, in Elmar H. Burack and Anant R. Negandhi (eds.), *Organization design* (Kent, Ohio: Comparative Administration Research Institute, Kent State University, 1977); Pradip N. Khandwalla, 'Some top management styles, their context and performance', *Organization and Administrative Science*, Vol. 7, 1976–77, pp. 21–51; Danny Miller and Peter H. Friesen, *Organizations: A quantum view* (Englewood Cliffs, N.J.: Prentice–Hall, 1984).
153. Pradip N. Khandwalla, 'Pioneering innovative management: An Indian excellence', *Organization Studies*, Vol. 6, No. 2, 1985, pp. 161–83.
154. See Pradip N. Khandwalla, 'Generators of pioneering—innovative management: Some Indian evidence', *Organization Studies*, Vol. 8, No. 1, 1987, pp. 39–59.
155. See M.J. Manimala, 'Managerial heuristics of pioneering–innovative (PI) entrepreneurs: An exploratory study', unpublished doctoral dissertation (Ahmedabad: Indian Institute of Management, 1988).

7. TURNAROUND DYNAMICS

Organisational dynamics are an exciting area of research, involving the study of how an organisation changes over a period of time, how events taking place in the organisation at different times are linked, and of the processes and phases by which it moves from one state of existence to another. Much of organisational research is cross-sectional or synchronic in character, while organisational dynamics require longitudinal or diachronic research. Organisational dynamics need to be studied to understand better the patterns of cause-effect or stimulus-response relationships in these organisations. Such better understanding would lead to more effective management decisions and interventions, and through better predictions, to more effective control of organisational behaviour. Organisational dynamics can help build useful organisational simulation models, and these in turn can help a decision-maker examine the consequences of alternative decisions by playing around with a computer.[1] This way the benefits of experimentation can be increased and its cost diminished.

If organisational dynamics have been relatively sparsely investigated, it is mainly because of the difficulty of tracking events over several years. Several attempts have, of course, been made to do so, though far more are needed. One approach has been to reconstruct organisational history by examining the past records of the organisation—minutes, correspondence, reports, annual reports, among others.[2] Another has been to analyse cases of decision-making in the organisations and try and sequence events.[3] A third approach has been to develop simulation models based on some field-work, and then try and trace through, on the computer, the consequences of changes in environmental or organisational parameters.[4] From these attempts have emerged some interesting models of how organisational structures change following changes in corporate strategy[5], how organisations negotiate transitions[6], how the organisational design and culture undergo a metamorphosis over its life cycle [7], how organisations grow over time[8], how they make strategic and other decisions,[9] how organisational innovations and changes are phased,[10] and so on.

Turnarounds offer a good opportunity to study organisational dynamics because most of the turnaround action is compressed in just a few years. Events flow thick and fast, and causal connections are easier to make. In this chapter several facets of organisational dynamics are examined. One facet examined is that of phasing in turnarounds: how different phases, especially the initial crisis management phase and the later growth, stabilisation, and institution-building phase, differ in terms of management actions and the elements that may be especially useful in each phase. Next, an attempt is made to examine the future consequences of turnaround actions, and the vast changes individual actions can trigger. Few turnarounds follow some pre-set textbookish sequence of actions. Most seem to be accomplished by experimenting and innovating, learning from the attempt, and trying again. In other words organisational learning is an important consequence of turnaround action. This learning results in skill acquisition which in turn powers the turnaround. Thus, the sorts of competence that arise from and contribute to turnaround are also explored.

An Illustrative Case

Ferranti's turnaround illustrates turnaround dynamics.[11] An old and family-controlled British producer of electronics and computers, by the mid-seventies Ferranti had become obsessed with technical leadership. Its management seemed to lack financial discipline and it could not convert inventions into marketable and profitable products. The management stuck to prestigious but non-profitable product-lines. It seemed to follow a policy of no growth. It was also excessively centralised. There were divisions but no divisional management. The company had taken on fixed-price contracts at a time of high inflation, and its transformer division was doing badly. The company was undercapitalised and had therefore become dependent on short-term debts. Industrial disputes and fires in factories also ravaged the company. As a consequence the company lost half-a-million pounds on sales of £86 million in 1975 and £4.1 million on sales of £108 million the next year. In November 1975

Mr Derek Alun–Jones of Burmah Oil was brought in as managing director after the government had stepped in to stave off collapse by injecting £15 million into the company.

Initial Actions

Alun–Jones introduced regular monthly meetings of the company's top managers. A task force was set up in the transformer division to come up with a diversification plan, and the management worked closely with government and labour to prevent plant shutdown. Alun–Jones instituted a weekly review of cash-flow and put a heavy emphasis on strict financial reporting by the units. He brought in centralised cash-control. At the same time profit responsibility was devolved upon the company's units. Target-setting and formalised planning and budgeting were emphasised. No large-scale lay-offs or major changes in top management were, however, made. There was some very modest retrenchment in the transformer plant. These actions during the first year centred around problem diagnosing and coordination at the top, enhanced management control, greater accountability, and roping in stakeholders like government and labour for the turnaround.

Middle Phase Actions

The diagnosis of what ailed the transformer division led to a physical reorganisation of the plant. There was also a major structural re-organisation. The company's business was organised into five operating groups—computer systems, instrumentation, electronic components, heavy engineering (transformers), and a regional group called the Scottish group. This represented a significant decentralisation. Consultative management was introduced into the troublesome transformer division (now called the heavy engineering group). For greater accountability the practice of biannual presentations by group managements to the board was introduced. One presentation was on the group's annual plan, the other on the updated five-year plan (this practice later lapsed). The company negotiated a £25 million loan from a consortium of banks to pay off heavy short-term borrowings and similar other liabilities. The company broke even in 1977 with a profit of £6 million on sales of £125 million.

Final Phase

The company began to diversify into other forms of mechanical engineering at its transformer division (later, however, the board decided to phase out the transformer business at a loss of £ 6 million). It acquired straddle carriers and an agricultural equipment company, while it sold off a Canadian subsidiary for £8 million and also a special components unit. The electronic components group sought to reform its business by going for niches in the micro-electronics market. The company set up Ferranti Measurements in partnership with Siemens. This phase was marked by divestiture, acquisitions, and other strategic moves like a joint venture and market refocussing. Ferranti's sales rose to £157 million in 1978 and further to £190 million in 1979, and profits rose to £9 million in 1978 and £10 million in 1979.

Notice the phasing in this turnaround: from an emphasis on fire fighting and diagnosing, top-level coordination, managerial accountability, control, and eliciting the help of stakeholders in the initial crisis management phase to a fairly massive structural reorganisation and plant reorganisation in the next phase to significant strategic action in the final phase. The actions were not random: they were linked to the causes of the company's sickness (such as excessive centralisation and a lack of financial discipline). The actions also had an organic linkage to one another—greater management control in the initial phase made possible a major reorganisation in the next; the support of stakeholders and the diagnosis by a task-force in the first phase made possible a major plant reorganisation in the next; business reorganisation in the middle phase facilitated major strategic moves in the final phase.

Notice also how the organisation changed: from one that was centralised, conservative, family controlled, obsessed with technological quality to a commercially oriented, professionally managed, decentralised organisation with a fairly clear strategic focus. The ability to compete (by identifying profitable niches), the ability to rope in stakeholders for the turnaround effort, the ability to operate efficiently by imposing strict financial discipline, the ability to decentralise without loss of accountability, and such other were the competencies the management picked up during the turnaround. These competencies helped the company transform itself.

Turnaround Phases

There has been some informed speculation (but little empirical work) on turnaround stages or phases.[12] Bibeault suggested five phases or stages of turnaround. These were: the management change phase of a new top management taking charge; the evaluation or diagnostic stage; the emergency stage of stopping bleeding, unloading losers and taking related measures; the stage of stabilising the retained and repositioned core business; and the return-to-normal-growth stage involving capital and organisational restructuring, assets redeployment, and overhaul of operations, strategies, and management systems. Of these five, the first three seem to represent crisis management, the last two, management stabilisation, growth, and institution building. Finkin postulated three turnaround phases: the start phase to breathe life into a dispirited organisation and re-impose management control; the awakening phase of focussing on the 20 per cent of the elements that contribute to 80 per cent of the costs and the making of bold, decisive, and significant improvements that get the staff excited; and the streamlining phase of forming a management team, upgrading staff with new skills, and linked actions. Khandwalla indicated that management change, establishing greater management control, quick pay-off actions and the like are early-phase phenomena in turnarounds while the building up of management systems and diversification are later-phase phenomena. The data from the turnaround cases examined in this volume provide, however, much more complex views of turnaround phasing.

An understanding of turnaround phasing was sought by categorising turnaround actions (as reported in the cases) in three phases: the early phase, lasting about a year from the time turnaround action was initiated (generally by a new top management); the middle phase, lasting generally from the end of the early phase to around the time the company broke even; and the final phase starting generally with the break-even and going on to the time the company resumed 'normal' profitability. Such an allocation of actions was possible only for the 42 complete turnarounds. Table 7.1 shows the usage frequencies (in percentages of the sample of 42 complete turnarounds) of the various turnaround elements for the three phases. As a point of clarification, a particular action could occur not just in one phase but in another one too, or indeed, in all three

Table 7.1

Use of Turnaround Elements in Three Turnaround Phases

Sample: *42 Complete Turnarounds*

	Early Phase	Middle Phase	Final Phase
A. Personnel Changes			
1. Changes in top management	88%	10%	8%
2. Fresh induction of managers, technical staff etc.	31%	7%	4%
Average	59%	8%	6%
B. Diagnosing and Troubleshooting			
3. Formal diagnostic activities	36%	5%	9%
4. Initiation of managerial meetings, problem-solving task-forces	22%	7%	1%
Average	29%	6%	5%
C. Stakeholder or People Management			
5. Credibility-building actions of management	17%	10%	4%
6. Garnering stakeholders' support	33%	17%	8%
7. Increased training of managers and staff	5%	17%	12%
8. Public articulation by management of mission, goals etc.	12%	7%	14%
9. Management communicating with staff, lower level managers etc.	31%	7%	5%
10. Incentives, motivation, grievance redressal	14%	31%	12%
11. Example-setting by top managers	14%	5%	5%
12. Disciplining	33%	19%	8%
13. Better organisational integration, participative management, emphasis on core values	19%	33%	10%
Average	20%	16%	9%
D. Operations Management			
14. Significant retrenchment	48%	31%	7%
15. Cost-reduction measures other than retrenchment	45%	29%	12%
16. Plant modernisation etc. for greater efficiency, quality, productivity	14%	41%	24%
17. Attempts to increase efficiency, quality, productivity other than through plant modernisation etc. and training	12%	24%	5%

Table 7.1 (contd.)

	Early Phase	Middle Phase	Final Phase
18. Marketing related changes	40%	62%	50%
Average	32%	37%	20%
E. Management Systems and Structure			
19. Management control-enhancing actions	43%	24%	10%
20. Professionalisation of manu-facturing management, personnel management, planning etc.	5%	19%	12%
21. Restructuring (decentralisation, fixing accountability, structural changes etc.)	29%	33%	12%
Average	26%	25%	11%
F. Financial Management			
22. Liquidation of current assets and liabilities	19%	10%	6%
23. Borrowings, raising equity finance etc.	16%	14%	12%
Average	17%	12%	9%
G. Strategic Management			
24. Diversification, product-line rationalisation, expansion etc.	36%	71%	74%
25. Divestiture and liquidation of fixed assets and long-term liabilities	17%	24%	12%
26. Innovation, new product development etc.	17%	33%	36%
Average	23%	43%	41%
H. Miscellaneous			
27. Miscellaneous actions	7%	7%	3%
Average for all 27 items	26%	22%	14%

phases. For example, price rise, a marketing action, may be resorted to in the early phase. The case may indicate, however, that it was resorted to in the middle phase, and also in the last phase. In that case, all three phases would be credited with marketing related actions. If, however, an action was initiated in one phase, such as the modernisation of a specific plant, but merely spilled over into a subsequent phase, the credit was given only to the earlier phase. On the other hand, if a different modernisation was taken up in another phase, the latter also got credit for modernisation. Seldom do cases provide specific dates on which actions are initiated, and so, the allocation of various initiatives to different phases was done on a best judgement basis. The judgement was formed by a careful reading of the text and after constructing a broad chronology of the actions of each case. Here too, two raters independently allocated actions to the three phases, and the degree of agreement was excellent (just about 90 per cent). In the few instances of disagreement due to ambiguity, the author used his judgement after close textual reading.

Table 7.1 discloses the expected and also the odd. Personnel changes, especially changes in top management, emerge unequivocally as an early phase phenomenon. In accordance with conventional wisdom, management attempts at increasing its control (item 19) also is largely an early phase phenomenon, as also retrenchment and cost-cutting (items 14 and 15). Formal diagnostic activity (item 3), where resorted to, is also an early phase turnaround tool, as also troubleshooting meetings and task-forces (item 4), garnering stakeholders' support (item 6), management communicating corporate problems and other relevant information to staff (item 9), and disciplining (item 12). These represent the core of the crisis management part of turnaround management.[13] Also, as per expectation, diversification (item 24), innovation (item 26), and plant modernisation (item 16) turn out to be middle and/or later phase initiatives, reflecting attempts at growth after successful crisis management. Marketing related actions (item 18) seem to peak in the middle phase, restructuring (item 21) seems to be invoked mostly in the early and middle phases, and motivating (item 10), participative management and such like (item 13) are largely middle phase phenomena (see Chart 7.1).

Chart 7.1

CRISIS VERSUS GROWTH, STABILISATION AND INSTITUTION-BUILDING PHASES OF TURNAROUND MANAGEMENT

Crisis Management	Management of Stabilisation, Growth, and Institution-Building
* Changes in top management and induction of senior level and technical personnel	* Modernisation of plant and facilities

Chart 7.1 (contd.)

Crisis Management	Management of Stabilisation, Growth, and Institution-Building
* Attempts at increasing management control over operations	* Technological innovation
* Retrenchment and other cost-cutting	* Diversification
* Aggressive marketing	* Marketing system related changes, basic changes in marketing strategy
* Formal diagnostic activities	* Restructuring for greater accountability (such as divisionalisation)
* Troubleshooting meetings of managers and use of task-forces	* Motivating the staff
* Garnering of external stakeholders' support	* Participative management and emphasis on core values
*Product-line rationalisation for greater profitability	
* Management communications about corporate problems to staff	
*Disciplining of staff	
* Some structural changes	

Phasing in Different Types of Turnarounds

In Chapters 3 and 4 two types of surgical turnarounds and two types of non-surgical turnarounds were identified. These differ substantially. Phase analysis of each could reveal the dynamics of how different sorts of turnaround evolve. Table 7.2 shows the usage frequencies of the Surgical Reconstructive and the Surgical Productivity/Innovation Oriented turnarounds; Table 7.3 shows these for the Non-surgical Innovation Oriented and the Non-surgical Transformational turnarounds.

There were some similarities and differences between the dynamics of the two types of surgical turnarounds. Personnel changes (items 1 and 2) were in the early phase in both cases, and retrenchment, other cost-reduction, and enhanced management control were middle-phase actions (see items 14, 15, and 19). However, restructuring (item 21) was very much a middle-phase action in the Surgical Reconstructive turnaround and more of an early-phase action in

Table 7.2

Use of Turnaround Elements in Three Phases in Two Types of Surgical Turnarounds

Samples: *14 Surgical Reconstructive Complete Turnarounds and 8 Surgical Productivity/Innovation Oriented Complete Turnarounds*

	Surgical Reconstructive Turnaround			Surgical Productivity/ Innovation Oriented Turnaround		
	Initial Phase	Middle Phase	Final Phase	Initial Phase	Middle Phase	Final Phase
A. Personnel Changes						
1. Changes in top management	86%	14%	0%	87%	0%	0%
2. Fresh induction of managers, technical staff etc.	35%	7%	0%	50%	0%	0%
Average	60%	10%	0%	68%	0%	0%
B. Diagnosing and Troubleshooting						
3. Formal diagnostic activities	21%	0%	0%	12%	0%	0%
4. Initiation of managerial meetings, problem-solving task-forces	0%	0%	0%	25%	0%	0%
Average	10%	0%	0%	18%	0%	0%
C. Stakeholder or People Management						
5. Credibility-building actions of management	7%	7%	0%	37%	12%	0%
6. Garnering stakeholders' support	14%	7%	0%	37%	12%	12%
7. Increased training of managers and staff	0%	0%	7%	25%	25%	12%
8. Public articulation by management of mission, goals etc.	7%	7%	7%	25%	12%	12%
9. Management communicating with staff, lower level managers etc.	14%	0%	7%	50%	0%	0%
10. Incentives, motivation, grievance redressal	0%	0%	0%	37%	50%	12%
11. Example-setting by top managers	14%	7%	0%	12%	0%	0%
12. Disciplining	14%	21%	0%	62%	25%	0%
13. Better organisational integration, participative management, emphasis on core values	0%	14%	0%	25%	12%	0%
Average	8%	7%	2%	34%	16%	5%
D. Operations Management						
14. Significant retrenchment	79%	50%	14%	100%	75%	12%
15. Cost-reduction measures other than retrenchment	43%	21%	0%	50%	50%	25%

Table 7.2 (contd.)

	Surgical Reconstructive Turnaround			Surgical Productivity/ Innovation Oriented Turnaround		
	Initial Phase	Middle Phase	Final Phase	Initial Phase	Middle Phase	Final Phase
16. Plant modernisation etc. for greater efficiency, quality, productivity	0%	7%	7%	12%	75%	50% -
17. Attempts to increase efficiency, quality, productivity other than through plant modernisation etc. and training	0%	0%	0%	25%	37%	12%
18. Marketing related actions	21%	36%	36%	37%	87%	50%
Average	29%	23%	11%	45%	65%	30%
E. Management Systems and Structure						
19. Management control-enhancing actions	50%	14%	14%	37%	37%	12%
20. Professionalisation of manufacturing management, personnel management, planning etc.	7%	14%	0%	0%	0%	27%
21. Restructuring (decentralisation, fixing accountability, structural changes etc.)	14%	50%	21%	25%	0%	0%
Average	24%	26%	12%	21%	12%	13%
F. Financial Management						
22. Liquidation of current assets and liabilities	7%	14%	0%	25%	12%	0%
23. Borrowings, raising equity finance etc.	14%	14%	0%	25%	25%	25%
Average	10%	14%	0%	25%	18%	12%
G. Strategic Management						
24. Diversification, product-line rationalisation, expansion etc.	57%	86%	71%	25%	75%	75%
25. Divestiture and liquidation of fixed assets and long-term liabilities	29%	36%	7%	12%	25%	12%
26. Innovation, new product development etc.	14%	28%	21%	12%	50%	62%
Average	33%	50%	33%	16%	50%	50%
H. Miscellaneous						
27. Miscellaneous actions	7%	7%	0%	12%	12%	0%

Table 7.3

Use of Turnaround Elements in Three Phases in Two Types of Non-surgical Turnarounds

Samples: *9 Non-surgical Innovation Oriented Complete Turnarounds and 11 Non-surgical Transformational Complete Turnarounds*

	Non-surgical Innovation Oriented Turnaround			Non-surgical Transformational Turnaround		
	Initial Phase	Middle Phase	Final Phase	Initial Phase	Middle Phase	Final Phase
A. Personnel Changes						
1. Changes in top management	78%	11%	0%	100%	9%	27%
2. Fresh induction of managers, technical staff etc.	22%	0%	11%	27%	18%	0%
Average	50%	5%	5%	63%	13%	13%
B. Diagnosing and Troubleshooting						
3. Formal diagnostic activities	22%	0%	0%	82%	18%	0%
4. Initiation of managerial meetings, problem-solving task-forces	33%	33%	11%	45%	27%	0%
Average	27%	16%	5%	63%	22%	0%
C. Stakeholder or People Management						
5. Credibility-building actions of management	0%	0%	0%	27%	18%	9%
6. Garnering stakeholders' support	22%	0%	0%	73%	45%	18%
7. Increased training of managers and staff	0%	11%	11%	0%	45%	18%
8. Public articulation by management of mission, goals etc.	11%	0%	11%	9%	18%	27%
9. Management communicating with staff, lower level managers etc.	22%	11%	0%	45%	18%	9%
10. Incentives, motivation, grievance redressal	0%	11%	11%	18%	73%	36%
11. Example-setting by top managers	0%	0%	11%	18%	9%	9%
12. Disciplining	11%	22%	0%	55%	27%	9%
13. Better organisational integration, participative management, emphasis on core values	22%	33%	11%	27%	73%	9%
Average	10%	10%	7%	36%	36%	16%
D. Operations Management						
14. Significant retrenchment	0%	0%	0%	0%	0%	0%
15. Cost-reduction measures other than retrenchment	33%	22%	22%	55%	27%	18%

Table 7.3 (contd.)

	Non-surgical Innovation Oriented Turnaround			Non-surgical Transformational Turnaround		
	Initial Phase	Middle Phase	Final Phase	Initial Phase	Middle Phase	Final Phase
16. Plant modernisation etc. for greater efficiency, quality, productivity	0%	45%	22%	36%	55%	36%
17. Attempts to increase efficiency, quality, productivity other than through plant modernisation etc. and training	11%	11%	11%	18%	55%	9%
18. Marketing related actions	45%	45%	78%	55%	100%	36%
Average	18%	25%	27%	33%	47%	20%
E. Management Systems and Structure						
19. Management control-enhancing actions	11%	0%	11%	64%	45%	0%
20. Professionalisation of manufacturing management, personnel management, planning etc.	0%	11%	11%	9%	45%	27%
21. Restructuring (decentralisation, fixing accountability, structural changes etc.)	33%	33%	11%	45%	55%	9%
Average	15%	15%	11%	39%	55%	12%
F. Financial Management						
22. Liquidation of current assets and liabilities	11%	11%	0%	36%	0%	0%
23. Borrowings, raising equity finance etc.	0%	11%	33%	9%	9%	18%
Average	5%	11%	16%	22%	4%	9%
G. Strategic Management						
24. Diversification, product-line rationalisation, expansion etc.	33%	56%	89%	27%	64%	64%
25. Divestiture and liquidation of fixed assets and long-term liabilities	0%	33%	22%	9%	9%	9%
26. Innovation, new product development etc.	33%	22%	45%	9%	36%	27%
Average	22%	37%	52%	15%	36%	33%
H. Miscellaneous						
27. Miscellaneous actions	0%	0%	0%	9%	9%	9%

the Surgical Reconstructive turnaround, it was very distinctly a middle and final-phase activity in the Surgical Productivity/Innovation Oriented turnaround. Also, marketing (item 18), plant modernisation (item 16), and innovation (item 26) were more decisively middle and final-phase actions in the Surgical Productivity/Innovation Oriented turnaround. While diversification and product-line realignment (item 24) was a measure taken in all three phases in the Surgical Reconstructive turnaround, it was very distinctly a middle and final-phase activity in the Surgical Productivity/Innovation Oriented turnaround. People-management was never important in the Surgical Reconstructive turnaround while several of its facets were important in the initial phase of the Surgical Productivity/ Innovation Oriented turnaround. In short, the Surgical Reconstructive turnaround tended to begin with personnel changes, cost-slashing, control-seeking, and realignment of the product portfolio, continued retrenching and diversifying in the middle phase, turned to restructuring too, in the middle phase, and ended the final phase with further diversification and product shuffling. People-management never assumed importance, nor diagnosing and troubleshooting, professionalising management systems, or financial management. In other words, there was reasonably effective crisis management in this type of turnaround but very little institution-building. The performance of this type of turnaround, it may be recalled from Chapter 4, was the worst of the four types. On the other hand, while the Surgical Productivity/Innovation Oriented turnaround too proceeded with personnel changes and cost slashing, there was also, in the early phase, a fair bit of people-management, especially in communication with staff and disciplining. While cost slashing continued into the middle phase, there was also, in this phase, a relatively frequent resort to motivating staff, plant modernisation, marketing, diversification, and innovation. In the final phase, too, marketing, plant modernisation, diversification, and innovation remained important. In this type of turnaround, crisis management seemed strong and institution-building stronger than in the Surgical Reconstructive turnaround.

Let us now look at the non-surgical turnarounds. Top management changes were an early-phase phenomenon in both types of non-surgical turnarounds. In both, diversification seemed to be mostly a middle and final-phase phenomenon, and plant modernisation a middle phase activity. The differences however, were striking.

Diagnosing and troubleshooting, especially formal diagnostic activity (item 3) was a pronounced initial-phase activity only in the Non-surgical Transformational turnaround, as also the garnering of stake-holders' support (item 6), disciplining (item 12), communicating with the staff (item 9), and enhanced management control (item 19). Thus, crisis management seemed far more vigorous and multi-fronted in the Non-surgical Transformational turnaround. Motivation (item 10), training (item 7), integration through partici-pative management (item 13), professionalisation of the manage-ment (item 20), and attempts to increase productivity (item 17) were distinctly used in the middle phase only by this type of turn-around. Also, while marketing initiatives (item 18) was a final-phase phenomenon in the Non-surgical Innovation Oriented turnaround, it was a middle-phase one in the Non-surgical Transformational turn-around. Institution-building was also much stronger in this type of turnaround than in that of the Non-surgical Innovation Oriented turnaround, and indeed, also more than the two surgical turnarounds. It may be recalled from Chapter 4 that the Non-surgical Transform-ational turnaround had the best performance of all four types.

Chart 7.2 shows the evolutionary profiles of the four types of turnarounds. For this purpose only turnaround items with usage frequencies of 50 per cent or more have been used.

Chart 7.2

EVOLUTIONARY PROFILES OF FOUR TYPES OF COMPLETE TURNAROUNDS

SURGICAL TURNAROUNDS		NON-SURGICAL TURNAROUNDS	
Reconstructive	Productivity/ Innovation Oriented	Innovation Oriented	Transformational
INITIAL PHASE			
1. Changes in top management	1. Changes in top management	1. Changes in top management	1. Changes in top management
2. Retrenchment	2. Retrenchment		2. Formal diagnostic activities
3. Diversification and product-line changes	3. Disciplining		3. Garnering stakeholders' support
4. Greater management control	4. Personnel changes		4. Greater management control
	5. Cost-cutting		5. Cost-cutting

Chart 7.2 (contd.)

SURGICAL TURNAROUNDS		NON-SURGICAL TURNAROUNDS	
Reconstructive	**Productivity/ Innovation Oriented**	**Innovation Oriented**	**Transformational**
	6. Communicating with staff		6. Disciplining
			7. Marketing changes

MIDDLE PHASE

1. Diversification and product-line changes	1. Marketing changes	1. Diversification and product-line changes	1. Marketing changes
2. Retrenchment	2. Retrenchment		2. Motivating the staff
3. Restructuring	3. Plant modernisation		3. Integration and participative management
	4. Diversification and product-line changes		4. Diversification and product-line changes
	5. Motivating the staff		5. Plant modernisation
	6. Cost-cutting		6. Productivity enhancement
	7. Innovation		7. Restructuring

FINAL PHASE

1. Diversification and product-line changes	1. Diversification and product-line changes	1. Diversification and product-line changes	1. Diversification and product-line changes
	2. Innovation	2. Marketing changes	
	3. Plant modernisation		
	4. Marketing changes		

Chart 7.2 reveals some interesting features of turnaround evolutions. The beginning and end points are common to all four: top management changes (beginning) and diversification and product-line changes (at the end). Secondly, seldom is the same turnaround element significantly deployed in more than one phase except in the case of the Surgical Productivity/Innovation Oriented turnaround. The only elements for which this happens are retrenchment

and diversification and product-line changes in the Surgical Reconstructive turnaround, diversification and product-line changes in the case of the Non-surgical Innovation Oriented turnaround, and marketing and diversification and product-line changes in the case of the Non-surgical Transformational turnaround. On the other hand, inter-phase recurrence of elements occurs for several elements in the Surgical Productivity/Innovation Oriented turnarounds: cost-cutting, retrenchment, diversification and product-line changes, marketing, plant modernisation, and innovation. Thirdly, there is considerable variation across the turnarounds *vis-à-vis* the number of elements that are salient in the three phases. In the Surgical Reconstructive turnaround four elements are salient in the first phase, three in the second and only one in the third; in the Surgical Productivity/Innovation Oriented turnaround the salient elements number six, seven, and four respectively. In the Non-surgical Innovation Oriented turnaround the salient elements number one, one and one, respectively, and in the Non-surgical Transformational turnaround these are seven, seven, and one, respectively. The tendency is for the number of salient elements to decline sharply from the first two phases to the last. In other words new turnaround initiatives begin to taper off sharply after break-even. Finally, though the beginning and end elements are similar, the evolutions of the four types of turnaround seem to be characterised by different mixes of elements. In particular, there is far greater reliance on people-management variables in the Surgical Productivity/Innovation Oriented and Non-surgical Transformational turnarounds than in the other two types, and in the former two turnarounds cost-slashing during the earlier part of the turnaround is softened by people-management actions.

Effective Turnaround Dynamics

An attempt was made to see if the use of turnaround elements in the three phases differed as between a group of companies experiencing rapid improvement in profitability and a group experiencing slow improvement in profitability. The rate of improvement in profitability was computed as described in Chapter 2 (basically, profitability one year after break-even minus worst loss situation, the difference divided by the period from the year of worst loss to the year after break-even). Those complete turnaround companies whose annual rate of change in profitability was *more* than 4 per cent on sales were categorised as part of the rapid improvement group while those complete turnaround companies whose rate was *below* 4 per cent were categorised as the slow improvement group. There were 18 in the rapid improvement group and 20 in the slow improvement group (there was insufficient information on two companies and two companies were not included because their score was 4 per cent). Table 7.4 presents a comparison of the two groups for the 27 turnaround elements in the initial, middle, and final phases.

In the initial phase, the group with a rapid improvement in profitability outscored the group that gained slowly in 20 of 27 elements, especially in formal diagnostic activities (67 per cent *versus* 10 per cent), garnering stakeholders' support (56 per cent *vs* 25 per cent), marketing related changes (61 per cent *vs* 15 per cent), and management control-enhancing actions (61 per cent *vs* 30 per cent). For these four elements the differences were statistically significant at the 95 per cent confidence level. Thus, effective crisis management by means of corporate diagnosis, an effort to win over stakeholders, aggressive marketing, and better control of operations in the early phase, are likely to accelerate the turnaround.

In the middle phase also, the group registering rapid improvement outscored the group showing slow improvement on 22 out of 27 turnaround elements. It outscored the slower group statistically significantly on incentives and motivation (50 per cent *vs* 10 per cent), integration through participative management and emphasis on core values (50 per cent *vs* 20 per cent), and miscellaneous ways of increasing productivity (44 per cent *vs* 10 per cent). Thus, emphasis on motivation, staff cohesion, and productivity—largely effective human resource management—in the middle phase may be especially useful in speeding a turnaround. In the final phase, aside from four ties, the group showing rapid improvement outscored the slower group on 15 elements. The lone statistically significant difference was *vis-à-vis* diversification and product-line changes, where the slow group outscored the rapid improvement group 90 per cent to 61 per cent. Thus, caution in diversification, even in the final phase of turnaround, seems called for.

Table 7.4

Turnaround Action in Three Phases in Fast versus Slow Improvement Samples

Samples: 18 fast increase in profitability (complete turnarounds) and 20 slow increase in profitability (complete turnarounds)

	Initial Phase			Middle Phase			Final Phase		
	Fast Turn-arounds	Slow Turn-arounds	Difference	Fast Turn-arounds	Slow Turn-arounds	Difference	Fast Turn-arounds	Slow Turn-arounds	Difference
A. Personnel Changes									
1. Changes in top management	94%	85%		6%	15%		17%	0%	0%
2. Fresh induction of managers, technical staff, etc.	33%	30%		17%	0%		0%	0%	
Average	63%	57%		11%	7%		8%	0%	
B. Diagnosing and Troubleshooting									
3. Formal diagnostic activities	67%	10%	Significant	11%	0%		0%	0%	
4. Initiation of managerial meetings, problem-solving task-forces	33%	15%		11%	5%		0%	0%	
Average	50%	22%		11%	2%		0%	0%	
C. Stakeholder or People Management									
5. Credibility-building actions of management	11%	25%		17%	5%		6%	0%	
6. Garnering stakeholders' support	56%	25%	Significant	28%	5%		6%	10%	
7. Increased training of managers and staff	6%	0%		28%	15%		11%	10%	
8. Public articulation by management of mission, goals, etc.	6%	20%		17%	0%		22%	10%	

Table 7.4 (contd.)

	Initial Phase			Middle Phase			Final Phase		
	Fast Turn-arounds	Slow Turn-arounds	Difference	Fast Turn-arounds	Slow Turn-arounds	Difference	Fast Turn-arounds	Slow Turn-arounds	Difference
9. Management communicating with staff, lower level managers, etc.	39%	25%		11%	5%		6%	5%	
10. Incentives, motivation, grievance redressal	28%	5%		50%	10%	Significant	17%	5%	
11. Example-setting by top managers	17%	10%		6%	5%		6%	5%	
12. Disciplining	39%	30%		17%	30%		6%	0%	
13. Better organisational integration, participative management, emphasis on core values	17%	20%		50%	20%	Significant	6%	10%	
Average	24%	18%		25%	11%		10%	6%	
D. Operations Management									
14. Significant retrenchment	39%	55%		17%	40%		6%	10%	
15. Cost-reduction measures other than retrenchment	50%	30%		17%	35%		6%	10%	
16. Plant modernisation etc. for greater efficiency, quality, productivity	22%	5%		39%	40%		28%	15%	
17. Attempts to increase efficiency, quality, productivity other than through plant modernisation etc. and training	22%	0%	Significant	44%	10%	Significant	11%	0%	
18. Marketing related actions	61%	15%		78%	50%		39%	50%	
Average	39%	21%		39%	35%		18%	17%	

Table 7.4 (contd.)

	Initial Phase			Middle Phase			Final Phase		
	Fast Turn-arounds	Slow Turn-arounds	Difference	Fast Turn-arounds	Slow Turn-arounds	Difference	Fast Turn-arounds	Slow Turn-arounds	Difference
E. Management Systems and Structure									
19. Management control-enhancing actions	61%	30%	Significant	33%	15%		6%	5%	
20. Professionalisation of manufacturing management, personnel management, planning, etc.	6%	5%		28%	10%		11%	5%	
21. Restructuring (decentralisation, fixing accountability, structural changes, etc.)	28%	35%		44%	30%		11%	10%	
Average	32%	23%		35%	22%		9%	7%	
F. Financial Management									
22. Liquidation of current assets and liabilities	33%	10%		6%	5%		0%	0%	
23. Borrowings, raising equity finance, etc.	22%	10%		17%	10%		17%	10%	
Average	27%	10%		11%	7%		8%	5%	
G. Strategic Management									
24. Diversification, product-line rationalisation, expansion, etc.	44%	30%		72%	65%		61%	90%	Significant
25. Divestiture and liquidation of fixed assets and long-term liabilities	17%	15%		11%	35%		6%	15%	

Table 7.4 (contd.)

	Initial Phase			Middle Phase			Final Phase		
	Fast Turn-arounds	Slow Turn-arounds	Difference	Fast Turn-arounds	Slow Turn-arounds	Difference	Fast Turn-arounds	Slow Turn-arounds	Difference
26. Innovation, new product development, etc.	11%	15%		44%	20%		33%	40%	
Average	24%	20%		42%	40%		33%	40%	
H. Miscellaneous									
27. Miscellaneous actions	11%	5%		11%	5%		6%	6%	

Note: Only difference significant at 95% confidence level have been highlighted.

The different types of turnaround described earlier may well be accelerated if they incorporate the seven initial and middle-phase turnaround accelerators discussed above. The fit is closest with the Non-surgical Transformational turnaround. All four initial-phase and all three middle-phase accelerator elements are salient in it in the appropriate phases (see Diagram 4.1). As was indicated in Chapter 4, this mode of turnaround had the best overall performance of the four. However, fairly radical changes in turnaround strategies may be needed in the other three types of turnaround. The four first phase accelerators of turnaround are wholly absent in the first phases of the Non-surgical Innovation Oriented and the Surgical Productivity/Innovation Oriented turnarounds and only one—management control—is present in the Surgical Reconstructive turnaround. The picture is broadly the same for the three middle phase turnaround accelerators—by and large these are, with the odd exception, absent from the middle phases of these three types of turnaround.

Futurity of Initial Actions

Turnarounds are likely to be shaped powerfully by the first actions of a new management. These give signals to the organisation of things to come and set in motion chain reactions of events. Some of the consequences of these first actions—their futurity—may be immediate, some somewhat delayed. Tracing these consequences could provide fresh insights into organisational dynamics.

In order to study the futurity of initial actions, the turnaround elements used in the initial crisis management phase (that is, the phase of about a year from the beginning of the attempt to turnaround) were correlated with elements within each of the three phases. The sample used was of the 42 complete turnarounds. Thus, for example, change in top management was correlated with the remaining 26 elements in the initial phase, all 27 elements in the middle phase, and all 27 elements in the final phase. Table 7.5 presents the data. Only substantial correlations—of 0.30 and above—are shown (a correlation of 0.30 would be statistically significant at the 95 per cent confidence level if the variables were normally distributed).

Table 7.5

Temporal Linkages of Initial Phase Turnaround Elements

Sample: 42 Complete Turnarounds			Correlation
1. Formal Diagnostic Activities			
Initial-phase correlates	:	Management communicating with staff, lower managers etc.	.36
	:	Garnering stakeholders' support	.32
	:	Significant retrenchment	−.31
Middle-phase correlates	:	Restructuring (decentralisation, fixing accountability, structural changes etc.)	.42
		Better organisational integration, participative management, emphasis on core values	.42
		Significant retrenchment	−.39
		Initiation of managerial meetings, problem-solving task-forces	.37
		Fresh induction of managers, technical staff etc.	.37
		Increased training of managers and staff	.34
		Garnering stakeholders' support	.33
		Formal diagnostic activities	.31
Final-phase correlates	:	Increased training of managers and staff	.35
		Changes in top management	.34
2. Garnering Stakeholders' Support			
Initial-phase correlates	:	Liquidation of current assets and liabilities	.43
		Initiation of managerial meetings, problem-solving task-forces	.37
		Formal diagnostic activities	.32
		Diversification, product-line rationalisation, expansion etc.	−.32
		Management control-enhancing actions	.30
Middle-phase correlates	:	Increased training of managers and staff	.37
		Attempts to increase efficiency, quality, productivity other than through plant modernisation etc. and training	.32
		Formal diagnostic activities	.31
		Professionalisation of manufacturing management, personnel management, planning etc.	.30
Final-phase correlates	:	Garnering stakeholders' support	.39
		Example-setting by top managers	.36
3. Credibility-building Actions of Management			
Initial-phase correlates	:	Public articulation by management of corporate mission, goals etc.	.45

Table 7.5 (continued)

		Sample: 42 Complete Turnarounds	Correlation
		Disciplining	.36
Middle-phase correlates	:	Initiation of managerial meetings, problem-solving task-forces	.39
		Management communicating with staff, lower managers etc.	.37
		Marketing related actions	.36
		Increased training of managers and staff	.31
Final-phase correlates	:	Garnering stakeholders' support	.63
		Liquidation of current assets and liabilities	.48
		Miscellaneous actions	.33
		Formal diagnostic activities	.32

4. Professionalisation of Manufacturing Management, Personnel Management, Planning etc.

Initial-phase correlates	:	Diversification, product-line rationalisation, expansion etc.	.30
Middle-phase correlates	:	Management control-enhancing actions	.40
		Innovation, new product development etc.	.32
		Changes in top management	.31
		Credibility-building actions of management	.31
		Liquidation of current assets and liabilities	.30
Final-phase correlates	:	Public articulation by management of corporate mission, goals etc.	.55
		Management communicating with staff, lower managers etc.	.47
		Management control-enhancing actions	.31
		Better organisational integration, participative management, emphasis on core values	.31

5. Initiation of Managerial Meetings, Problem-solving Task-forces

Initial-phase correlates	:	Plant modernisation etc. for greater efficiency, quality, productivity	.45
		Incentives, motivation, grievance redressal	.45
		Garnering stakeholders' support	.37
		Restructuring (decentralisation, fixing accountability, structural changes etc.)	.36
Middle-phase correlates	:	Better organisational integration, participative management, emphasis on core values	.61
		Increased training of managers and staff	.54
		Professionalisation of manufacturing management, personnel management, planning etc.	.34
		Public articulation by management of corporate mission, goals etc.	.30
Final-phase correlates	:	Incentives, motivation, grievance redressal	.36

Table 7.5 (contd.)

Sample: 42 Complete Turnarounds	Correlation

6. Plant Modernisation etc. for Greater Efficiency, Quality, Productivity

Initial-phase correlates	: Initiation of managerial meetings, problem-solving task-forces	.45
	Restructuring (decentralisation, fixing accountability, structural changes etc.)	.34
Middle-phase correlates	: Attempts to increase efficiency, quality, productivity other than through plant modernisation etc. and training	.41
	Increased training of managers and staff	.36
	Professionalisation of manufacturing management, personnel management, planning etc.	.32
	Incentives, motivation, grievance redressal	.31
Final-phase correlates	: Miscellaneous actions	.36
	Credibility-building actions of management	.33

7. Increased Training of Managers and Staff

Initial-phase correlates	: Miscellaneous actions	.37
	Management communicating with staff, lower managers etc.	.33
Middle-phase correlates	: Borrowings, raising equity finance etc.	.55
	Innovation, new product development etc.	.32
	Liquidation of current assets and liabilities	.30
Final-phase correlates	: Example-setting by top managers	.47
	Plant modernisation etc. for greater efficiency, quality, productivity	.40
	Better organisational integration, participative management, emphasis on core values	.31

8. Diversification, Product-line Rationalisation, Expansion etc.

Initial-phase correlates	: Garnering stakeholders' support	−.32
	Disciplining	−.32
	Incentives, motivation, grievance redressal	−.30
	Professionalisation of manufacturing management, personnel management, planning etc.	.30
Middle-phase correlates	: Credibility-building actions of management	.43
	Attempts to increase efficiency, quality, productivity other than through plant modernisation etc. and training	−.42

Table 7.5 (contd.)

Sample: 42 Complete Turnarounds			Correlation

		Plant modernisation etc. for greater efficiency, quality, productivity	−.32
		Borrowings, raising equity finance etc.	−.30
Final-phase correlates	:	Nil	

9. Attempts to Increase Efficiency, Quality, Productivity other than through Plant Modernisation etc. and Training

Initial-phase correlates	:	Incentives, motivation, grievance redressal	.48
		Fresh induction of managers, technical staff etc.	.43
Middle-phase correlates	:	Miscellaneous actions	.47
		Incentives, motivation, grievance redressal	.39
Final-phase correlates	:	Fresh induction of managers, technical staff etc.	.39
		Credibility-building actions of management	.38
		Plant modernisation etc. for greater efficiency, quality, productivity	.31

10. Management Communicating with Staff, Lower Managers etc.

Initial-phase correlates	:	Marketing related actions	.39
		Public articulation by management of corporate mission, goals etc.	.38
		Formal diagnostic activities	.36
		Increased training of managers and staff	.33
Middle-phase correlates	:	Garnering stakeholders' support	.39
		Increased training of managers and staff	.39
Final-phase correlates	:	Diversification, product-line rationalisation, expansion etc.	.42

11. Incentives, Motivation, Grievance Redressal

Inital-phase correlates	:	Attempts to increase efficiency, quality, productivity other than through plant modernisation etc. and training	.48
		Initiation of managerial meetings, problem-solving task-forces	.45
		Diversification, product-line rationalisation, expansion etc.	−.30
Middle-phase correlates	:	Increased training of managers and staff	.55
Final-phase correlates	:	Garnering stakeholders' support	.41
		Miscellaneous actions	.36
		Credibility-building actions of management	.33

Table 7.5 (contd.)

Sample: 42 Complete Turnarounds	Correlation

12. Example-setting by Top Managers

Initial-phase correlates	:	Management control-enhancing actions	.33
Middle-phase correlates	:	Increased training of managers and staff	.55
		Cost-reduction actions other than retrenchment	.49
		Professionalisation of manufacturing management, personnel management, planning etc.	.32
Final-phase correlates	:	Garnering stakeholders' support	.41
		Credibility-building actions of management	.33
		Innovation, new product development etc.	−.30

13. Disciplining

Initial-phase correlates.	:	Fresh induction of managers, technical staff etc.	.40
		Credibility-building actions of management	.36
		Diversification, product-line rationalisation, expansion etc.	.32
Middle-phase correlates	:	Diversification, product-line rationalisation, expansion etc.	−.33
		Disciplining	.30
Final-phase correlates	:	Professionalisation of manufacturing management, personnel management, planning etc.	.32
		Credibility-building actions of management	.31

14. Marketing Related Actions

Initial-phase correlates	:	Management communicating with staff, lower managers etc.	.39
Middle-phase correlates	:	Garnering stakeholders' support	.41
		Marketing related actions	.35
		Significant retrenchment	−.34
Final-phase correlates	:	Diversification, product-line rationalisation, expansion etc.	−.39
		Restructuring (decentralisation, fixing accountability, structural changes etc.)	−.31

15. Management Control-enhancing Actions

Initial-phase correlates	:	Example-setting by top managers	.33
		Liquidation of current assets and liabilities	.32
		Disciplining	.31
		Garnering stakeholders' support	.30

Table 7.5 (contd.)

		Sample: 42 Complete Turnarounds	Correlation
Middle-phase correlates	:	Nil	
Final-phase correlates	:	Marketing related actions	−.39

16. Restructuring (Decentralisation, Fixing Accountability, Structural Changes etc.)

Initial-phase correlates	:	Initiation of managerial meetings, problem-solving task-forces	.44
		Plant modernisation etc. for greater efficiency, quality, productivity	.34
Middle-phase correlates	:	Example-setting by top managers	.35
		Innovation, new product development etc.	−.33
Final-phase correlates	:	Innovation, new product development etc.	−.36

17. Fresh Induction of Managers, Technical Staff etc.

Initial-phase correlates	:	Disciplining	.40
Middle-phase correlates	:	Changes in top management	.48
		Significant retrenchment	.34
		Professionalisation of manufacturing management, personnel management, planning etc.	−.33
		Garnering stakeholders' support	−.30
Final-phase correlates	:	Nil	

18. Divestiture and Liquidation of Fixed Assets and Long-term Liabilities

Initial-phase correlates	:	Nil	
Middle-phase correlates	:	Disciplining	.43
		Significant retrenchment	.37
		Marketing related actions	−.33
		Liquidation of current assets and liabilities	.31
Final-phase correlates	:	Restructuring (decentralisation, fixing accountability, structural changes etc.)	.42

19. Liquidation of Current Assets and Liabilities

Initial-phase correlates	:	Garnering stakeholders' support	.43
		Management control-enhancing actions	.32
Middle-phase correlates	:	Disciplining	.38
		Attempts to increase efficiency, quality, productivity other than through plant modernisation etc. and training	.30
Final-phase correlates	:	Nil	

20. Significant Retrenchment

Initial-phase correlates	:	Formal diagnostic activities	−.31
Middle-phase correlates	:	Significant retrenchment	.49

Table 7.5 (contd.)

	Sample: 42 Complete Turnarounds	Correlation
	Better organisational integration, participative management, emphasis on core values	−.37
	Changes in top management	−.30
Final-phase correlates :	Nil	

21. Public Articulation by Management of Corporate Mission, Goals etc.

Initial-phase correlates :	Credibility-building actions of management	.45
	Management communicating with staff, lower managers etc.	.38
	Cost-reduction actions other than retrenchment	−.34
Middle-phase correlates :	Nil	
Final-phase correlates :	Garnering stakeholders' support	.48

22. Miscellaneous Actions

Initial-phase correlates :	Increased training of managers and staff	.37
Middle-phase correlates :	Borrowings, raising equity finance etc.	.68
	Formal diagnostic activities	.37
	Attempts to increase efficiency, quality, productivity other than through plant modernisation etc. and training	.30
Final-phase correlates :	Nil	

23. Cost-reduction Actions other than Retrenchment

Initial-phase correlates :	Public articulation by management of corporate mission, goals etc.	−.34
Middle-phase correlates :	Attempts to increase efficiency, quality, productivity other than through plant modernisation etc. and training	.39
	Fresh induction of managers, technical staff etc.	.31
Final-phase correlates :	Nil	

24. Changes in Top Management

Initial-phase correlates :	Nil	
Middle-phase correlates :	Nil	
Final-phase correlates :	Formal diagnostic activities	−.42
	Liquidation of current assets and liabilities	−.35

25. Borrowings, Raising Equity Finance etc.

Initial-phase correlates :	Nil	
Middle-phase correlates :	Innovation, new product development etc.	.36

Table 7.5 (contd.)

Sample: 42 Complete Turnarounds			Correlation
Final-phase correlates	:	Innovation , new product development etc.	.48
26. Better Organisational Integration, Participative Management, Emphasis on Core Values			
Initial-phase correlates	:	Nil	
Middle-phase correlates	:	Plant modernisation etc. for greater efficiency, quality, productivity	.46
		Incentives, motivation, grievance redressal	.33
Final-phase correlates	:	Nil	
27. Innovation, New Product Development etc.			
Initial-phase correlates	:	Attempts to increase efficiency, quality, productivity other than through plant modernisation etc. and training	.43
Middle-phase correlates	:	Nil	
Final-phase correlates	:	Fresh induction of managers, technical staff etc.	.39

Table 7.5 is revealing. First of all, the futurity of turnaround elements varies widely. Formal diagnostic activities (item 1) has 13 substantial correlates among the three phases, the garnering of stake-holders' support (item 2) 11, credibility-building actions of the management and professionalisation of management systems (items 3 and 4) 10 each, and initiation of meetings and task-forces (item 5) 9, *versus* less than 5 correlates for each of 9 variables (items 19-27), such as liquidation of current assets and liabilities, borrowings and raising of equity, significant retrenchment, articulation of mission and goals, and better organisational integration through core values and participative management.

Secondly, there is a distinct tendency for substantial correlates of initial-phase actions to peak in the middle phase. The average number of initial-phase action correlates with initial-phase actions was just about 2, of middle-phase action correlates with initial-phase actions was 2.7, and of final-phase action correlates with initial-phase actions was 1.5. Thus, futurity tends to rise for a while and then declines, instead of being maximum initially and then declining. There are, of course, many exceptions to this general trend. For instance, management communication with staff members (item 10) had 5 initial-phase correlates and only 2 middle-phase correlates, and professionalisation of management systems (item 4) had 4 final-phase correlates *versus* only one initial-phase correlate. In other words, turnaround elements differ quite a lot on how immediate *versus* how remote their futurity is.

Thirdly, initial-phase elements seem to have two kinds of futurity: unidirectional or asymmetric futurity (the element is correlated with another element in the subsequent phase but the other element as an initial phase element is not correlated with the former element in the subsequent phase) and reciprocal or symmetric futurity (A at time 1 → B at time 2 and B at time 1 → A at time 2, where the arrow signifies correlation). For instance initial-phase formal diagnostic activity was correlated with middle-phase garnering of stakeholders' support and initial-phase garnering stakeholders' support was correlated with middle-phase formal diagnostic activity (this is an example of reciprocal or symmetric futurity). On the other hand, initial-phase formal diagnostic activities was correlated with middle-phase increased training of managers and staff, but initial-phase increased training of managers and staff was not correlated with middle-phase formal diagnostic activities (example of unidirectional or asymmetric futurity). Reciprocal futurities may have a more constrictive influence on the evolution of turnarounds than those unidirectional. That is to say, turnarounds with many reciprocal futurities would tend to have recurring sets of salient elements in different phases while turnarounds with a preponderance of asymmetric futurities would tend to have differing sets of salient elements in different phases. The vast majority of relationships were, however, unidirectional, suggesting that in turnarounds there are seldom powerful feedback loops from consequences back to the originating actions. Turnarounds tend to become ever-widening networks of elements as actions trigger other, different actions, which in turn trigger still further actions. This may be the reason why, starting with a few decisive actions, many turnarounds quickly tend to resemble revolutions, bringing change to many facets of the functioning of the organisation.

An example of how turnaround actions can proliferate is provided by examining the correlates of a moderately linked element like disciplining (element 13 in Table 7.5). As its correlates suggest, management's action in disciplining staff is likely to be accompanied simultaneously or within a short time by the ingestion of fresh managerial blood into the organisation, some credibility-building action by management, and an attempt at reshuffling the product-line (usually this amounts to the dropping of unprofitable products and taking on profitable ones). Each of these actions in turn are likely to trigger other actions later. For example, credibility building (item 3) has four middle-phase correlates (meetings and task forces, communications, marketing initiatives, and increased training); product shuffling (item 8) also has four, including plant modernisation, raising capital, and attempts at increasing productivity; fresh managerial blood (item 17) also has four correlates including seeking the support of stakeholders, retrenchment, and professionalisation of management systems. These dozen or so consequences in turn could trigger other turnaround elements. Thus, a simple act of disciplining could well unleash a maelstrom of management actions in a year or two.

This has an important implication, namely that while it is possible for a single individual to initiate a turnaround, for the turnaround to pick up momentum a lot more people must get into the act. There is no way a single individual can take decisions and see to their implementation in areas ranging from the induction of new staff to modernisation, diversification, participative management and the lot, and that too, in a relatively short period. The sooner therefore, that the change-agent draws people into the turnaround sport, the faster the tunaround could become a multi-faced corporate revolution. Hence the great importance of collective diagnosing, meetings, task forces, communications, mission articulation, participative decision-making and other 'people management' actions. And this pays. Evidence presented in Chapter 2 indicates that the larger the number of activated turnaround elements, the faster the improvement in corporate performance.

Another implication is for the change agent. What should a chief executive wishing to turnaround a sick organisation do early on in the game to get a turnaround going at a fast clip? Actions that accelerate turnarounds *and* have high futurity should ideally be the priorities of the change agent. Two such actions are an effective diagnosis of what ails the organisation to identify the steps that must be immediately taken, and talking to stakeholders to get them involved in the turnaround. Both these are accelerators of turnaround (see previous section), and both also have high futurity (see Table 7.5). If these two jobs are done well, the direction of the turnaround effort would become clearer, there could be support to this direction from the stakeholders, and the turnaround get raring ahead.

Turnaround Learning

Turnarounds are times of hectic organisational learning,[14] of cycles of querying, contacting, experiencing, groping, testing, reflecting, conceptualising, choosing and implementing something new. Initially, this learning is confined mostly to a few at the top. Later, however, it must percolate to the many at lower levels. Indeed, it is when significant cognitive and behavioural changes have stabilised among many members at most levels. that the organisation can be said to have truly learned. Learning involves the acquisition of competencies. In the turnaround context, these competencies are picked up in the organisation's struggles with its manifold initiatives. Once internalised, these competencies transform the organisation and its performance.

Potts and Behr reviewed the transformations wrought at such previously ailing American corporations as General Electric, Martin Marietta. Gould. RCA, National Steel, AT and T, Coca Cola, Walt Disney, Borg-Warner and General Motors.[15] They found that underlying these transformations were such learnings as the ability to anticipate environmental changes and to react quickly to them, the ability to harness technology for generating new products and services and for lifting productivity, the ability to enter into beneficial alliances with other corporations, the ability to create a partnership between management and employees, the ability to create an entrepreneurial culture of calculated risk taking, the ability to throw up a visionary leadership, and the ability to be future oriented without losing contact with present realities. Their stories of corporate transformation suggested that these are the competencies vast corporations must acquire if these leviathans are to survive the sharks.

These stories of big US corporations tell a provocative but partial story of turnaround learning. A fuller picture could emerge by surmising learnings from a more global sample of turnarounds.

The major lessons from turnarounds that emerged from the 65 cases examined in this volume are briefly described below:

Learning to be a Sober Entrepreneur

Conservatism as well as reckless growth (especially *via* acquisitions) are significant causes of corporate sickness.[16] Learning to blend caution with enterprise, although apparently a contradiction in terms, is an important turnaround lesson. The crux of the learning is calculated risk taking: acquiring the competence to thrust into underexploited products, technologies, and markets but with solid preparation and orchestration of effort. General Motors offers a good example of this sort of competence acquisition.[17] GM wished to develop a highly computerised car of the future, an expensive and risky proposition because of the huge development costs and uncertain markets. So GM entered into partnerships with Suzuki and Fanuc for access to sophisticated robotics and other car manufacture technologies; it acquired a company specialising in artificial intelligence; a consulting organisation; a data processing company; and an electronics company to get hold of all the esoteric technologies it needed to make headway. Effective intra-preneuring and internal corporate venturing to generate a stream of tested potential future "stars" may also be essential for acquiring the competence of sober entrepreneurship.[18] In essence the organisation learns to take big risks that it can whittle down to manageable levels of risk by solid preparation.

Learning to Compete

Many large, monopolistic corporations go to pot when competition catches up with them. This is especially true of public enterprises, and also of private enterprises in oligopolistic industries or protected markets. Learning how to compete is an important competence for such organisations. Here again, frantic cost cutting or niche hunting or an acquisition spree is not the heart of learning how to compete. What is critical is for the organisation as a whole to become intensely aware of the marketplace, the needs of customers, the strategies of competitors, and the realistic strategic options available to the company. Lucas provides a good example of how this can be done.[19] Lucas asked each of its business units to compare itself with its best international competitor, and to develop competitive action plans to catch up with the competitor. Toyo Kogyo learned to compete with its national and international competitors through a variety of other means: research to replace an uneconomical car engine; partnership with Ford to market each other's products in their respective strongholds; the development of speciality cars for specific niches, such as cars specially designed for the handicapped and for female drivers; assault on the internal Japanese market with better customer service and a stronger sales force.[20] An important part of learning to compete is to learn to market service packages rather than just products. ICL created business centres to serve different sectors with total service, a move from marketing computer mainframes to marketing hard and soft ware integrated systems tailor-made to the needs of each business sector.[21]

Learning to Collaborate

In highly competitive societies competition comes more naturally to corporate managers than collaboration with other organisations. Also, opportunities for collaboration tend to be shunned because of the stigma attached to collusion. But in a globalised economy, the costs of innovation, the scale of production, and the costs of entry into markets are so high that the skill of entering into productive technological and marketing joint ventures becomes important for survival and growth. This is especially so when the corporation is sick and starved of resources. A number of turn-around cases illustrated the corporation learning to collaborate with others through joint ventures. Italtel entered into a number of technical know-how agreements with foreign companies, and coordinated its R and D effort with leading European producers of digital switching equipment.[22] ICL sought collaboration with Fujitsu of Japan, MITEL of Canada, and others, and started collaborative research with academic institutions, and other commercial organisations among others.[23] IRI entered into partnerships with foreign companies to develop new products.[24] Olivetti linked up with such "high tech" organisations as AT & T, Toshiba, and Xerox.[25] Essential are the skills of identifying distant "high tech" growth opportunities, suitable technological partners, and of building on each other's strengths and compensating for each other's weaknesses rather than letting these weaknesses wreck the venture.

Learning to be Efficient

Inefficiency, and the high costs that go with it, is an important cause of sickness in competitive situations. While many companies confuse efficiency with indiscriminate cost slashing, what is important is to institutionalise tools of efficiency and bring into the organisation a culture of efficiency. Sylvania and Laxman offers a good example of this.[26] In the initial phase of its turnaround, the company imposed greater control over purchases, inventory, cash collections, sales office expenses, and inter-departmental transfer of goods. The budgetary control system that had fallen into disuse was revived and made more sophisticated. Monthly preparation of comprehensive performance reports was instituted. Emphasis was put on planning cash-flow and operations, and a finance director was appointed. Apollo Tyres provides another example of learning to institutionalise efficiency.[27] It offered monetary incentives pegged to capacity utilisation and bonus linked to productivity. It imposed control over raw material consumption and other variable costs to increase efficient use of resources. Quality control was beefed up to reduce rejects. Productivity norms were strictly enforced. Overtime was abolished.

Learning to Practice a Mix of Management Styles

Past success with a specific style tends to freeze it into management. But both internal and external circumstances change, and what may have worked once may do so no longer. This rigidity has been identified as a cause of corporate sickness.[28] Since turnarounds are characterised by multiple phases, each requiring a different style of handling, learning to practise several styles in different phases or different situations becomes critical. For instance, a highly result oriented, organic style may be needed in the initial crisis management phase of the turnaround. This may occasionally also need to be supplemented by a capacity to seize control and impose discipline on a recalcitrant staff through an authoritarian mode; or, alternatively, a charismatic mode involving the evocation of a great mission, a vision of excellence and so forth, that peps up demoralised employees. During the next phase a participatory style may be needed to encourage decision-making, reach lower levels, reconcile differences, coordinate operations and breed similar attitudes. During the final phase a blend of management professionalism and entrepreneurship may be required with emphasis on management systems and bold, long-term growth and diversification strategies. Thus, the management needs to be able to practise, as dictated by circumstances, any one or a combination of the organic, authoritarian, charismatic, participatory, entrepreneurial, or professional modes of management.[29] SAIL provides a good example of this ability to practise different styles in different phases of the turnaround.[30] The new chief executive began by practising "management by moving around"; he also sought to mobilise the rank-and-file by focussing on priorities for action and SAIL's mission in the Indian economy. Next he installed a structure of participative decision-making in the organisation. In the final phase he institutionalised a good deal of management professionalism, in the areas of human resource development, project management, perspective planning, responsible decentralisation, marketing, and so on. An important skill is to practise synergistic blends of styles, as for example to blend the organic with the entrepreneurial, the professional with the participative.[31] Another skill is to manage the transition to a different management mode without creating a loss of credibility or too much dissonance.[32] It is useful to prepare the staff for the coming change in style with cues and explanations.

Learning to Mobilise the Stakeholders for Turnaround

Sick organisations are often beset by cynicism, demoralisation, conflicts, self-centred behaviour, 'finding' scapegoats, and similar attitudes. Few like to be part of a sinking ship or to take responsibility for a failing organisation. There is also the spectre of being cast on the street. In this murky situation the turnaround change agent has to flash a beacon, show the way, empower people, and get them excited about the possibility of a collective rescue. He/she has to provide transformational leadership.[33] This is an important skill to learn because as we noted in Chapters 4 and 6, it may vastly reduce the costs of turnaround and speed the turnaround appreciably.

To be able to mobilise a disgruntled and apathetic crowd the change agent must have credibility. He/she must do something heroic or off beat, such as bring in own cash in a sinking ship

(Evans at Macmillan increased his stake in the company,[34] as did Fiat's owning family,[35] and De Benedetti brought in his own $17 m. in an effort to turn around Olivetti)[36]; or break a strike (as at Richardson and Cruddas)[37]; or get the owners to agree to a hefty pay hike (Prodi did this at IRI)[38]. Credibility building may not be as fortuitous as it may sound. Hundreds of things are wrong in a sick organisation and dozens of these may be remediable fairly quickly with a determined and intelligent effort. It is for the turn-around change agent to pick the most fertile turf, make a success of it, and get himself or herself some publicity for it.

Another skill needed for mobilising an apathetic staff is personal contact, management by moving around, and interaction in small groups to "hear" what people have to say. This works for a variety of reasons. First, it is cathartic. Secondly, it is informative to both parties—the top boss gets some photos of reality he/she would otherwise never get to see. People lower down get a feel for what the boss is really like and the perspectives he/she may be carrying. Thirdly, a lot of good ideas get generated. This sort of interaction was attempted at SAIL with spectacular success,[39] as also at Rockware.[40]

A third skill needed for mobilising the staff is the articulation of something that is meaningful, something that grabs people. This may be a mission, a vision of excellence, an issue, a commitment. At BHEL national priorities and what BHEL could do to contribute to them were emphasised.[41]. ICL made a world-wide communication of its determination to succeed.[42] At RFD the importance of the life saving equipment produced by the company was dramatised.[43] Jaguar publicised internally its uphill struggle to remain afloat.[44] Olivetti emphasised its mission of making itself the global leader in automated office equipment of the future.[45]

A fourth mobilisation related skill is communication to the staff of goals, priorities, mission, vision, issues, operating problems, progress etc. etc. It is important that the communication is in a language the intended audience can understand. At Travancore Cochin Chemicals communications to workers were made in their mother tongue rather than in the official language of the company.[46] The message must reach everyone. At SAIL the company's priorities for action were mailed to each one of its quarter million employees.[47] Communication must be continuous. At IRI the management went out of its way to have a continuous dialogue with unions about the company's reorganisation, the industrial policies of the sector holding companies, and the retrenchment packet.[48]

A fifth skill for mobilising people involves engaging them in collective diagnosis and troubleshooting. SAIL set up briefing groups in each plant and organised shift meetings to brainstorm on how to improve the functioning of the plant.[49] At Travancore Cochin Chemicals suggestions were sought from lower level managers.[50] Lucas set up a large number of interdisciplinary task forces to redesign its plants.[51]

Credibility building, wide interaction and networking, articulation of the significant and the meaningful, communication of organization related information, and collective diagnosis and troubleshooting make sense not just for mobilising managers and other staff; these make sense also for mobilising other stakeholders for turnaround, such as bankers, suppliers, customers, unions, the press, and the government. Italtel, Chrysler,[52] British Steel,[53] and several other turned around enterprises used these mechanisms to advantage in mobilising one or more of their stakeholders. Without the support of major stakeholders perhaps none of these could have turned around, or turned around as effectively as it did.

Learning to Institutionalise a Culture of Innovative Professionalism

Turnarounds may not last unless a culture of innovative professionalism gets institutionalised in the organization. Forceful chief executives and forceful top management actions may push the organisation to break-even or even beyond. But power and charisma create dependency on the Great Person. Unless the rank-and-file learns to lead, the system will tend to collapse once the Great Person is not on the scene. At Richardson and Cruddas for example, Sharangpani was able to get the company to break-even within a year and a half of his joining as chief executive. But once he left the company again lost ground.[54] The same thing happened at a company called Bharat Pumps and Compressors.[55] K.L. Puri galvanised the company to improve its performance from net operating earnings of 3% on sales to 13% of sales. But after he left there was once again a collapse. Chrysler kept lurching between profits and losses in the seventies and early eighties until Iacocca came along and changed the work culture of Chrysler.[56]

The culture needed for turnaround is one of innovationism *and* professionalism. Innovationism implies experimentation, bold new initiatives, creative responses to problem situations, a higher order of flexibility, opportunism, etc. Professionalism means a high order of competence, a systematic analysis of problems and opportunities, reliance on trained and qualified staff, use of tested and effective tools of management, and the institutionalisation of sound management systems. Innovationism and professionalism are uneasy bed fellows, but given high levels of environmental and internal turbulence and complexity, they must learn to live together synergistically.[57] In the turnaround situation, especially the post-breakeven situation, a fusion of innovationism and professionalism makes good sense. Like a fusion reaction, it would continue to power the organization even when the Great Person has gone.

How is the culture of innovative professionalism to be instituted? The turnaround cases provide several clues. First of all, example setting by the top management is a good way to introduce a new culture. At several organizations the chief executive initially showed the way to effective operations. At Docutel the president engaged in personal selling,[58] and Iacocca went on television hawking Chrysler cars.[59] De Benedetti at Olivetti started holding his management meetings at 6 a.m.[60] At Travancore Cochin Chemicals the chief executive made a fetish of keeping promises.[61]

Motivating appropriate staff behaviour is another mechanism for instituting the right culture. At Bharat Heavy Plate and Vessels a monthly esteem prize scheme was instituted to reward the workers with the best productivity records.[62] At Volkswagen the management involved workers in the planning and designing of a fully automated assembly line.[63] At State Timber Corporation the chief executive made it a practice to pick up promising persons at lumber sites for managerial jobs at the head office.[64] A number of companies linked bonus, incentives, etc. to productivity, capacity utilization, quality, profitability and so forth.

Training is yet another tool for consolidating the right culture. At Zambia Railways a 5-year training programme was instituted.[65] At Lucas, training in systems engineering was given to members of task forces with the mission of redesigning factories.[66] SAIL instituted a programme for training tens of thousands of workers and managers a year.[67] Travancore Cochin Chemicals started capsule training programmes for managers in managerial and organizational effectiveness.[68] BHEL began various skill development programmes.[69] Non-formal training is another device for bringing in the right culture. Job rotation can be useful here. BHEL rotated some 300 executives between divisions just in one year.[70] General Motors temporarily transferred 7000 workers to a dynamic, innovative subsidiary so that they could pick up its culture.[71]

Suggestion schemes and quality circles can strengthen the culture of innovative professionalism. Jaguar introduced quality circles on the shop floor and strengthened its suggestion scheme—it received 8000 suggestions in just one year.[72] Induction of creative people, and placing them in strategic posts, can help institutionalise a culture of innovation, as at NBC Radio.[73]

The institution of good management systems strengthens a culture of professionalism. At SPIC, a management services group was set up to help top management monitor performance and formulate and implement plans.[74] SAIL revamped its performance appraisal, human resource development, and project management systems.[75] BHPV computerised production planning and scheduling and brought in budgetary control over the larger orders it was executing.[76] Travancore Cochin Chemicals introduced career and succession planning for managers.[77] Searle beefed up project management.[78] Fiat went for the Just in Time system.[79] Redman Heenan buttressed its product and market development functions.[80] ICL improved its business forecasting.[81]

Finally, culture change can be facilitated by using some of the tools of organization development (OD).[82] Particularly useful are tools like survey feedback and sensitivity training.[83] Survey feedback involves taking stock of the organization's work culture through structured instruments and providing of feedback of the results to the staff. Usually, several dimensions of the organization's culture are assessed, such as the organizational climate, cooperation and conflict, work values, job satisfaction and dissatisfaction, superior-subordinate relationship, leadership style, etc. At the time of feedback an attempt is made to brainstorm on how emerging areas of concern can be tackled and the work culture improved. Sensitivity training is an unstructured, agenda-less, prolonged group meeting in which people are encouraged to give and receive feedback, experiment with frankness, and learn to be interpersonally competent. It is a powerful tool for unfreezing a group and make it see the reality of seething human feelings, motives, and values beneath the tidy veneer of formal work relationships. It is also a powerful tool for redesigning superior-subordinate and peer relationships so that they become more open and dynamic, and thereby facilitate more mature professional relationships at work. Some of the other techniques that can help a culture of innovative professionalism take root, such as brain-storming, action research, SWOT, zero-based budgeting, and value engineering have already been briefly reviewed in Chapter 6.

Learning to Look within for El Dorado

Strategic gaming has become glamorous in recent decades. How to pick up and drop businesses for greater glory and lucre has become the favourite pastime of corporate statesmen and academic entre-preneurs.[84] Turnarounds indicate the limitations of this obsession. Indeed, as was noted in Chapter 2, the element diversification, product line rationalisation, expansion, etc. was *negatively* cor-related with the rate of gain of profitability for the sample of 42 complete turnarounds (the correlation was -.33). At least during turnarounds strategic gaming generally does not work well. Instead, what yields dividends seem to be internal scanning for opportunities for motivating people, cutting costs, increasing productivity, simplifying structure, improving management systems, improving the process and quality of decision-making, etc.—what some economists have called X-efficiency.[85] It is worth recalling from Chapter 2 (see Table 3 in that chapter) that the sizeable positive correlates of the rate of gain in profitability included such items as attempts to increase productivity (correlation of .49), formal diagnostic activities (.42), incentives (.39), participative management (.38), managerial meetings (.32), and management control related actions (.30). The reason is obvious. If top manage-ment gets conditioned to looking mostly outward for profitable opportunities it may fail to notice large internal opportunities for improving corporate performance. Besides, the internal systems and culture in large organizations may so degenerate in the absence of top management attention that even the external opportunities seized by management will be hamstrung by poor execution. Very many turnaround examples are available of spectacular pickings from an internal focus. British Steel could raise its productivity by 15% a year[86] and Lucas,[87] SAIL,[88] Toyo Kogyo[89] and Chrysler[90] also posted comparable gains. An especially fertile area—because it tends to be neglected—is the production area. Relatively insulated both from the turbulence of the external environment and the gaze of top management, this heartland of the organization may accumulate an enormous potential for greater X-efficiency. A top management incursion in this area of operations, backed with consultants and fresh blood may yield exceptional results in many turnaround situations.[91] The critical management competencies required are diagnostic skills, people mobilisation skills, change agentry and management system building and culture building skills.

Concluding Comments

In this chapter we have examined organisational dynamics during turnaround, that is, how actions are linked together, the different phases of turnaround, and the dynamics of effective *versus* less effective ways of changing a sick organisation. We have also taken a look at organisational learning, which is both an outcome of organisational dynamics as well as its fuel. It is very likely that organisational learning, like creativity or transformational leadership, is an important key to effective turnaround management. Organisational learning is not only important; in the context of turnaround management it is also intriguing. This is because most successful turnarounds are engineered by newcomer chief executives. For newcomers to learn enough about a sick organisation in a short time and to learn the sorts of lessons that power spectacular turnarounds, is a tribute to human resourcefulness and learning ability. How such prodigious learning, comparable to the rate at which infants learn, take place, how it is transformed into collective learning, are mysteries worth probing for benefit not only to management but also to anthropology and psychology. Buried in its mysteries may be gems of insight for human transformation and retrieval from the staggering wilderness in which the human species finds itself five thousand years after it began its exodus from a different kind of wilderness.

Notes and References

1. See Kalman J. Cohen and Richard M. Cyert, 'Simulation of organizational behaviour', pp. 305–34, in James G. March (ed.), *Handbook of organizations* (Chicago: Rand McNally, 1965).

2. See Alfred D. Chandler, *Strategy and structure* (Cambridge, Mass.: MIT Press, 1962), D. Channon, *Strategy and structure in British enterprise* (Boston: Harvard University Press, 1973).

3. See Henry Mintzberg, Duru Raisinghani, and Andre Theoret, 'The structure of "unstructured" decision processes', *Administrative Science Quarterly*, Vol. 21, 1976, pp. 246–75.

4. See Richard M. Cyert and James G. March, *A behavioral theory of the firm* (Englewood Cliffs, N.J.: Prentice–Hall, 1963). See also C.F. Smart, W.A. Thompson, and I. Vertinsky, 'Diagnosing corporate effectiveness and susceptibility to crises', pp. 53–92, in C.F. Smart and W.T. Stanbury (eds.), *Studies on crisis management* (Toronto: Inst. for Research on Public Policy, 1978).

5. See Chandler, 1962, op. cit., Channon, 1973, op. cit.; Lawrence W. Foster, 'From Darwin to now: The evolution of organizational strategies', *Journal of Business Strategy*, Vol. 5, No. 4, 1985, pp. 94–98.

6. See Danny Miller and Peter H. Friesen, *Organizations: A quantum view* (Englewood Cliffs, N.J.: Prentice–Hall, 1984).

7. See Malcolm Salter, 'Stages of corporate development', *Journal of Business Policy*, Vol. 1, No.1, 1970, pp. 23–37; J. Kimberly and R.H. Miles (eds.), *The organizational life cycle* (San Francisco: Jossey–Bass, 1980).

8. See Willam H. Starbuck, 'Organizational growth and development', pp. 451–533, in James G. March (ed.), *Handbook of organizations* (Chicago: Rand McNally, 1965), and L.E. Greiner, 'Evolution and revolution as organizations grow', *Harvard Business Review*, July-August 1972, pp. 55–64.

9. See D.J. Hickson, R.J. Butler, D. Cray, G.R. Mallory, and D.C. Wilson, *Top decisions: Strategic decision making in organizations* (Oxford: Blackwell, 1986).

10. See Donald C. Pelz, 'Quantitative case histories: Are there innovating stages?' *IEEE Transactions on Engineering Management*, EM–30, Vol. 2, 1983, pp. 60–67; see Patrick E. Connor and Linda K. Lake, *Managing organizational change* (New York: Praeger, 1988).

11. See David Mansfield, 'How Ferranti fought back', *Management Today*, January 1980, pp. 66–70 and p. 128. Also see Stuart Slatter, *Corporate recovery: Successful turnaround strategies and their implementation* (Harmondsworth. Middlesex: Penguin, 1984, pp. 354–66).

12. See Donald B. Bibeault, *Corporate turnaround* (New York: McGraw-Hill, 1982, chapter 10); Eugene Finkin, 'Company turnaround', *Journal of Business Strategy*, Vol. 5, No. 4, 1985, pp. 14–24; Pradip N. Khandwalla, 'Strategy for turning around complex sick organizations', *Vikalpa*, Vol. 6, 1981, pp. 143–66.

13. See Smart and Stambury, 1978, op. cit., for perspective on crisis management.

14. See C. Argyris and D.A. Schon, *Organizational learning: A theory of action perspective* (Reading. Mass.: Addison–Wesley. 1978), and Frank Friedlander,

'Organizations and individuals as learning systems' in Suresh Srivastava (ed.), *The executive mind* (New York: Jossey–Bass, 1983).

15. See Mark Potts and Peter Behr, *The leading edge* (New Delhi: Tata McGraw–Hill, 1987).

16. See Manjunath C. Hegde, 'Western and Indian models of turnaround management', *Vikalpa*, Vol. 7, No. 4, 1982, pp. 289–304.

17. See O.P. Kharbanda and E.A. Stallworthy, *Company rescue: How to manage a company turnaround* (London: Heinemann, 1987, pp. 115–27); B.O'Reilly, 'Is Perot good for General Motors?' *Fortune*, Vol. 110, No. 6, August 1984, pp. 84–85; G.G. Burck, 'Will success spoil General Motors?' *Fortune*, Vol. 108, August 1983, p. 94.

18. See Ian C. MacMillan and Robin George, 'Corporate venturing: Challenges for senior managers', *The Journal of Business Strategy*, Vol. 5, No. 3, 1985, pp. 34–43.

19. See Anita van de Vliet, 'Where Lucas sees the light', *Management Today*, June 1986, pp. 38–45.

20. See *Business Week*, 'Toyo Kogyo: A sure loser stages a turnaround', 25 January 1982, pp. 74–76. For some interesting suggestions on how to compete, see Ian C. Macmillan and Patricia E. Jones, 'Designing organizations to compete', *Journal of Business Strategy*, Vol. 4, No. 4, 1984, pp. 11–26.

21. See D.C.L. Morwood, 'ICL: Crisis and swift recovery', *Long Range Planning*, Vol. 18, No. 2, 1985, pp. 10–21. Also see Simon Caulkin, 'ICL's Lazarus act', *Management Today*, January 1987, pp. 56–63; and Kharbanda and Stallworthy, 1987, op. cit., pp. 158–65.

22. See Marisa Bellisario, 'The turnaround at Italtel', *Long Range Planning*, Vol. 18, No. 1, 1985, pp. 21–24.

23. See note 21 above.

24. See Dilip Thakore, 'How the world's largest public sector company has been turned around', *Business World*, 22 June–5 July 1987, pp. 34–47. See also K.K. Roy, 'Italy's non-oil public sector: Prodi(gious) turnaround', *Economic Times*, 19 June 1987, p. 5.

25. See Kharbanda and Stallworthy, 1987, op. cit., pp. 142–53; and G. Turner, 'Inside Europe's giant companies—Olivetti goes bear hunting', *Long Range Planning*, Vol. 19, 1986, pp. 13–20.

26. See Pradip N. Khandwalla, *Effective turnaround of sick enterprises (Indian experiences): Text and cases* (London: Commonwealth Secretariat, 1989, pp. 173–82).

27. See K.G. Kumar, 'Apollo Tyres Ltd: No more skidding', *Business India*, 18–26 June 1988, pp. 61, 63, 67, and Pradip N. Khandwalla, 1989, op. cit., pp. 231–44.

28. See W.H. Starbuck, A. Greve, and B. Hedberg, 'Responding to crises: Theory and the experience of European business', pp. 107–34, in C.F. Smart and W.T. Stanbury (eds.), *Studies on crisis management* (Toronto: Inst. on Research for Public Policy, 1978).

29. See B. Hedberg, P. Nystrom, and W. Starbuck, 'Camping on seesaws: Prescriptions for a self-designing organization', *Administrative Science Quarterly*, Vol. 21, 1976, pp. 41–65.

30. See V. Krishnamurthy, 'SAIL blazes a new trail', *The Economic Times*, 19 November 1987. See also Subrata Roy, 'Spotlight on SAIL', *Business World*, 1–14 March 1986, pp. 43–51; 'SAIL rolling plan for 1989–90',

The Economic Times, 29 December 1989, p. 1; 'Steel price hike unlikely', *The Economic Times*, 1 March 1989, p. 1; T.N. Ninan, 'SAIL: Dramatic turn-around', *India Today*, 30 April 1986, pp. 106–7; 'SAIL to enter chemicals', *The Economic Times*, 2 April 1987, p. 1; Subrata Roy, 'SAIL: Will it succeed?' *Business India*, 10–23 August 1987, pp. 42–52.

31. See Pradip N. Khandwalla, 'Some top management styles, their context and performance', *Organization and Administrative Science*, Vol. 7, 1976–77, pp. 21–51.

32. For models of effective transition management, see Danny Miller and Peter Friesen, 'Archetypes of organizational transition', *Administrative Science Quarterly*, Vol. 25, 1980, pp. 268–99.

33. For transformational leadership in a Western context see Warren Bennis and Burt Nanus, *Leaders: The strategies for taking charge* (New York: Harper and Row, 1985). For transformational leadership in a Third World context, see Pritam Singh and Asha Bhandarkar, *Corporate success and transformational leadership* (New Delhi: Wiley Eastern, 1990). For skills of change agent, see Pradip N. Khandwalla, *Fourth eye: Excellence through creativity*, 2nd ed. (Allahabad: A.H. Wheeler, 1988, ch.9).

34. See *Business Week*, 'Macmillan: Back to the school house to sustain a textbook turnaround', 28 November 1983, pp. 67–68.

35. See Fabrizio Galimberti, 'Getting FIAT back on the road', *Long Range Planning*, Vol. 19, No. 1, 1986, pp. 25–30; Kharbanda and Stallworthy, 1987, op. cit., pp. 146–47.

36. See note 25 above.

37. See Pradip N. Khandwalla, *Excellent management in the public sector: Cases and models* (New Delhi: Vision, 1990, chapter B. 2).

38. See note 24 above.

39. See note 30 above.

40. See Anita van de Vliet, 'Why Rockware was recycled', *Management Today*, September 1985, pp. 62–69.

41. See V. Krishnamurthy, 'Management of organizational change: The BHEL experience', *Vikalpa*, Vol. 2, No. 2, 1977, pp. 113–19; Ravi Ramamurti 'National Machinery Corporation of India', a disguised case BHEL (Boston: Northeastern University, undated).

42. See note 21 above.

43. See Stuart Slatter, 1984, op. cit., pp. 296–301.

44. See David Chambers, 'Consumer orientation and the drive for quality', paper presented at the Roundtable on Public Enterprise Management: Strategies for Success', held at New Delhi, 6–11 March 1988, under the auspices of the Commonwealth Secretariat, London, and Indian Institute of Management, Ahmedabad.

45. See note 25 above.

46. See Pradip N. Khandwalla, 1989, op. cit., pp. 183–96.

47. See note 30 above.

48. See note 24 above.

49. See note 30 above.

50. See note 46 above.

51. See note 19 above.

52. See *Business Week*, 'Can Chrysler keep its comeback act rolling?' 19 February 1983, pp. 53–62; see also *Business Week*, 'The next act at Chrysler', 3 November 1986, pp. 48–52; and Maynard M. Gordon, *The Iacocca management technique* (New York: Bantam, 1987).

53. See Ian MacGregor, 'Recovery at British Steel', *Journal of General Management*, Vol. 7, No. 3, 1982, pp. 5–16. See also David Chambers, 1988, op. cit. Also Kharbanda and Stallworthy, 1987, op. cit., pp. 62–69.

54. See note 37 above.

55. See Pradip N. Khandwalla, 1990, op. cit., Part D.

56. See note 52 above.

57. See Pradip N. Khandwalla, 'Organizations of the future: A strategic organization perspective', pp. 159–76, in *Productivity through people in the age of changing technology* (New Delhi: National Productivity Council, 1987).

58. See *Business Week*, 'Docutel: Born again and counting on new vigor in automatic tellers', 27 July 1981, pp. 48 and 50.

59. See note 52 above.

60. See note 25 above.

61. See note 46 above.

62. See Pradip N. Khandwalla, 1990, op. cit., Part C.

63. See Kharbanda and Stallworthy, 1987, op. cit., pp. 214–29.

64. See Ravi Ramamurti, 'State Timber Corporation of Sri Lanka (A) and (B)', cases 0–382–018 and 0–382–019. Boston: President and Fellows of Harvard College, 1981.

65. See Emanuel Hachipunka, 'Zambia Railways Limited', paper presented at the Roundtable on 'Public Enterprise Management: Strategies for Success', New Delhi, 6–11 March 1988, held under the auspices of the Commonwealth Secretariat, London, and Indian Institute of Management, Ahmedabad.

66. See note 19 above.

67. See note 30 above.

68. See note 46 above.

69. See note 41 above.

70. See note 41 above.

71. See note 17 above.

72. See note 44 above.

73. See Geoffrey Colwin, 'Freddie Silverman's secret success', *Fortune*, 14 July 1980, pp. 123–24.

74. See Sushila Ravindranath, 'SPIC bounces back', *Business India*, 23 April–5 May 1985, pp. 110, 111, 113, 115, 117, 119 and 120.

75. See note 30 above.

76. See note 62 above.

77. See note 46 above.

78. See *Business Week*, 'Searle: Rallying a drug company with an injection of new vitality', 8 February 1982, pp. 50 and 52.

79. See note 35 above.

80. See Stuart Slatter, 1984, op. cit., pp. 279–87.

81. See note 21 above.

82. See W.L. French and C.H. Bell, Jr., *Organization development* (Englewood Cliffs, N.J.: Prentice Hall, 1978).

83. See D.A. Nadler, *Feedback and organization development* (Reading, Mass.: Addison–Wesley, 1977); R.T. Golembiewski and A. Blumberg, *Sensitivity training in the laboratory approach* (Ill.: F.E. Peacock, 1977). See also Dharni Sinha, *T–group team building and organization development* (New Delhi: Indian Society for Applied Behavioural Science, 1986).

84. See Michael Porter, *Competitive strategy* (New York: Free Press, 1980); Boston Consultancy Group Staff, *Perspectives on experience* (Boston: BCG Group, 1968; Michael J. Stahl and Thomas W. Zimmerer, 'Modelling strategic acquisition policies: Simulation of executives' acquisition decisions', *Academy of Management Journal*, Vol. 27, No. 2, 1984, pp. 369–83.

85. See Harvey Leibenstein, 'Allocative efficiency vs "X–efficiency" ', *American Economic Review*, Vol. 56, 1966, pp. 392–415; also Harvey Leibenstein, 'On the basic proposition of X–efficiency theory', *American Economic Review*, Vol. 68, No. 2, 1978, pp. 328–32.

86. See note 53 above.

87. See note 19 above.

88. See note 30 above.

89. See note 20 above.

90. See note 52 above.

91. For examples of top management interventions in the area of operations that contributed to turnaround, see V. Padaki and V. Shanbhag (eds.), *Industrial sickness: The challenge in Indian textiles* (Ahmedabad: ATIRA, 1984).

8. TURNAROUND MUSINGS

It is conventional to summarise findings of research in the concluding chapter and end it with some rousing platitudes. Instead, in this chapter the attempt is to muse, to encounter the data and respond to them speculatively and indeed, to go beyond corporate findings to deeper layers of organisational, occasionally societal, anthropology. Some of these musings have jelled into hypotheses.

Flawed Immortality

For quite some time the biological metaphor has been influential in organisation theory.[1] The parallels between the organisation and the living organism are there: birth, sentience, maturation, crises. Death, however, is not a commonality. All living things must die; that is the law of nature. But all organisations need not, and do not. Organisational deaths are few and far between. True, a few organisations do go into liquidation every year, mostly small, marginal ones. Few sizeable, complex organisations do. They may change ownership or identity, they may decline, they may be swallowed up by bigger fish, they may get dismembered, they may undergo structural or strategic metamorphoses. But very, very few die, that is, wholly cease operations. In their immortality complex organisations resemble redwoods rather than humans. Biology-oriented organisation theorists have missed this point. They, such as the population ecology theorists,[2] have constructed models of organisational mortality when what we need are models of organisational immortality.

Equally visible is the pervasiveness of organisational pathology. All manner of organisations fall sick or decline for all manner of reasons. In India alone the amount of capital tied up in sick enterprises seems to be rising at around 15 per cent a year, that is, it is doubling every five years.[3] In Britain and the USA too, sickness is rampant, with one of three or four corporations getting sick in any decade.[4] There has been some perceptive work on organisational sickness and decline.[5] There is, however, relatively little work on why sick organisations do not die. Turnaround processes indicate why they may not.

The 65 cases listed in Table 1.1 of Chapter 1 demonstrate the universality of turnarounds. Small as well as big organisations, organisations in the consumer as well as capital and producer goods industries, organisations in Western as well as Third World societies, private sector as well as public sector organisations, high-tech as well as low-tech organisations, relatively young as well as old organisations, deeply sick as well as marginally sick organisations are listed in the Table. The cases given are most likely only a small percentage of all the organisations that experienced revival after a decline during recent years (many turnarounds were not published; only a fraction were published in English; many turnarounds were excluded because they were not revivals from a loss situation, or were not detailed enough).

Not just corporations, other collectivities are also known to re-generate. There are examples of not-for-profit organisations that have been regenerated,[6] communities,[7] and indeed, whole societies[8] (the Soviet system is a spectacular example) that have been turned around. Not only can collectivities other than corporations also regenerate themselves, they seem to use very similar processes, such as the placement of a dynamic transformational change agent in a powerful post, credibility-building efforts, attempts to garner the support of various stakeholders in the regeneration effort, undertaking a large number of quick pay-off activities, and mobil-isation of members of the collectivity through mission and vision of excellence, intrinsic motivation, collective diagnosis, conscientisation and troubleshooting, participative decision-making, setting an example, and so on. The ability to regenerate may be intrinsic to human collectivities, just as the tendency to sicken is also intrinsic to their nature. That is, it is collectively human to fail as it is col-lectively human to revive.

A collectivity (such as a formal organisation) is potentially immortal because of the enormous redundancy that is built into it: multiple problem solvers and decision makers, information processors, operatives, machines, sites, energy sources, sources of finance, among others. The death or destruction of any member or machine can be inconvenient, but very rarely fatal to the organisation. Another reason is the stake of many diverse constituencies in the continuation of the collectivity—of employees or members, customers, suppliers, the government, the financial institutions, the shareholders or owners, and others. A great many stakeholders need to agree to the demise of a collectivity before it can pass on.

But the very complexity of the collectivity and the diversity of stakeholders can be sources of sickness. Highly differentiated organisations, for example, often fall prey to excessive specialisation, sub-optimisation, and inter-functional conflict, excessive centralisation or decentralisation, incapacity to adapt to environmental or internal pressures, and similar malaise.[9] Diverse stakeholders can tear collectivities apart through their contradictory demands, such as in union–management conflicts. Added to all these may be pressures from rivals. Thus, collectivities, especially organisations, continually teeter over the brink of chaos due to poor management of internal complexity and/or contextual complexity.

When they do go over the hill, however, the means of regeneration lie precisely in the instrumentalities of their fall—in the mobilisation and orchestration of the organisation's varied resources, and in the alignment of the interests of the stakeholders for preventing the destruction of the collectivity. The turnaround data indicate the powerful meliorative effect of efforts to mobilise the organisation for turnaround and of the effort to woo stakeholders for supporting the turnaround. It may be recalled from Table 2.3 of Chapter 2 that some of the strongest correlates of the rate of improvement in profitability of complete turnarounds were such actions as attempts to increase productivity, formal diagnostic activities, attempts to garner the support of stakeholders, professionalisation of management systems, attempts to motivate the staff, attempts to improve organisational integration, and attempts at collective diagnosis and team effort at problem solving. Furthermore, as shown in Table 2.6 of the same chapter, several of these were also 'strategic' turnaround elements, that is, they were relatively highly linked with other turnaround elements and therefore more likely than others to get the turnaround roaring.

The preceding discussion suggests some hypotheses for complex collectivities (including complex organisations):

H1 The more complex the collectivity and its stakeholder system, the greater will be the collectivity's longevity and the more precarious its health.

H2 For a given level of sickness, the more complex the collectivity and its stakeholder system, the greater will be the contribution of efforts to mobilise the collectivity and its stakeholders for turnaround to regenerating the collectivity.

Constrained Choices

In these chapters several turnaround choices have been encountered. A basic choice is between surgical and non-surgical turnarounds. Within each choice there is a further choice between a primarily technical/commercial turnaround (changes in capital, product line, cost structure, technology, marketing, and organisational structure) and one that also emphasises mobilising the stakeholders. Another basic choice seems to be between creative versus conventional turnaround actions. These are strategic choices, for they seem to affect the cost of turnaround, the speed of turnaround, the magnitude of turnaround, and the design, culture, and functioning of the organisation. The data suggest that humane, mobilisation-oriented, creative turnarounds tend to outperform harsh, technical, conventional turnarounds. What shapes these choices?

Strategic choices are believed to be affected by the exigencies of creating/maintaining a dominant coalition, by the norms and values of the organisation, by the operational context of the organisation, by past commitments, by the structure and technology of the organisation, and similar factors.[10] In many, perhaps most turnarounds, the basic choices—whether to fire people or not, whether to be innovative or not, whether to be participative or authoritarian—appear to be made at least initially by one or two persons, and that too by individuals who are often newcomers to the organisation. Thus, the initial strategic choices are likely to reflect the perceptions and priorities of the change agent rather than the organisation's power structure as a whole. This is possible because in sick organisations this power structure is commonly paralysed through a shared perception of helplessness.

Turnaround situations are often curious blends of widespread cynicism *and* widespread hope for a saviour. The challenge before a change agent is to respond to these contradictory stances. The commonplace response is to do what is expected. The creative response is to blend the familiar with the unfamiliar—the familiar to assure and the unfamiliar to unfreeze. That is to say, 'right' noises and actions are blended with the shocking, the miraculous, or the novel to achieve deep rather than superficial changes in the system. The right noises and actions tend to be managerially accept-able moves concerning production, product line, marketing, structure, finance, and so on. Unfreezing, however, tends to be attempted through relatively uncommon actions, such as surgery, participation, and/or innovation. Which of surgery, participation, or innovation (or what combination of these) will be attempted by the change agent is likely to depend upon the personality of the change agent, his/her diagnosis of the organisational system, and more fundamentally, upon his/her perception of waht is permissible in the organisational culture.

In several societies surgery is either not feasible for legal reasons or not very acceptable for social reasons. This is broadly true of many Third World societies like India, socialistic Scandinavian countries, and possibly also of communist states. The absence of social security in societies plagued by unemployment, or the presence of a social commitment to providing employment to all, makes surgery for turnaround an unacceptable or unlikely proposition in these societies. This may have interesting consequences for turn-arounds. Participation and/or innovation are likely to be employed as the major unfreezing mechanisms. As Table 5.1 of Chapter 5 indicates, such participatory elements as garnering stakeholders' support, integration through participative management, and initiation of managerial meetings and task forces were far more common in non-Western (mostly Indian) turnarounds, while surgery was more commonly employed in Western turnarounds. Tables 6.1 and 6.2 in Chapter 6 show that Indian high scorers on turnaround creativity were seven while there was only one low scorer and while there were only two American high scorers, there were as many as eight low scorers.

It is tempting to extend the argument to collectivities other than corporate organisations, such as not-for-profit and commonwealth organisations, communities, and societies. It is tempting to offer the following hypotheses:

H3 Given sufficient resolve to revive a sick collectivity, the stronger the cultural or legal proscription of surgical means, the greater will be recourse to participatory and innovative means for regenerating it.

H4 Given sufficient resolve to revive a sick collectivity, the stronger the cultural or legal proscription of surgical means, the faster will be its regeneration.

From Public Ignominy to Glory

A great divide in the organisational universe is ownership of the organisation.[11] An early American study indicated that the sharpest difference among 75 assorted organisations were between privately owned business organisations and the rest (many of which were publicly owned.[12] Government owned organisations tended to be more centralised and bureaucratic, and experienced less competition. Comparative Indian studies of government owned versus privately owned enterprises indicate poorer personnel relations, poorer organisational climate, poorer work culture, greater authoritarianism, more restricted diversification, and poorer performance of government owned enterprises.[13] Poor financial performance of public enterprises has been a global phenomenon.[14] Many reasons have been advanced for the relatively poorer functioning of public sector organisations: mix of commercial and social goals, fuzzy goals, bureaucratic control, political interference, public accountability, 'security-proneness' of the staff, smugness due to size and monopoly power, and so on.[15] As a consequence, the incidence of sickness tends to be high in the public sector—in India, the percentage of loss-making public enterprises is three to four times higher than the percentage of loss-making large private enterprises.[16]

There is, however, a lot at stake in the health of public sector organisations. In most countries public sector organisations provide vital public goods and services. Many public sector organisations are the progeny of market failure. In many Third World, socialistic and communist societies they perform strategic developmental functions like pioneering into the country new products and technologies and spearheading development of backward regions.

Mastering the art of regenerating moribund public sector organisations may have enormous beneficial multiplier effects affecting a great many facets of life.

How should grave sickness in vitally important public institutions be handled? One answer is privatisation, a simplistic clarion call that ignores the social missions of public sector organisations and offers an unproven panacea.[17] The other answer is more effective turnaround management. It is significant that Table 1.1 in Chapter 1 lists as many as 20 cases of successful turnarounds of public enterprises operating in a variety of Western and Third World countries. There are several additional cases known to the author but not included because of insufficient information.[18]

Table 5.3 of Chapter 5 shows the sharp differences in the turnaround management of public *versus* private sector enterprises. Although public enterprises resorted less frequently to surgical means than private enterprises, the difference was not statistically significant. But in 13 other turnaround elements, however, the differences were statistically significant. As was noted in Chapter 5, public sector turnarounds were built around wooing stakeholders for support, human resource development, more professionalised systems of management, diagnosis and team effort at problem solving, participative management, recourse to motivating the staff and inspiring it with a mission, and emphasis on plant modernisation, besides the elements shared with private sector enterprises (restructuring, marketing related actions, cost reduction other than through retrenchment, diversification, changes in top management, and related actions). What is interesting is that the turnarounds of public sector enterprises were more broad based, that is, utilised many more turnaround elements, than those of private enterprises. Public enterprises scored 50 per cent or more on 19 turnaround elements *versus* the 10 on which private enterprises scored 50 per cent or more. Why should public enterprises need to be more comprehensive in their turnaround effort than private enterprises?

One possibility is that public enterprises get sicker than private enterprises because of absence of competition and/or poor performance feedback through pursuing many fuzzy goals on which feedback is weak or long delayed. There is just more to do to clean up the mess. The second reason may lie in the way the turnaround is pursued—the collectivist, diagnosis-based mode discloses many areas of action. The third reason may be the professionalist bias of public enterprise top managers—faith in training, planning, elaborate management systems among others—that predisposes them to draw up comprehensive rather than piecemeal plans of action.

Another intriguing feature of public enterprise turnarounds was their greater reliance on creativity than private enterprises. Half each of the high creativity turnarounds were of public and private enterprises (see Table 6.1, Chapter 6) while only 10 per cent of the low-creativity turnarounds were of public enterprises and 90 per cent were of private enterprises (see Table 6.2, Chapter 6). Why should public enterprises, widely believed to be wooden and bureaucratic, display so much creativity during turnaround?

Crozier, in his study of French bureaucracies, noted the tendency of government organisations to get rigid and resist change until malfunctioning reaches crisis proportions, and then open the floodgates of changes and innovations.[19] The phenomenon is like that of damming adaptation until the dam bursts. Thus, bureaucracies seem to experience long periods of ossification and short bursts of innovation. His reason for this behaviour was a cultural one, the propensity of the French to avoid confrontation and negotiation in superior-subordinate relations, leading to great operating rigidity at the interface of two hierarchical levels. Another reason for organisational paralysis, particularly in authoritarian cultural settings, may be a dependency-proneness of employees.[20] The dependency of employees on their bosses and on rules and regulations may lead to excessive centralisation at the top. Consequently, the sorts of local or incrementalist adaptations needed at lower levels are made only if the big boss gives the nod. Since his/her capability for attention is limited, a large queue of unattended adaptations piles up. This is likely to happen more in the public than in the private sector because of the security consciousness of public sector employees and the fear of being questioned for deviating from orders or procedures.

The foregoing, however, is not a very satisfactory explanation because, during turnaround, the same apparently dependency-prone individuals seem to take initiative and implement changes and innovations on their own. One possibility is that people, especially those in societies transiting from the traditional to modernity, internalise two different identities, one passive and dependent, rooted in childhood upbringing, and the other proactive, learnt through exposure to modern institutions, ideas and mores.[21] Thus, which set of behaviours is evoked at work will depend on what cues are emitted at work: to conform and obey, or to take initiative and be dynamic. Public enterprises being centralised and rule-bound, tend generally to evoke feudal and servile behaviour. But during turnarounds the dynamic change agent seeks ideas, delegates, rewards initiative, and so forth, and thus cues proactive behaviour. Thus, public enterprises are creative during turnarounds because (a) they are non-innovative and rigid in normal times thus building up a large queue of needed changes and innovations and (b) the proactive facet of schizoid identities is evoked during turnaround by dynamic change agents at the top.

The preceding discussion prompts the following hypotheses:

H5 The more constrained the functioning of a collectivity preceding turnaround by regulations, conventions, and/ or timidity, the more comprehensive and innovative will be turnaround action, when initiated in earnest.

H6 The more constrained the functioning of a collectivity preceding turnaround by regulations, conventions, and/or timidity, the faster will be the improvement in performance during turnaround.

H7 In collectivities whose members are socialised into both passivity and proactivity, the more bureaucratic and/or authoritarian the top leadership, the sicker will the collectivity become, and the more dynamic and participatory the top leadership, the faster will be its regeneration.

Turnaround Change Agentry Traits

Most successful turnarounds are powered by new chief executives. Of the 65 turnarounds listed in Table 1.1 of Chapter 1, some 90 per cent were accomplished by new heads. Not all new heads are, of course, successful in bringing about a turnaround. In a British study, 27 out of 30 successful turnarounds were shepherded by new chiefs but six out of 10 unsuccessful turnarounds were also headed by new top managements; and in an Indian study in which all ten sick companies had a change of top management, in only five could the turnaround be considered successful.[22] Thus, a change of leadership may be necessary for most sick organisations but may not be enough. Whether the new chief succeeds or not is likely to depend a lot on the person's personality, skills, and tactics.

Students of turnaround have made some perceptive comments about the kind of person needed. Donald Bibeault, based on experience with American turnarounds, suggested that the architect of turnaround requires 'entrepreneurial skills, broad business experience, analytical ability, creativity, and self-awareness. In a few cases, in larger corporations, these requirements are completed with a sensitivity to society's expectations regarding the businessman's broader social responsibilities.'[23] As implementor of strategy he/she must be a good manager. He/she must be 'tough minded and have objective orientation, self-confidence, decisiveness, good negotiating skills, good interviewing skills, high standards of evaluation, and most importantly, an impatience to get something done'.[24] As a leader, he/she must inspire self-confidence in others, be flexible as to means but firm as to ends, be able to attract high achievers, be tough and competitive. 'Successful turnaround leaders seem to sense which task merits the highest priority, are able to seize initiative, and devote enormous energy to driving the organisation and themselves to task-completion. They are consistently dogged in their pursuit of objectives and the accomplishment of goals, while maintaining the flexibility to change intermediate goals as the situation develops. They are very determined people.'[25] Kharbanda and Stallworthy, drawing on turnarounds in the USA, Europe, India and Japan, suggested that turnaround leaders bring out, develop, and use the best in others.[26] They also suggested that such leaders should be able to create a culture of freedom and autonomy but with a reasonably rigid framework set by company policy and culture. Potts and Behr, scanning the turnarounds of giant US companies, indicated that turnaround managers tend to be hands-on managers who have risen from the ranks.[27] They tend to be flexible and they move quickly in a fast-changing environment. They tend to be aggressive and unafraid to make needed changes. And most of all, they are driven by a far-reaching vision for their companies, that can carry legions of employees with them. He/she should be all of a dreamer, a businessman, and a son-of-a-bitch!

Most of the traits mentioned above fit the requirements of operating in an environment assumed to consist of tough competitors, union leaders, bankers, customers, suppliers, government agencies, staff members, and such like. The descriptions abound in masculine characteristics. But the world is not only tough; it is also tender, emotional, sensitive, a world of apparent ineptitude but great competence given the right nurturance. The fist-pounding emphasis on the masculine for changing collectivities may give good short-term results but may also further militarise human consciousness. Many turnarounds we have encountered in this book—at BHEL, SAIL, Italtel, IRI, Can Cel, Rockware, Tinplate, Travancore Cochin Chemicals, NBC Radio and others—indicate the efficacy of such traits as empathy, ability to listen, ability to dialogue with the weak as well as the strong, nurturance, ability to touch the conscience, ability to evoke expression to hostile and other pent-up feelings, ability to share power rather than hog it, sincerity, warmth, intuitive judgement, equanimity, transparency, altruism, and creativity. These are 'feminine' traits that have remade the world again and again, let alone rescued ailing corporations—Buddha, Jesus, and Gandhi as world change agents come readily to mind. The best results are likely to be secured by a change agent who is both tough and tender, masculine and feminine, Yin and Yang.[28] Lest it be forgotten, the creative and humane turnarounds vastly outperformed the brashly surgical ones (see Table 3.6 of Chapter 6).

Scarcely any human has all the masculine and feminine traits needed for turnaround. The strategy therefore must be to rapidly increase the pool of traits and skills by coopting into the turnaround others who complement the traits of the chief and compensate for his/her weakness. That is to say, the Great Person model of turnaround maker has to be replaced by the growing Great Team model of turnaround facilitation. A person may start a turnaround, but unless others are coopted into the effort the turnaround may abort. This is especially true where the collectivity is complex, or is operating in a complex context. To paraphrase Marx, the strength of a hundred can exceed that of a thousand-strong mob when the hundred operate as a team. We need to add team-building as a critical skill to the list of masculine and feminine traits outlined earlier—critical because it is the open sesame to a treasure of needed skills and traits.

The discussion points to the following hypotheses:

H8 Given a complex collectivity or operating context, the higher the turnaround change agent on 'masculinity' as well as 'femininity' the faster and cheaper would be the turnaround; the greater the imbalance between 'masculinity' and 'femininity' the slower and dearer would be the turnaround.

H9 Given a compelx collectivity or operating context, the greater the turnaround change agent's capacity to build an effective turnaround team, the faster and cheaper the turnaround.

Change Agent's Strategies

Besides the personality and competencies of turnaround change agents, their change heuristics also contribute significantly to turn-arounds. Since turnaround change agents are usually new helmsmen, and commonly outsiders to the sick collectivity, they need to pursue a familiarisation strategy, that is, a strategy for getting to know quickly the essentials of the collectivity and its operating context. They also need to follow a strategy for gaining the acceptance of stakeholders. There must also be a system change strategy. And finally, they must think up a consolidation and institution building strategy.

Familiarisation

The newcomer change agent needs to know—fast—the culture, business, operating problems, strengths, weaknesses, constraints and related factors, of the collectivity, and also the power structure and priorities of the significant external and internal stakeholders. Meeting stakeholders individually and/or in groups is a most useful element of any familiarisation strategy, exemplified so effectively by SAIL's Krishnamurthy, a rank newcomer to the giant steel-maker.[29] Then there are balance sheets and annual reports and other documents to pore over, diagnostic surveys to initiate, and so on. One Indian government servant, often called upon to head sick public enterprises, initiates a SWOT (strength, weaknesses, opportunities and threats) exercise within days of becoming the chief. The SWOT instrument is sent to all managers. The response is often poor; but the information is often rich, including the information on who has what ideas and who potentially can be a member of the turn-around team. A periodic performance review meeting of department heads chaired by the new chief may be another powerful familiar-isation heuristic. Frequent office and plant tours, and 'management by moving around' can also be a familiarisation tool. A few manage-ment weekend retreats in some elysial place can yield to the change agent a good deal of crucial data about what is embedded deep in the managers' hearts. Lunch and tea with different sets of stake-holders daily can economise on time and generate the informationally rich gossip that is the inevitable fall out of filling stomachs.

Acceptance

A newcomer also has to get acceptance. Social get-togethers of stakeholders, preferably with family members, is one simple mechanism. More solid perhaps are initial credibility building actions—stopping wastage, imposing quality control, clearing long-pending requests, dismissing corrupt officials, disciplining re-calcitrant workers, landing orders, getting fresh infusion of funds, resolving a conflict, and so on. Catharsis inducing actions can also help, such as 'bitching' sessions. Articulating publicly a stirring mission and some challenging but achievable concrete goals can also win acceptance. Sharing information about the collectivity, taking stakeholders into confidence, as at Italtel,[30] also works. At the malfunctioning Damodar Valley Corporation, Luther, the new chief, learnt that thousands of unattended staff grievances had accumulated.[31] Nobody wanted to touch them because these grievances were filed by workers who were not members of re-cognised unions. Luther was advised by his lieutenants to keep these grievances under the rug, at least initially. Instead, Luther sent teams of managers to the sites to investigate the grievances, made a public commitment to dispose off the complaints within six months, and kept his word. So great was the acceptance he gained that a militant union leader who had earlier paralysed the manage-ment tried thrice to call a strike but failed each time, and Luther was able to increase productivity by 30 per cent in a single year.

Change Strategies

Pointing the organisation in the right direction, that is the change strategy, requires the change agent to identify points in the system where he/she wishes to initiate action with a view to achieve some larger, long-term changes in the character of the collectivity. These points may relate to specific tasks performed in the system, or the way they are performed; or change in some critical performance parameters like growth rate, capacity utilisation, or profitability, eliminating an obsolete or harmful but well-entrenched practice, correcting a dysfunctional but critical relationship with a stakeholder, a quick pay-off opportunity, and so on. The change agent not only seeks to make an improvement, he/she also seeks to help the collectivity learn some important lesson or skill that transforms the way it functions. The change agent therefore tries to pick points of intervention where the action may have not only immediate pay-offs but also long-term systemic consequences for the collectivity. The new chief at Hindustan Photo Films, a state monopoly, recalled defective shipments which earlier it used to dump on customers, as a means of signalling to the external as well as internal stakeholders a major shift towards a culture of quality.[32] At SAIL the new chief appointed a top executive in charge of training and another to be in charge of projects to bring in the new culture of human resource development and effective project management.[33] At Jaguar Motors, customer complaints were shared with the workers to develop a new awareness of the importance of quality.[34]

A hypothesis is:

H10 In a complex, sick collectivity, the greater the symbolic and futurist significance of concrete turnaround actions, the faster and cheaper the turnaround.

There are many modes of transformation the change agent can draw upon.[35] Rewarding appropriate behaviour and penalising inappropriate behaviour is a commonplace mechanism for creating direction change in a collectivity. Creating or strengthening profit centres and rewarding those heads of profit centres that perform well and punishing those that fail was tried by the new chief executives of several organisations. Setting a personal example—influencing by creating a role model—is another state-altering mechanism.

This too was tried widely, such as at Chrysler,[36] where Iacocca personally tried to market new models, and at Olivetti where De Benedetti started his meets at six in the morning.[37] A variant is to create heroes by playing up outstanding performers within the system and thereby create additional role models. Influencing through publicised performance feedback or open sharing of performance is a third mechanism for system change. At Hindustan Photo Films, for example, the performance of various sections was publicly displayed.[38] At Richardson and Cruddas, performance review meetings were started at which each head of department presented the performance of his/her department, which then was discussed by the whole group.[39] Subtle peer pressure thus got used to sting laggards into improving their performance. Persuasion through mass contact to get people to accept the unpalatable is another useful change heuristic, one that was tried successfully at British Steel,[40] Rockware,[41] and Chrysler.[42] The so-called Pygmalion effect can be harnessed by the change agent through pep talks and communication of high expectations to the managers, the 'I-know-you-can-do-better' mode used commonly by sports coaches and captains.[43] The turnaround change agent can also administer shock to unfreeze—fire or demote some exalted ones, 'clean up' a plant à la Neutron Jack of General Electric,[44] and 'send a message' by such means. Where there have been many past mistakes, mass catharsis—through bitching or breast beating sessions—can occasionally be tried out to cleanse the psyche of long festering sores or dissatisfactions before getting on with renewed vigour to doing the needful. Setting people to 'see' a new perspective—change through insight—is worth trying. This can be done by setting up debates, by 'conscientisation' or getting people to confront their reality and the forces that oppress them,[45] and also by getting them to experience a contradiction or anomaly or dissonance, such as facing up to the consequences of their carelessness, as at Jaguar Motors.[46] Market surveys, organisational surveys, international, inter-industry or other comparisons—employed creatively at Lucas, for example[47]—can also force people to confront what they like to evade and thereby restructure their perceptions of reality. Indoctrination and brainwashing, done so well at some Japanese corporations,[48] is still another tool for system change. This can be tried through training, newsletters, speeches, video shows and the like. At SAIL, for example, the human resource development ideology was sought to be diffused through training;[49] and video shows, in-plant speeches, and such like were used to telling effect at Jaguar to communicate the message of efficiency.[50] Activating dormant needs and yearnings (as they do in advertising) is also a mode of system change. The trick is to activate needs that can be met by meeting system requirements. Internal communication can be directed at evoking dormant needs for autonomy, self-actualisation, or even making a significant social contribution, and then opportunities can be provided to 'earn' a chance to realise these through better performance. 'The sky is the limit for a high achiever' may be an effective message in a previously stultifying clime. Confidence-building in the demoralised, giving them challenging but achievable assignments, is an additional mechanism for system change. The trick is to excite demoralised people through challenging assignments that seem risky, but then provide the moral and material support to ensure success. This sort of success can unleash a positive cycle of higher achievements and aspirations. Setting up numerous task forces to tackle a system's problems, and then giving them the necessary support to implement the suggested changes can powerfully build up confidence, as at Enfield,[51] Hindustan Photo Films,[52] Lucas,[53] and several other organisations. The mode is that of change through making people dare and succeed. Where a culture of unscrupulousness has arisen, a possibility for change lies in harnessing the force of conscience, by emphasising the ethical over the expedient, and by holding up the mirror to people to see how ugly their behaviour is. Finally, change through a new mission and vision of excellence is possible. A vivid, superior, inspiring but credible alternative to the status quo needs to be identified and communicated to the rank-and-file and other stakeholders, not once but again and again, affirmed in small acts and decisions as in large, until that social mission and/or vision of collective excellence seizes people's imagination and pushes them to strive for glory. The process is one of restructuring the Freudian superego, and involves the use of what Burns has called transformational leadership[54] and what Bennis and Nanus have called leadership through vision.[55]

So many are the ways of changing, and so many creative combinations are possible that given enough will and ingenuity the turnaround of almost any sick collectivity may approach certainty. The death of any complex collectivity may be much less a function of inexorable ecological pressures than of insufficient ingenuity or avoidable human failure.

Which of these change modes should be invoked would obviously depend upon many factors—the nature of sickness and the context of the collectivity, the skills and preferences of the change agent, and the nature of change needed. But quite possibly more change modes need to be utilised in differentiated, complex collectivities than in simpler ones. Also, the deeper the sickness, the more effective may be the evocative, emotive, rousing, 'deeper' mechanisms of change, such as catharsis, conscientisation, empowerment, insight, brainwashing, and vision, and the less effective may be the more 'surface' means such as rewards and punishment, role-modelling, information and feedback, the Pygmalion effect, or manipulative activation of dormant needs. The profound changes wrought in such once somnolent societies as Russia, India, and China might not have been possible without the call to the core by change agents like Lenin, Gandhi, and Mao, and more recently, Gorbachev. Rewards, penalties, and propaganda, however, may be enough for fine-tuning societies, such as Reaganite USA and Thatcherite Britain. To come back to sick corporations, the profound and comprehensive turnaround action in sick public sector organisations may have been possible in part because change agents in such organisations could credibly employ calls to the core—they could speak of major social missions, for example, and a vision of corporate excellence beyond mere profitability. More earthy, more surface change strategies tended to be emphasised (with some exceptions, however) at sick private sector enterprises because the change agents there were predisposed to use more surface, pecuniary, and punitive instrumentalities of change.

Three hypotheses are proposed:

H11 Given deep sickness of a complex collectivity (or of one operating in a complex context), the greater the use of emotive, gestalt-changing, transcendental, or mystical means of change (call to the core), the faster and less expensive would be the turnaround.

H12 The more modest the sickness of a collectivity, complex or otherwise, the more effective are 'surface' means of change expectations, role-modelling, information and performance feedback, and manipulative activation of dormant needs.

H13 Given a newcomer turnaround change agent, the more effective his/her familiarisation, acceptance, and change strategies, the faster and cheaper will be the turnaround.

What we call modern, professional management, the sort that is taught in schools of management, is largely the technical elaboration of 'surface' means of change and optimisation. In societies where revolutions are needed in many spheres of socio-economic and political existence, and change agents are needed to trigger these revolutions, the technology of surface change may have to be supplemented by the technology of radical change, one that can effectively reach the crores of people.

Consolidation

Mere change for the better is an unfinished business for the change agent. He/she must become dispensable; that is, the collectivity must internalise the skills of remaining healthy even without the change agent. What needs to be institutionalised is a culture of innovative professionalism (see Chapter 7) and strategy, structure, and management systems that reflect this culture and are appropriate to the operating context of the collectivity. Culture, strategy, structure, systems are the subject matter of organisational design.[56] The what of design is less important in consolidation attempts than how the design is emplaced. This is where the 'surface' tools of change may be critically important: a reward and sanctions system, a performance monitoring and feedback system, a system of continuous promotion (through publicity) of desirable and undesirable behaviours and their consequences, a system of mentoring, training, and socialising newcomers into the collectivity, and a system of review, reflection, and learning. The turnaround change agent's role is not that of parenting these systems but of assisting in their birth and nurturance. These systems are likely to last if they are evolved, like folklore and folk art, through mass parenting, that is, through consensus processes.

A hypothesis is:

H14 The more participatory the change agent in institutionalising a culture of innovative professionalism and appropriate strategy, structure, and management systems, and the greater the attention to supportive systems of reward, sanction, performance monitoring and feedback, sanctification of good practices, publicising of desirable and undesirable behaviours, socialisation of newcomers, and collective learning, the more likely would a turnaround graduate into durable excellence.

The acquisition of certain skills by the collectivity as a whole—not just by a few individuals—also helps the consolidation of effectiveness. Many of these were reviewed in Chapter 7 as turnaround learnings. The ability to compete with and also to cooperate with other collectivities, is one such skill. How to mobilise stakeholders to aid the collectivity in a crisis situation is another skill. How to live with heterogeneity (mix of cultures and styles) is a third skill. How to get the most out of not only the external context or environment of the collectivity but also its innards is a fourth skill. How to maintain a culture of innovative professionalism in the face of bureaucratic pressures is a fifth skill.

H15 The greater the emphasis on collective learning, especially learning to cope with and utilise other collectivities, mobilise support for the collectivity, live with internal differentiation, tap X-efficiency, and maintain a culture of innovative professionalism in the face of bureaucratic press, the more likely would a turnaround graduate into a durable collective excellence.

Training for Turnaround

Given the vastness of corporate, institutional, and societal sickness, a much larger number of turnaround change agents is globally needed. True, social forces would anyhow eventually increase their supply given a strong enough demand for them. But so distinctive are the traits, competencies, and needed turnaround know-how that a short-term increase—by a factor of ten, say, and that too in cultures where such traits and competencies are distant from the cultures' central thrusts—is unlikely without some form of social engineering. The question must therefore be faced: is it possible to train a large number of turnaround change agents in a relatively short time?

At a technical level the problem seems tractable. After all, an analogous type, the entrepreneur, has been trained in thousands, with at least a fair degree of success.[57] Also, the behavioural sciences have developed the technologies for strengthening such elusive traits and skills as the achievement drive, creativity, interpersonal competence and empathy, communicative ability, leadership, problem structuring and solving skills, ability to take stress, among others such that are critical in turnaround change agents.[58]

A whole lot of existing tools of management can be useful in turnaround work. In Chapter 6 we discussed such tools as brainstorming, SWOT, action research, value analysis, and zero-base budgeting that can be helpful in generating many innovative options in many areas of operations and, therefore, could be taught to potential turnaround change agents. In Chapter 7, OD was indicated as a useful bag of tools for unfreezing systems, particularly survey feedback and sensitivity training. Stock-in-trade management tools like budgeting, information systems, planning, market research, human resource development, are also useful, especially in the penultimate stages of the turnaround. The point is that these tools are widely known and teachable.

Most of the nuts and bolts of turnaround are already known. Twenty-seven of these have been described in Chapter 2. Any turnaround training must seek to familiarise the trainees to these, the alternative actions that are feasible within each element, and the different sorts of turnaround that can be engineered out of them (see Chapters 3 and 4)

Several turnaround learnings were listed in Chapter 7, such as learning to be a sober entrepreneur, learning to compete, learning to collaborate, learning to be efficient, learning to practice a mix of styles, learning to mobilise the stakeholders for turnaround, learning to institutionalise a culture of innovative professionalism, and learning to look within the system for gold. Many of these are not taught or not taught well in management schools.

These learnings will need to be amplified, elaborated, and refined to facilitate the teaching of how to turnaround. The emphasis, however, will have to be not on developing mechanistic tools, but rather, on identifying broad approaches with alternatives in each area so as to facilitate the designing of collectivity-tailored action paths.

A further area that needs to be included in a training syllabus is turnaround phasing (see Chapter 7). The actions that are important in the initial phase of turnaround are not necessarily important in the middle and ultimate phases, and actions that are important in the middle or ultimate phases are not necessarily important in the initial phase. Also, a feel for the futurity of turnaround actions also needs to be inculcated.

Judging by what we do know about how to turnaround sick corporations, and about the sorts of traits and skills that are needed, it should not be impossible to develop packages for training turnaround change agents not just for sick corporations but also for sick not-for-profit institutions, political institutions, communities, and societies.

Concluding Comments

To extrapolate the learnings from corporate turnarounds to all sizeable collectivities is scientific sin, but given the need for revitalising so many other collectivities, it is a necessary first step. Obviously, research on the regeneration of collectivities ranging from group to society must be undertaken to sharpen the capacity to intervene in them. But far too much of social science remains compartmentalised, so that insights from studying the family or group are seldom used by organisation theorists or macro-sociologists, and vice versa. Within reason, such insights from one kind of collectivity can, at least, supply provocative hypotheses for other kinds of collectivities. Let us not forget that the moving spirit of all collectivities and their *raison d'etre* too is the human. A deliberate attempt was therefore made in this concluding chapter to move from the terminology of corporate management to that of collectivity. And that is where the offence rests.

Notes and References

1. See Gareth Morgan, *Images of organization* (Beverly Hills: Sage, 1986, ch. 3).
2. See Michael T. Hannan and John H. Freeman, 'The population ecology of

organizations', *American Journal of Sociology*, Vol. 82, 1977, pp. 929–64; W.H. Starbuck and Paul C. Nystrom, 'Designing and understanding organizations', pp. ix–xxii, in Paul C. Nystrom and W.H. Starbuck (eds.), *Handbook of organizational design*, Vol. 1 (London: Oxford University Press, 1981); B. McKelvey and H. Aldrich, 'Populations, natural selection and applied organizational science', *Administrative Science Quarterly*, Vol. 28, 1983, pp. 101–28.

3. See Pradip N. Khandwalla, 'What can financial institutions do to prevent corporate sickness?' *Vikalpa*, Vol. 13, No. 2, 1988, pp. 11–23.

4. See Donald B. Bibeault, *Corporate turnaround* (New York: McGraw–Hill, 1982), and Stuart S. Slatter, *Corporate recovery* (Harmondsworth, Middlesex: Penguin, 1984).

5. For a recent review, see William Weitzel and Ellen Jonsson, 'Decline in organizations: A literature integration and extension', *Administrative Science Quarterly*, Vol. 34, 1989, pp. 91–109.

6. See, for example, Anil Bhatt, 'Creation out of calamity: The case of a training institution', *Vikalpa*, Vol. 9, 1984, pp. 374–78; J.M. Deo and M.B. Prasad, 'Cooperative turnaround strategy' (mimeo.), Patna: A.N. Sinha Institute of Social Studies, 1988; Padma Ramachandran, 'Effective management in government: The case of the Ahmednagar Collectorate', *Vikalpa*, Vol. 9, No. 2, 1984, pp. 191–95.

7. See, for example, Eric Trist, 'QWL and community development: Some reflections on the Jamestown experience', *Journal of Applied Behavioral Science*, Vol. 22, pp. 223–38; A.D. Jedlicka, *Organization for rural development* (New York: Praeger, 1977).

8. See Arnold Toynbee, *A study of history* (abridgement of volumes 1 to 4 by D.C. Somervell) (New York: Dell Publishing, 1946); Jan Berting and Wim Blockmans (eds.). *Beyond progress and development: Macro-political and macro-societal change* (Aldershot: Arebury, 1987).

9. See Michel Crozier, *The bureaucratic phenomenon* (Chicago: University of Chicago Press, 1964) for structural causes of sickness.

10. See John Child, 'Organizational structure, environment and performance: The role of strategic choice', *Sociology*, Vol. 6, 1972, pp. 2–22.

11. See Krishna Kumar, *Organization and ownership* (Delhi: Macmillan India, 1982).

12. See R.H. Hall, J. Eugene Haas, N.J. Johnson, 'An examination of the Blau-Scott and Etzioni typologies', *Administrative Science Quarterly*, Vol. 12, 1967, pp. 118–39.

13. See Pradip N. Khandwalla, 'Organizational effectiveness', pp. 97–215, in Janak Pandey (ed.), *Psychology in India: The state-of-the-art* (New Delhi: Sage, 1988).

14. See A.M. Choksi, 'State intervention in the industrialisation of developing countries: Selected issues'. Washington, D.C.: World Bank staff working paper No. 341; Commonwealth Secretariat, *Performance evaluation of public enterprises*, London: Commonwealth Secretariat, 1978; M. Vanamala and T.S. Rasool Saheb, 'Profitability of public enterprises in developing countries', *IPE Journal*, Vol. 7, No. 1, 1980, pp. 105–7.

15. See Liaquat Ahmed, 'A functional review of public enterprises in Bank reports', staff working paper (Washington, D.C.: The World Bank, 1978);

Pradip N. Khandwalla, *Excellent management in the public sector: Cases and models* (New Delhi: Vision, 1990).

16. See Pradip N. Khandwalla, 'Dynamics of corporate regeneration', *RVB Research Papers*, Vol. 9, No. 1, 1989, pp. 1–13.

17. See Richard Hemming and Ali M. Mansoor, *Privatization and public enterprises* (Washington, D.C.: IMF, 1988); T.L. Sankar and Y. Venugopal Reddy (eds.), *Privatisation: Diversification of ownership of public enterprises* (Hyderabad: Institute of Public Enterprises and Booklinks Corporation, 1989).

18. Indian cases include Damodar Valley Corporation, Bharat Electronics, Burn Standard, Hindustan Copper, REMCO, Mysore Porcelain, INPB, Coal India, etc. Pakistani cases include Pakistan Industrial Development Corporation and State Engineering Corporation (see A.M. Mufti, 'Policy and prospects of public manufacturing enterprises in Pakistan', paper presented at the 'International Seminar on Public Sector Manufacturing Enterprises' at Bangalore, July 1982). A case from Venezuela is of Instituto Venezolano de Petroquimica (See Pedro J. Pick, 'Managing state owned enterprises more effectively: The Venezuelan case', *Annals of Public and Cooperative Economy*, Vol. 54, No 4 pp. 387–96).

19. See Crozier, 1964, op. cit.

20. See J.B.P. Sinha, *The nurturant task leader: A model of the effective executive* (New Delhi: Learning Concept Press, 1980).

21. See Pulin K. Garg and Indira J. Parikh, 'Indian organizations: Value dilemmas in managerial roles', pp. 175–90, in Alfred, M. Jaeger and Rabindra N. Kanungo (eds.), *Management in developing countries* (London: Routledge, 1990).

22. See Slatter, 1984, op. cit. See also Pradip N. Khandwalla, *Effective turnaround of sick enterprises (Indian experiences) : Text and cases* (London: Commonwealth Secretariat, 1989).

23. See Bibeault, 1982, op. cit., p. 149.

24. See Bibeault, 1982, op. cit., p. 150.

25. See Bibeault, 1982, op. cit., p. 151.

26. See O.P. Kharbanda and E.A. Stallworthy, *Company rescue: How to manage a business turnaround* (London: Heinemann, 1987, p. 238).

27. See Mark Potts and Peter Behr, *The leading edge* (New Delhi: Tata McGraw–Hill, 1987, p. 200).

28. See Geert Hofstede, *Culture's consequences: International differences in work-related values* (Beverly Hills, Cal.: Sage, 1980) for the dimension of masculinity-femininity in organizational cultures.

29. See V. Krishnamurthy, 'SAIL blazes a new trail', *The Economic Times*, 19 November 1987.

30. See Marisa Bellisario, 'The turnaround at Italtel', *Long Range Planning*, Vol. 18, No.1, 1985, pp. 21–24.

31. Information provided by Mr. P.C. Luther during a talk at the Indian Institute of Management, Ahmedabad. For information on the revival of Damodar Valley Corporation, see D. Thakore and G. Gupta, 'Miracle at DVC', *Business World*, 12–25 October 1981, pp. 26–35.

32. See C.K. Prahlad and P.G. Thomas, 'Turnaround strategy: Lessons from HPF's experience', *Vikalpa*, Vol. 2, 1977, pp. 99–112.

33. See note 29 above.

34. See David Chambers, 'Consumer orientation and the drive for quality', paper presented at the Roundtable on 'Public Enterprise Management: Strategies for Success', held at New Delhi, 6–11 March 1988, under the auspices of the Commonwealth Secretariat, London, and Indian Institute of Management, Ahmedabad.

35. See Somnath Chattopadhyay and Udai Pareek (eds.), *Managing organizational change* (New Delhi: Oxford and IBH, 1982); Robert T. Golembiewski, *Approaches to planned change,* Vols. 1 and 2 (New York: Marcel Dekker, 1979).

36. See Maynard M. Gordon, *The Iacocca management technique* (New York: Bantam, 1987).

37. See Kharbanda and Stallworthy, 1987, op. cit., pp. 142–53; and G. Turner, 'Inside Europe's giant companies—Olivetti goes bear hunting', *Long Range Planning*, Vol. 19, 1986, pp. 13–20.

38. See note 32 above.

39. See Pradip N. Khandwalla, 1990, op. cit., Part B.

40. See Ian MacGregor, 'Recovery at British Steel', *Journal of General Management*, Vol. 7, No. 3, 1982, pp. 5–16. See also David Chambers, 1988, op. cit. Also Kharbanda and Stallworthy, 1987, op. cit., pp. 62–69.

41. See Anita van de Vliet, 'Why Rockware was recycled', *Management Today*, September 1985, pp. 62–69.

42. See note 36 above.

43. See J. Sterling Livingstone, 'Pygmalion in management', *Harvard Business Review*, July-August 1969, pp. 81–89.

44. See Potts and Behr, 1987, op. cit., chapter 2.

45. See Paulo Freire, *Pedagogy of the oppressed* (Harmondsworth, Middlesex: Penguin, 1983).

46. See note 34 above.

47. See Anita van de Vliet, 'Where Lucas sees the light', *Management Today*, June 1986, pp. 38–45.

48. See *Management Japanese style*, compiled and condensed by the editors of World Executive's Digest (Bombay: India Book House, 1981).

49. See note 29 above.

50. See note 34 above.

51. See Dharani Pani, 'Enfield: Revving up again', *Business India*, 5–18 December 1983, pp. 84, 85, 87, 89, 91, and 92, and Pradip N. Khandwalla, 1989, op. cit.

52. See note 32 above.

53. See note 47 above.

54. See James M. Burns, *Leadership* (New York: Harper and Row, 1978).

55. See Warren Bennis and Burt Nanus, *Leaders: The strategies for taking change* (New York: Harper and Row, 1985).

56. See Pradip N. Khandwalla, *The design of organizations* (New York: Harcourt Brace and Jovanovich, 1977); John Child, *Organization* (New York: Harper and Row, 1984); Ralph Rowbottom and David Billis, *Organizational design: The work-levels approach* (Aldershot, UK: Gower, 1987).

57. See V.G. Patel, *Innovation in banking: The Gujarat·experiments* (Bombay: IDBI, 1981).

58. See Udai Pareek, T.V. Rao, and D. Pestonjee, *Behavioural processes in organizations* (New Delhi: Oxford IBH, 1981). For achievement-motivation training, see David McClelland and D. Winter, *Motivating economic achievement* (New York: Free Press, 1969); for creativity training, see Pradip N. Khandwalla, *Fourth eye: Excellence through creativity*, 2nd edition (Allahabad: A.H. Wheeler, 1988); for leadership training, see John Adair, *Effective leadership: A modern guide to developing leadership skills* (London: Pan Books, 1983); for training in stress tolerance, see L.J. Warshaw, *Managing stress* (Reading, M.A. Addison-Wessley, 1979); for training in interpersonal competence, see Gary Dessler, *Applied human relations* (Reston, Virginia: Reston Publishing, 1983); for team-building, see Udai Pareek, *Organizational behaviour processes* (Jaipur: Rawat Publications, 1988, pp. 190–263); for communication skills, see William V. Haney, *Communication and organizational behavior: Text and cases* (Homewood, Ill.: Richard D. Irwin, 1967); for effective problem-solving, see C. Kepner and B. Tregoe, *The rational manager: A systematic approach to problem solving and decision making* (New York: McGraw-Hill, 1965).

INDEX OF AUTHORS
AND COMPANIES

SUBJECT INDEX